WHO WE ARE IS WHERE WE ARE

WHO WE ARE IS WHERE WE ARE

MAKING HOME IN THE AMERICAN RUST BELT

AMANDA McMILLAN LEQUIEU

Columbia University Press   *New York*

Columbia University Press
Publishers Since 1893
New York   Chichester, West Sussex
cup.columbia.edu

Copyright © 2024 Columbia University Press
All rights reserved

Library of Congress Cataloging-in-Publication Data
Names: Lequieu, Amanda McMillan, author.
Title: Who we are is where we are : making home in the
American rust belt / Amanda McMillan Lequieu.
Description: New York : Columbia University Press, [2024] |
Includes bibliographical references and index.
Identifiers: LCCN 2023050926 | ISBN 9780231198745 (hardback) |
ISBN 9780231198752 (trade paperback) | ISBN 9780231552790 (ebook)
Subjects: LCSH: Deindustrialization—Middle West. | Middle West—
Economic conditions. | Economic development—Middle West.
Classification: LCC HC107.A14 L37 2024 |
DDC 338.977—dc23/eng/20240212
LC record available at https://lccn.loc.gov/2023050926

Printed and bound by CPI Group (UK) Ltd, Croydon, CR0 4YY

Cover design: Noah Arlow
Cover image: Jennifer Manzella, *Skylines 4*,
multiple woodblock print.

To all of us who live in—and love—places that are changing beneath our feet.

CONTENTS

PREFACE AND ACKNOWLEDGMENTS

PREFACE

The audience for my book has always been clear to me: my interviewees, nibbling on homemade molasses cookies (my mom's recipe) at kitchen tables or in local parks and showing me their scrapbooks, monuments, and hopes for the future. I also see my parents and my neighbors reading this book: people naming what is lost in their beloved places when the new coal mine wrecks their water supply or when the new high-rise goes up next door. "Just moving" away from home isn't an option. I want you to know you are not alone. My intended audience is also my academic colleagues, who have moved every few years for the past decade, as have I. Maybe you, too, are questioning where and what exactly home *is* anymore.

Ultimately, this book is for all of us. It is a rare person who does not live in or love a place that has been turned upside down because of economic crisis or earthquakes, rising sea levels or desertification, new Amazon warehouses or power plants, and nuclear fallout or war. Just as the causes of these crises are not located at the individual level, neither can their solutions be. We all deserve to make choices and live in place we would like to call home.

A brief note to readers about names and places. All places are real—names unchanged, with historical information fact-checked. However, this is not strictly a history of two communities. Instead, this is a work of sociology—an approach to social science research that searches for broader patterns and cross-cutting lessons learned from groups of people interacting in specific times and places. Historical facts structure the book, but individuals' memories of history propel its arguments. Unlike a historical account, I present interviewees' personal stories through a veil of pseudonyms. I link descriptors of race, age, gender, and residential longevity to interviewees' quotes and life histories, but I change their names. Pseudonyms grant speakers a modicum of privacy, useful for life narratives like these, where people are sharing about family, friends, and significant (and sometimes very personal) life events. Their quotations have not been altered—when in double quotation marks, I am directly quoting from interviews that I recorded, with the speaker's oral or written permission. When in single quotation marks, I am quoting my closest approximation of what was said during an on-the-move interview or unrecorded conversation with a larger group of people.

ACKNOWLEDGMENTS

Qualitative social science research is a relational project. Interviews, ethnography, and historical data collection were possible only with the support of people and organizations in my two case locations. The Iron County Historical Society and the Southeast Chicago Historical Museum were starting places and home bases for me in Wisconsin and Illinois, respectively.

I am grateful for interactions with the Iron County Development Association, the Iron County Extension office, and Sam at WJMS AM, who broadcast my oral history project that constitutes part of this research on the local radio station. In Chicago, the members of the tenth ward's chapter of retired United Steelworkers union members welcomed me in, and representatives from nonprofits and city-based organizations offered me helpful information. Two community members fact-checked the historical information presented in the first two chapters of this book: the indomitable Rod Sellers in Southeast Chicago and the insightful Julie Morello in Iron County. These two local experts are deeply familiar with community history and local archives. Any errors that remain are certainly my own.

Telling the sociological story of these two communities also required a cloud of supporters. At the University of Wisconsin, where I completed my PhD in Sociology in 2019, Michael Bell, Jane Collins, Gary Green. Chad Goldberg, Bill Cronon, Jess Gilbert, and Josh Garoon fundamentally shaped my approach to research. Mike's curiosity about my interviewees' sense of home, Gary's clarity of thought about community change, and Jane's big-picture questions about the relationships between people and places sparked my imagination and honed my arguments. Chad Goldberg brought me into the literatures on labor, the welfare state, citizenship, and Charles Tilly. Bill Cronon's mentorship granted me a historical perspective and patience for thinking about place, space, story, and narrative in ways too often hurried past by sociologists. Josh Garoon's clear feedback and vast knowledge of social scientific literature pushed me in the right direction, every time. And Jess Gilbert's kind and historically-tempered perspective on the sociology of agriculture and natural resources continues to influence my writing and teaching on land, the economy, and the state. I workshopped the earliest versions of this project with participants from the

Department of Sociology's brownbags in Politics, Culture, and Society and Sociology of Economic Change and Development, along with the Nelson Institute for Environmental Studies' Center for Culture, History, and Environment. Troy Reeves at UW's Oral History Program gave me invaluable advice about the public sociology components of my research. Rebecca Rodgers thought through home and interview narratives with me, and Daanika Gordon read portions of early analyses.

I completed much of this book while visiting other institutions. While living in Chicago and making weekly trips to the Southeast Chicago Historical Museum and retired steelworkers' union meetings, I was fortunate to sit in on Dan Slater's Comparative Historical Analysis class at the University of Chicago. Yaniv Ron-El and Wan-Zi Lu kindly invited to workshop my most unwieldy and risky chapter at the University of Chicago's Money, Markets, and Governance workshop. These scholars brought me into their writing community and gave clarifying feedback on data analysis that became one of the key arguments in the book. I am grateful for my time as a visiting scholar in the Department of Environmental Studies at the University of California-Santa Barbara, as well as a fruitful visit to the Max Planck Science Po Center for Instability in Society in Paris.

At Drexel University, where I am an assistant professor, my colleagues Kelly Underman, Anil Kalhan, and Diane Sicotte provided valuable feedback on chapters from the book. The interdisciplinary Science and Technology Studies Works-in-Progress workshop participants asked compelling questions on the book project as a whole, as well as adjacent projects from this data. Joseph Larnerd and Lillian Walkover cheered me on through all the stages of writing and revision. Developmental editing from Emma Warnken Johnson set my earliest book draft on a solid foundation. Funds from Drexel also enabled me to hold a workshop with three remarkable scholars who gave my draft book a close, incisive, and generous read. The synergy, brilliance, and warmth of my book workshop participants—David Pellow, Hillary Angelo, and Colin Jerolmack—made my final round of revisions an exciting and emboldening process.

Undergraduate research assistants brought energy to my data analysis and writing process. Many thanks to my four stellar undergraduate research assistants from the University of Wisconsin–Madison: Yoki Wang, Claire Morse, Constance Chang, and Hannah Chouinard. Once at Drexel, the book benefited from the time and commitment of Devesh Chainani, Aurora Wiley, and Grace Zaborski.

Finally, this book wouldn't exist without the indefatigable insights of two remarkable people. First, katrina quisumbing and I have exchanged drafts of academic research and writing projects every two weeks since 2014. She has read multiple iterations of this much-revised book—some parts more than once. When I lost sight of the big picture in the morass of revisions, katrina pulled me back to the core of my argument and my personal motivation for this project. I credit much of my growth as a writer and professionalization into academia to our consistent meetings and mutual support.

Second, I offer weighty thanks to my husband, Josh. Because we met in graduate school, this project has paralleled our relationship. Josh joined me on my earliest research trips to Iron County, and we lived in Chicago together. His support showed up in meals cooked, chapters read, ideas rebutted, and encouragement sincerely given. My interviewees asked after him when I returned to the Southeast Side and Iron County for fact-checking and follow-up interviews. And in poetic conclusion, Sophia was born as I finished revising this book. May we keep making our home together, again and again.

WHO WE ARE IS WHERE WE ARE

INTRODUCTION

"**C**ome walking with me. People come, and they look, but they don't see, because they don't know what to look for." With a quick push, Marcos extracted himself from the car and beelined for Lake Michigan.[1] His friend Jesús climbed from the driver's seat and buttoned his coat against the cold November wind. Only a few minutes earlier, Marcos and I were standing in Jesús's house, immersed in laughter, music, cinnamon cookies, and cups of hot tea. With a meaningful glance at the clock and a jangle of his car keys, Jesús had summoned us out of the warm house and to our established errand. Bundled in his small sedan, we had driven a half mile to an open field in Southeast Chicago where U.S. Steel South Works used to stand—a place I'd passed unawares during my past visits to the neighborhood.

I had met these men at a monthly meeting for retired steelworkers. When they heard of my interest in the region's history of steel, they offered to drive me through their neighborhood for their version of a history lesson. This was the place that Marcos and Jesús wanted me to see first. The lifelong friends moved with familiarity through wind-whipped prairie grass growing between boulders and disused railroad tracks. "We're from the neighborhood called the Bush," Marcos said. He turned his back to Lake Michigan to orient us with a gesture toward a row of wooden-frame houses just visible beyond a wide road. "I was born right across the street. I come from a family of steel-workers." Climbing to the peak of some rubble, Marcos offered a genealogical tour of the region's blue-collar steelwork with broad, directional gestures. "My brothers, my uncles, my dad worked forty years at U.S. Steel." He paused to indicate the rubble that used to be that mill then pointed south and west. "My uncles, at Wisconsin, Republic, Acme. My wife's family worked in Indiana in the steel mills." Jesús nodded, his salt-and-pepper hair standing on end in the wind as he added, "*This* is the oldest Mexican neighborhood in the whole city of Chicago. Before Pilsen, before Eighteenth Street, before Back of the Yards . . . this is the first and oldest. Why? Because of the steel mills."

For Jesús and Marcos, home was indistinguishable from steel. The "good life" took place in neighborhoods organized around eight steel mills that, between 1875 and 1990, dominated these marshy lowlands fifteen miles south of downtown Chicago. Jesús's and Marcos's grandfathers had immigrated from Mexico in the early twentieth century as part of a wave of strikebreakers lured by steel managers' promises of consistent employment. By the mid-twentieth century, these immigrants and their children had joined the tens of thousands of locals who were full-time steelworkers. This was a rare breed of work: unionized, blue-collar jobs that paid middle-class wages, with starting salaries in the 1960s at nearly three times the minimum wage. Opportunities for promotion, double-pay overtime, full benefits, and secure job tenure allowed workers to buy houses, put away savings, and send their kids to college or into a new generation of steelwork. Industry not only organized the spatial and social relations of this neighborhood but also set everyday people's expectations for work and home in midcentury Southeast Chicago.

As young men, Jesús and Marcos both worked for a few years in the mills, keen to reap the rewards of these highly paid jobs. Standing on the rubble of what was once the largest steel mill in the city, however, it was clear to me that Marcos's and Jesús's youthful hopes had been disappointed. Beginning in the 1980s, the U.S. steel industry crumbled and took the neighborhoods of Southeast Chicago with it. The causes were macroeconomic and global—technological change, trade deals, environmental regulations, and increased competition—but the effects were local. Rather than benefiting from well-paid, blue-collar jobs, Jesús and Marcos found themselves in want. They joined neighbors standing in lines at the welfare office, collecting food from charities, and staring down notices for unpaid rent, over-leveraged mortgages, or repossessed cars. Between 1980 and 2000, they watched as the very landscape of the neighborhood changed before their eyes. Steel mills were flattened by bull-dozers; houses in the Bush and other neighborhoods adjacent to the mills were vacated; property values plummeted; unemployment rates doubled; and thousands of former steelworkers moved away from Southeast Chicago in search of better jobs. Those left behind found themselves living through an economic crisis that persists today. For five decades, incomes on the Southeast Side have stubbornly remained in the city's lowest quartile ($16,000–$20,000). Depending on the census block, unemployment has consistently ranged from 17 to 25 percent. Today, nearly a quarter of local families live well below the federal poverty line.[2]

Certainly, *this* isn't the home that Marcos and Jesús expected to inhabit when they were young. But, against all odds, this place, this neighborhood, and this rubble still matters to these two men and thousands of their friends and neighbors. The hard landscape of the Southeast Side still contains fifteen thousand people—approximately half of the population present during the steel industry's midcentury peak. Of those residents, I estimate that approximately one-third are long-term residents—people who witnessed boom and did *not* out-migrate after bust.[3] Although the Southeast Side's economy utterly changed, there is some remnant of community.

At the former U.S. Steel site, Jesús and Marcos led me to something else that's resisted erasure—forty-foot-high walls that stored ore, lime, and other steelmaking components until 1979. Jesús placed his hand on one wall. "Mostly [the mill] is gone, except for the mighty ore walls," he said with a smile. Crunching through loose gravel, taconite pellets, and dried grass, Marcos climbed toward a crumbled gap in one wall. With a bark of laughter, he hollered back to us how the city of Chicago once tried—and failed—to knock down these walls with wrecking balls. These "dinosaurs," Marcos declared with glee, wouldn't fall. Just like him and Jesús, he suggested with a wink and an elbow as he rejoined us. Jesús stepped back to take in the vastness of the two-thousand-foot-long structures. "Being an artist and a sculptor," he said, "I see the ore walls in a completely different form." Marcos waggled his eyebrows at his friend and took the bait. "What do you see?" Jesús flung his hand toward the water, the grass of a city park behind us, and the walls casting deep shadows overhead. "I see them as a kind of a Mount Rushmore. . . . to draw people *here*."

Where I see cracks, Marcos and Jesús see a gem waiting to be rediscovered. Where the city sees rubble, *they* see resistance. They see a future that builds something livable on the rearranged vestiges of the past economy, community, and geography.

They see because they stayed. And they want others to admire Southeast Chicago—their home—as much as they do.

Look north with me five hundred miles as the crow flies. In one of the Lake Superior towns that once supplied iron ore to the steel mills in Chicago, Rupert and I sat bundled against blustery autumn winds seeping through the windows of a century-old city hall. This is Iron County, Wisconsin—population six thousand. Four schools and two grocery stores are scattered across seven hundred and fifty square miles. The closest cities are Green Bay, Milwaukee, and Duluth—all at least a hundred miles south and west and accessible only via narrow, unlit highways that wind through dense forests. Rupert and his wife, Nan, live in this very rural place only because, like most Iron Countians, their predecessors migrated here from Canada, Wales, northern Europe, or Italy in the late nineteenth century to be iron miners. Propelled by dreams of wealth, thousands of immigrants exchanged demanding physical labor for good wages, functional infrastructures, and, in many locations, company housing and social services financed directly by their employers. Home—as both housing and a sense of belonging—was quite literally built by iron companies. Rupert recalled an idyllic midcentury childhood of playing in the collective garden space and stopping by the company doctor's office whenever he or his sisters needed a bandage. As in Southeast Chicago, midcentury miners' incomes were solidly middle-class and more than enough to support a family of five. Rupert said, "My dad worked hard, my mom was able to stay home, raise myself and my three sisters. We lived the dream there, one person working. I had the best life in the world, then, because we were able to afford a new car, and my mother was able to get some appliances in the house!" He grinned at the memory.

But this version of home is just that—a memory. The postwar economic contractions that shuttered Southeast Chicago's steel mills in the 1970s and 1980s hit the extractive side of the steel commodity chain first. Between 1952 and 1965, all of Iron County's mines closed as raw iron ore was sourced from cheaper international sources and mined through new technologies. A quarter of the population out-migrated by 1990. Without the economic connections that fueled Iron County's small towns, the region has faced its own form of erasure. Since 1965, Iron County's residents have consistently been older, poorer, and much more likely to be unemployed than the average Wisconsin citizen.[4] Today, nearly a third of Iron County residents rely on fixed incomes, like pensions and social security, while those who are working age are employed in jobs that pay between a third to half of the state average wage for comparable work.[5] Locals are haunted by this contrast between the good past and an economically tenuous present. With a shake of his head, Rupert stated, "We keep on losing population here. We've got the highest unemployment in the state. We've got the lowest . . . you name it . . ." His voice trailed off into a groan.

In Iron County—a place named after a natural resource that no longer sustains its population—it is easy to focus on what's absent. But what and who remains defines home in Iron County today. People want to call this place home even though economic stagnation might motivate escape. Like in Southeast Chicago, Iron County claims a little more than half of its peak population. Through the open door of the old city hall where Rupert and I talked—now the county historical society—we heard the echoes of dozens of footsteps as volunteers and visitors navigated the winding corridors. The hallway bulletin boards flutter with layers of announcements for community meetings and winter sports activities. Through the window, I watched a car coast down Hematite Street and turn into the Iron Nugget restaurant's crowded parking lot. Outside, the crisp October air was already heavy with the promise of snow. Soon, thousands of tourists will arrive to Iron County's public forests and fourteen feet of annual snowfall. Outdoor tourism provides seasonal jobs and significant income to the county. But when those visitors leave, permanent residents are left scrambling to make ends meet between seasons. Rupert wants more for himself and his neighbors than an annual struggle to pay the bills.

"*That's* why I was for the new mine," Rupert continued, shrugging. Between 2012 and 2014, Rupert lobbied his political representatives, argued with journalists, and regularly spoke at public meetings hosted by Wisconsin's Departments of Environmental Protection and Natural Resources in favor of a four-mile-long strip mine proposed by a corporate conglomerate based in Florida. In a rural county whose motto is still "live li*Fe*"—emphasis on the chemical abbreviation for iron—this proposed iron mine was met with enthusiasm. "I wasn't going to gain from it—I'm sixty-seven years old!" Rupert exclaimed. "But I look at the community, I look at the young people losing out. I wanted good jobs for our people here. I was for it for freedom for our people here. If a family has a good job, that's freedom—they can educate their kids, they can go on their vacations." He paused with a frown, working out the right words to respond to a frequent debate he would have with opponents at public meetings. "They're going to have to work hard. . . . Like I told all these politicians and all these writers—we're not looking for handouts here. All we want is a good job." Iron Countians are weary of economic struggles, of losing their working-age youth to faraway cities, and of feeling geographically invisible in these remote forests. With a sigh, Rupert gathered himself to leave for his own delayed dinner at the Nugget. With his heavy coat half-pulled onto his shoulders, he concluded with a tired smile, "It's a great place to live but a hard place to make a living. But," he continued, "I tell you something. I wouldn't move from here."

Across popular culture and scholarly literature from social psychology, economic development, and environmental change, there's a common assumption that *stability* is required for a person to feel at home or be attached to a place or community. Home needs contextual familiarity, it's argued—a recognizable physical location, a social collective built through regularized interactions or at least an element of predictability.[6] Crisis erodes this stability, either through the displacement and dispersion of a place's people or the physical degradation of neighborhoods, landscapes, and social institutions. The deindustrialization of communities that were literally constructed around a single industry was one such crisis.

The mid- to late-twentieth-century mass industrial closures upended locals' taken-for-granted sense of home, belonging, and security. From New York to Minnesota, towns and cities that grew up around industries that extracted iron and manufactured steel suddenly lost the core of their blue-collar employment. This Rust Belt region has experienced five decades of Great Depression-scale unemployment—an entire generation troubled by double-digit losses akin to those that devastated the United States only briefly in the 1930s. In the wake of these industrial closures, hundreds of thousands of unemployed people packed up their houses and sought their fortunes elsewhere—in the American south and west or anywhere far away from the sucking vortex of economic depression and the ghostly remnants of their postindustrial regions. Public writers and academic researchers have since suggested that without the smoke of the mills, the creak of mine shaft elevators, and the perpetual wages of multiple generations of industrial work, deindustrialized places lost their grip on their people and their place in the American story.[7]

And yet.

And yet for people like Jesús, Marcos, Rupert, and thousands of others who did not leave Iron County, Southeast Chicago, or similarly deindustrialized places, home remains. Not merely an idea or moment frozen in time, home is *here*: a physical place and social world layered with complicated residues of boom and bust. And here, without stability and within significant economic, social, and environmental constraints, home is being reshaped by people who stayed. On landscapes still punctuated by the solidity of ore walls or the sheer remoteness of rural villages, the people who have become long-term residents not only survived higher-than-average rates of poverty, joblessness, and economic depression but also, through their prolonged presence and many small decisions, they have pursued a good life. Marcos ran for local government; Jesús built an art studio; and Rupert joined a local citizens' board to advise the county on economic development projects.

This book defines the capacious but powerful concept of home using interview, ethnographic, and historical data from two sites of economic transformation in the American Midwest. Deindustrialized communities, like Southeast Chicago and Iron County, are exemplary microcosms within which to probe narratives of American progress, loss, disenfranchisement, and resilience. Across the two urban and rural communities central to this book, I ask three entangled questions: How is a place organized into a cohesive site of home? Why do people make the seemingly inexplicable decision to stay after the processes that created home have devolved into crisis? And how does the continued presence of long-term residents interact with past vestiges and future possibilities of home?

Scaffolding these specific questions is a pervasive and deeply sociological puzzle: How is home socially constructed in a world characterized more by economic and environmental transformation than stability? After all, home persists not only on landscapes wracked by economic crisis but also sites of environmental and social upheaval—on islands quickly disappearing beneath rising waters, adjacent to hazardous waste sites, straddling fire lines, bridging tectonic plates, lodged between warring factions, and hidden within nuclear fallout zones. So while common sense suggests that home needs stability, it is clear that home is nonetheless malleable, responsive to the realities of living life in a changing world and constantly being reshaped by the people who lay claim on it. While crisis undermines institutional structures that enable social thriving in certain places, it also creates space within which long-term residents reimagine their priorities, actions, and stories about what home can be. Home is both a physically specific place, comprising material and cultural signifiers that are tied to that location, *and* a fluid source of identity for individuals and their social groups. Questions of "who we are" are always tangled up with questions of "where we are."

To theorize how home is constructed and reimagined over space and time, this book builds a malleable definition of home through the case of boom and bust. By attending to how home was historically constructed, why and how people stayed after the companies closed, and how long-term residents navigate the residues of the original industrial organization of home today, I offer a definition of home as comprised of three components: geography, community, and economy. These three categories—which I will define shortly—illuminate material and cultural resources that residents leverage to make sense of what home means and how it changes over time. Over the next six chapters, I demonstrate the utility of this definition of home through analysis of detailed life stories, close reads of archival documents, and time spent on the ground with residents in their communities.

This introduction places my study in conversation with other public and scholarly thinkers concerned with home, place, identity, and social change. In the next section, I consider how boom and bust help us understand the social construction of home and define the tripartite conceptualization that I derived from my data. Then, I introduce my cases and explain how my qualitative methodology and study design are key to answering the questions motivating this project.

HOME IN CRISIS, HOME AS TRANSFORMATION

Americans have a fascination with the transience of home. From settler-colonist narratives of westward expansion to Great Depression journeys to recent enthusiasm for untapped gas in the West, centuries of essays, movies, memoirs, and novels celebrate the promise and sacrifice of pulling up roots in pursuit of wealth. On the dark side of boom, declining action follows heartsick workers and disappointed entrepreneurs as they disentangle themselves from a dying place and strike out for the next opportunity.

Both common understanding and scholarly research on these landscape-scale crises often presume either the rationality of residential mobility or emphasize the cultural tragedies awaiting those who stay in their dying home.[8] Without jobs, the first argument goes, the most resilient people uproot and flee beyond the reach of economic crisis. When considered purely from an economic perspective, physical distance from hubs of financial crisis is correlated with job seekers attaining better earning opportunities. In 1979, the poverty scholar John Kenneth Galbraith declared that "migration . . . is the oldest action against poverty. . . . What is the perversity in the human soul that causes people to resist so obvious a good?"[9] James Fallows, a journalist writing in an 1985 issue of the *Atlantic*, inadvertently echoed this sociological claim by praising the "proud steelworker who gets laid off in Youngtown" and who, like the generations of people unemployed by the Great Depression before him, took to the road in response to "today's changing economy."[10] Even today, migration and labor researchers consistently find that residential mobility leads to better economic and educational outcomes for both migrants and the people back home they financially support.[11] The data support a commonsense argument: since staying in a geography of "bust" will suffocate their potential, resilient people should seek their fortunes far from home.[12]

But for every jobseeker who chased the economic boom away from deindustrialization in the American industrial corridor, someone stayed.[13] A second prevalent story about company closures focuses on cultural and economic tragedies faced by those "left behind."[14] "As markets and capital go global," the sociologist Thomas Gieryn mused, "rusted steel mills and ghostly impoverished towns stay behind."[15] Certainly the flight of capital away from places utterly transformed them. Across the United States, the "systematic disinvestment in the nation's basic productive capacity," as the political economists Barry Bluestone and Bennett Harrison described deindustrialization, directly caused crumbled infrastructures, persistent poverty, and relentless unemployment in cities and towns stripped of their central industries.[16] Given these challenging circumstances, observers wonder if people living in post-industrial contexts resisted outmigration because limited opportunity structures were holding them hostage. Few jobs, withering social networks, and declining educational opportunities might structurally trap people in tough circumstances.[17] Other scholars suggest cultural reasons for residential immobility—collective trauma or sluggish cultural scripts that are propelling self-defeating political choices or freezing people in place and in time.[18]

These two interpretive lenses about boom and bust tell true—but partial—stories about transforming places and their people. The first, which focuses on the wins of mobility, overlooks remnant populations. Very few places in the world are truly ghost towns devoid of people. And where there are people, social science must attempt to make sense of their experiences. The second lens, which draws attention on the accrued losses of residential stability, tempts scholars to propose solutions that reek of structural or cultural determinism. Scholars concerned with the disintegration of the structures of daily life (infrastructures, employment relations, or policy-making practices) tend to call for a complete overhaul of social institutions through aggressive gentrification,[19] while researchers focused on culture not-so-subtly suggest that there are places in America that should be canceled because local morale has soured into racialized populism or out-of-touch nostalgia.[20] These arguments not only discount the individual and collective choices made by those who stay but also impoverish observers' understanding of how or why remnant populations negotiate structural constraints, like geographic disconnection or lack of economic opportunity. In short, by attending only to the benefits of leaving or the problems with staying, we lose track of home: what it is beyond a vague notion of white picket fences, how people make choices and understand trade-offs within its material structure, and how people's experiences and expectations of the past and future transform in the face of crisis. If we fail to understand how home is constructed and reimagined, we—as researchers, social scientists, and citizens of a changing world—cannot speak to what is lost when economies shatter or environments rebel.

To theorize home throughout this book, I pull from academic and popular literatures that discuss the meanings and materiality of place, belonging, culture, and structure in a constantly changing world. Geographers like Doreen Massey and David Harvey argue that what a place means often becomes *more* powerful in the face of globalization because residents and community leaders are spurred to define what makes their places special.[21] Historians and rural sociologists establish how, in resistance to exploitation or in reaction to disaster, remnant populations collectively build creative strategies of informal work, find clever land tenure loopholes, and develop mutual aid networks to make functional a home in crisis.[22] I join microsociology and place attachment discussions on how crisis or disaster intensifies people's sense of belonging and affection for that place.[23] These literatures show that the longer that residents live in a place, the more they are attached to that place.[24] Crisis or disaster might upend certain taken-for-granted structures, but loss may also create space for people to leverage place-specific resources and create coherent sets of action and story in the face of threat. Lacking status quo explanations or self-evident rationales, long-term residents have to actively articulate their motivation to stay.[25] Depending on the context, these motivations range from maintaining stability for families or children; adhering to familiar gender, class, or racial scripts; retaining financial investment in property;[26] or simply liking where they live.[27]

These academic ideas catalog what many of us already know from personal experience. For decades, public thinkers have offered language that captures the tangled meanings of home, place, identity, and loss. For instance, the mid-twentieth-century writer Wallace Stegner observed that most Americans seemed to live in one of two camps—either they were "boomers" primed for frontier life, anxious to make a profit, and willing to "pillage and ruin" a place before moving on or "stickers" who "settle, and love the life they have made and the place they have made it in." One of Stegner's students, the poet and essayist Wendell Berry, mused that as a "sticker," his continued presence on his multigenerational farm in Kentucky derived from how tied up his identity was with that place. "Because I have never separated myself from my home neighborhood, I cannot identify myself to myself apart from it. . . . It is present in me, and to me, wherever I go."[28] The writer Terry Tempest Williams's complicated love of her Utah home located downwind of nuclear testing sites counters common assumptions that purely positive attachment to place is required for a place to shape a person's sense of self.[29] And in her memoir reflecting on the ebbs and flows of home's claim on her, the social theorist bell hooks draws attention to the quiet strategies of survival, resistance, and reimagined meaning leveraged by out-migrants and returnees.[30] Such diverse literatures offer new ways of thinking about home in crisis. When brought to bear on two community studies in the American Midwest, these concepts frame my questions about how—and by whom—home was built, eroded, and reimagined.

TOWARD A SOCIOLOGY OF HOME

Propelled by data from my two cases, this book synthesizes perspectives on place and belonging and builds a typology of home. I use narratives from long-term residents in urban and rural communities alongside on-the-ground observations of community life and archival data tracking environmental and social histories to explore how home was constructed, what characteristics of home are threatened in disaster, crisis, and movement, and how residents' choices redefine home in the face of situational constraints. Across this book, I build a flexible definition of home that captures three categories of persistent material and cultural resources: geography, community, and economy. There is certainly overlap and blurring of boundaries between these three; however, distinguishing and naming these themes establishes a much-needed vocabulary for discussing *what* about home is lost, retained, or renegotiated during large-scale crises.

First, home is *geography*—by this I mean a place's material resources and connection to other places. Neither an aspatial idea (home is "where the heart is") nor a generic and interchangeable place, home is meaningful because of its physical specificity.[31] Home is a tangible place "to which one withdraws and from which one ventures forth," as the geographer Yi-Fu Tuan mused.[32] As the first and final chapters of this book show, these geographic components accrete over time and calcify physical boundaries, institutional connections, and collective identities. Geography is what makes home *here*, not *there*.

Second, when people talk about home, they're signaling a sense of belonging to *community*. Individual identity is embedded in some geographically located, collective social world. Put simply, home is often a place where we know who we belong to—be they family, community, workmates, employers, or friends.[33] At the same time, community is more than sentiment; social life takes place in material ways and comprises political or commercial institutions, infrastructure such as housing and roadways, and policies that regulate and organize interactions between people.[34] As cued by Marcos, Jesús, and Rupert in the opening vignettes, historically, both the ideas and material practices of community in Southeast Chicago and Iron County were organized by outside forces. The first half of this book discusses how industrial companies played a core role in managing conflicts, creating racial and gendered hierarchies through policies and infrastructures, and providing context for nonemployment social relations.[35]

Finally, home is always tangled up with the *economic* practicalities of everyday life, like paying a mortgage and making ends meet. Seemingly, they are simply material relations between people and places, ranging from the interconnections of commodity chains to the links between firms and their workers' wages. At the same time, work means something beyond profits—it's a way to be human, express creativity, and belong to a collectively valued "middle class."[36] Whether perceived as monochromatically material or tangled up with identity, economics roots people to place. Each chapter discusses how the presence and absence of economic opportunity shapes how people talk about home.

These three components of home map onto real-world cases in myriad and conflicting ways, dependent on historical moments and macroscale structures. As chapter 1 will demonstrate, industrial organizations organized and inscribed the sole purpose of the places and people of early-twentieth-century Southeast Chicago and Iron County, Wisconsin. In these extreme cases of cultural construction, iron and steel companies exercised remarkable control over the norms of collective behavior, axes of conflicts, experiences of economic thriving, and the distribution of material or political resources. Chapters 2 through 6 articulate how and why, even after the disintegration of these institutions, the earliest definitions of where, when, and for whom home exists are sticky. The very real, material legacies of industrial pasts constrain how contemporary residents of my two cases traverse their landscapes, negotiate social relationships, and make ends meet. Continuing to live in their deindustrialized geographies requires intentionality and choice, as residents daily navigate remnants of structural and cultural pasts created generations ago for long-defunct purposes and very different interests. Yet in the final chapters of the book, we will see that while historical structures matter, over time, their meanings and imprints on specific places are negotiable. Within the space created by the crisis of deindustrialization, residents leveraged what remained of geography, community, and economy to collectively reimagine their priorities, actions, and identities.

This book demonstrates how definitions of home are simultaneously durable and fluid, structured and yet negotiable across time, crisis, and context. By breaking home down into these three elements, it becomes evident not only how powerful actors constructed home in the image of industry but also why and how people who became long-term residents worked hard to reorganize those components in the wake of crisis. Through story and strategic choice, postindustrial community members offer new motivations for their residential persistence grounded in reinterpretations of their home's landscapes, social relations, or economic opportunities. Whether propelled by internalized values, declared in rebellion to institutional failures, or pursued as the only viable option, choices to stay in the troubled *here* of a home in transition energize new transformations of that place. Grappling with changing meanings of the *who* and *where* of home enables new insights into how history and choice collide to shape economic and environmental futures for entire regions.

STUDY DESIGN AND RESEARCH METHODS

The Logic of Incorporated Comparison

The two cases core to my study—Iron County, Wisconsin, and Southeast Chicago, Illinois—could certainly be studied separately.

Both are complex and capture spatially distinct parts of the national story of boom and bust (see figure 0.1). Why consider the two together? What insights can be gained from comparing two locations? Quite simply, I study two ends of a defunct commodity chain because place matters. Most other studies of deindustrialization or other crises impacting peoples' homes quietly assume that the resources, contexts, and demographic orientation of rural *or* urban locations are integral to people's feelings of belonging or choice.[37] Throughout this book I emphasize how the geographic position of a community along the rural-urban spectrum shapes the stories that long-term residents tell and the material resources available to them in the long aftermath of crisis. Bounding one study geographically, temporarily, or

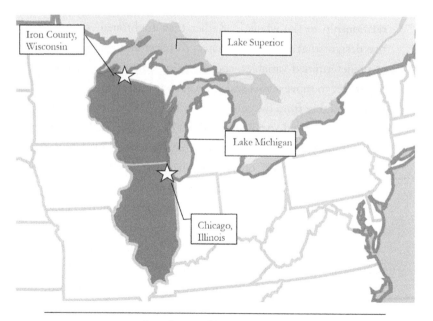

FIGURE 0.1 Iron County, Chicago, and the Great Lakes.

Source: OpenStreetMap, edited by author

methodologically hinders the analytical capacity of these studies. For instance, often data interpretation from single case studies involves comparing findings to cases from other locations. Similarities that stand out, particularly in cases of deindustrialization, tend to be themes of economic loss and out-migration. While, in my study, economic crisis was certainly common to my two cases, cross-case comparison enables me to ask deeper questions about how residents' historical and contemporary responses to such crisis leveraged the benefits of place. Paired cases enable me to explain how *where* people call home shapes identities, choices, and structural possibilities for revitalization.

I build here on what the sociologist Charles Tilly called an *encompassing comparison*—comparisons that "begin with a large structure or process, select locations, and then explain similarities or differences among those locations as consequences of their relationship to the whole."[38] Rather than traditional comparative designs that require researchers to select and contrast a set of predetermined variables, encompassing comparisons allow a researcher to move across scale, space, and time to answer questions emerging from the comparison itself. Within development and environmental sociology, Phil McMichael offered a pragmatic application of this approach that he termed *incorporated comparison*—a method of analysis that gives "substance to a historical process (a whole) through comparison of its parts."[39] I seized the opportunity to use these integrated approaches to comparison to merge community studies—in-depth analyses of on-the-ground social relations within a geographically specific region—with commodity chain analysis—a meso-scale accounting of the processes and interconnections required to transform raw materials into marketable final products.[40] Studying two communities five hundred miles apart but incorporated into the same process illuminates how people constitute home in light of very different social relations, geographic contexts, and economic and material resources.[41]

The cases central to my study share certain characteristics in part *because* of their historical integration into the same economic process, timeframes for community development, and geographically interconnected industrial flows. Shared analysis makes sense because these places are integrated into the same economic and environmental history, as William Cronon discusses in his analysis of Chicago's ecological past. If "city and country have a common history," Cronon proposed, "their stories are best told together."[42] Even with their obvious contradictions in population densities, scales of remoteness, land use needs, and presence in popular imagination, rural and urban should be considered part of "community in its broadest sense," as the environmental sociologist Michael Bell suggests.[43] The interconnections, linkages, flows, and movement within the same economic process might contribute to similarities or differences across geography and community. Through comparative research design, I ask new questions about how, exactly, economies and environments have been intertwined across those blurry lines of individual and macroscale, past and present, or wilderness and metropolis. Tracking the conditions in which people with different levels of geographic, social, and economic resources make ends meet and make meaning allows me to identify the causes and consequences of remaking home in the American Rust Belt.

Case Description

In 2015, I saw a map webbed with economy, community, and geography. With only the barest state or county boundaries visible, this 1940s map—"The Last of the Free Seas"—was alive with lines marking railways, roads, and trade routes for massive Great Lakes freighters that entangled rural extractive sites with urban markets for grain and steel (see figure 0.2). While most iron flowed from Minnesota, a small but strong line linked the northern half of Iron County, Wisconsin, to steel docks located in the southeastern corner of the city of Chicago. This map catalyzed my imagination of how home could be connected and compared across space and time. In both locations, *here* depended on *there*. An iron mining community deep in the Upper Midwest's forests only functioned because of the demand of urban steel mills and the material, economic, and cultural scaffolding that enabled their connection. Their dissolution, then, would also be integrated. And indeed, when deindustrialization hit the Midwest—Iron County's mines closed in the 1960s, some twenty years before steel mills shut down in Chicago—the processes that had instigated the construction of home unraveled. But even in a place that with every passing decade looked less and less like its origin story, people remained.

Deindustrialization changed the ways that residents in both locations experienced the geographies of home. As the majority of American iron ore production shifted to open-pit mines in Minnesota and Michigan in the late twentieth century, Iron County became even more remote (see figure 0.3). Railroad companies pulled up their underutilized tracks and the county's population shrank by 40 percent. In Southeast Chicago, closure escalated infrastructural declines as city bus routes were reduced, promised expansions of regional light rail lines never came to pass, and the Illinois-Indiana Skyway toll road was built to lift drivers over the least densely populated residential ward in the city.[44] From the shores of Lake Michigan in Southeast Chicago, an observer looking north can see the downtown skyline fifteen miles away, and to the east, the smokestacks of the last remaining

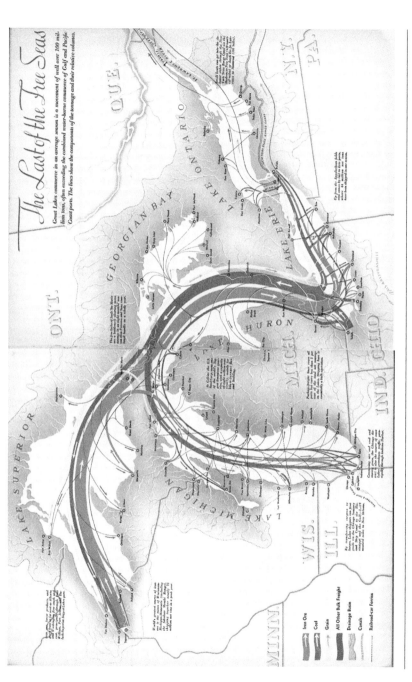

FIGURE 0.2 "The Last of the Free Seas," by Boris Artzybasheff, published in *Fortune* magazine in July 1940.

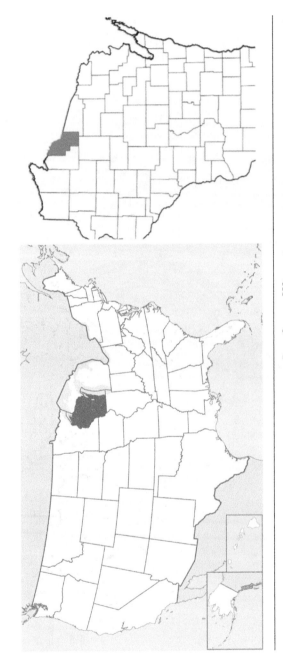

FIGURE 0.3 Iron County, Wisconsin.

Source: Rcsprintcr123, Creative Commons Attribution 3.0. OpenStreetMap, edited by author.

steel mill in Gary, Indiana (see figure 0.4). What this geographic remoteness means for both cases is contingent on other material resources endemic to rural and urban locations—resources I explain later in this book. Yet even with such dramatic shifts of fates, both communities still claim remnant populations—the people who came to be the basis for this study. Based on demographic, employment, and homeownership data, I estimate that at least one third of people living in both sites are long-term residents, and they composed the majority of my interviewees.

For all these similarities, the social and physical contexts of Southeast Chicago and Iron County are different in several important ways. Today, Iron County is, by all measures, much more sparsely populated, demographically homogenous, and geographically remote than its urban cousin. A third of the county's population of six thousand lives in two towns once central to the iron industry—fifteen hundred live in the county seat of Hurley, and eight hundred live two miles down the road in the former mining company town of Montreal. The remainder of the population lives in unincorporated villages either clustered around picturesque lakes or scattered along the abandoned iron deposit. In between towns, there is ample space to spread out—more than 90 percent of Iron County's land is forested and, when calculated per capita, each permanent resident of the county can claim their own thirty-seven acres of publicly accessible forest land.[45] In contrast, Southeast Chicago's twenty-five square miles are home to ten times more people. While Southeast Chicago's millgate neighborhoods do host one of the largest proportions of parkland in the city, they are also rimmed by waste deposit sites and warehouses. Three-quarters of the region remains zoned for industrial uses, including the Calumet River, which flows with waste from both defunct and active industrial projects. Contemporary industries provide some employment,

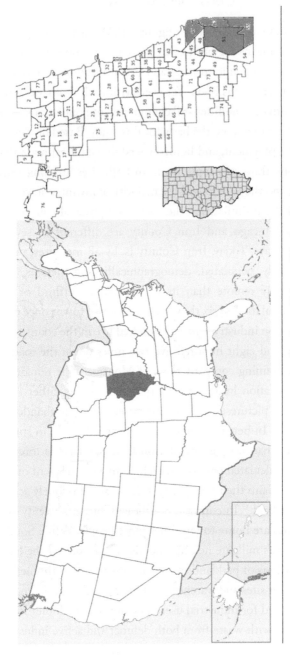

FIGURE 0.4 Southeast Chicago, Illinois.

Source: Creative Commons Attribution 3.0. OpenStreetMap, edited by author.

but these jobs are hazardous to environmental and human health and fail to replace the middle-class wages that fueled this blue-collar community for generations.

Who lives in these postindustrial communities differs across cases as well. While the average Iron Countian is a fifty-five-year-old white ethnic (second- or third-generation descendant from European immigrants), a Southeast Chicagoan walking down Commercial Avenue is more likely be a thirty-five-year-old African American or Latino resident.[46] As one of the largest metropolitan areas in the United States, Chicago attracts and retains more young people than Iron County. In fact, since the 1990s, only 43 percent of young people born in Iron County stay there to adulthood and only half of the population is within the federal category of "working age" of fifteen to sixty-five.[47] Across the arc of the book, readers will see how these demographic and geographical contrasts interact with macroeconomic changes to shape long-term residents' perceptions of the past, strategies for the present, and visions for the future of their home.

METHODS

Using archival and contemporary records, ethnography, and 120 interviews, I braid together these two ends of the steel manu-facturing commodity chain into one story. I pulled local and regional histories from tidy neighborhood historical societ-ies and dusty shelves in locals' houses to learn more about how the economic boom and bust of Iron County and Southeast Chicago was enacted and explained by residents and on-the-ground observers in the nineteenth and twentieth centuries. I read autobiographies by iron miners and oral histories of steel-workers gathered by a high school history class in Southeast

Chicago in the early 2000s. Over multiple visits during three years—2015–2017—I conducted a "patchwork ethnography."[48] I attended meetings for retired steelworkers in Chicago and high school reunions in Wisconsin; I asked locals to show me important documents in economic development offices and historical museums; I rode along with interviewees in their cars and climbed over rubble with them on foot. Through these visits, I observed how geographically located were people's stories, memories, and diagnoses of problems.

But the interviews with people who lived through the boom and bust are what propel this book's argument. I conducted sixty interviews in each community, each following an approximation of the same set of questions about their residential histories and connections to place and industry. I prioritized interviewing long-term residents but also spoke with neighbors who were visiting local family or celebrating community events, regional political leaders, and volunteers and activists for nonprofit organizations. Some interviews were brief, and others were half-day experiences involving photos and field trips. I triangulate interviewee narratives with historical sources, ethnographic observations, and regional, economic histories.

I go into more detail on the choices I made as I gathered and analyzed my data in appendix A. Before transitioning to the chapters based on primary data, however, I want to discuss two components of my methodology that inform how a reader may understand this book—how I interpreted my data as story and how the process of data gathering iteratively refined my research questions.

First, I anchor this book in interviewees' interpretations of historical events and their perceptions of those events' implications for the structures and cultures of home today. In some chapters, interviewees wrestle with choices they made within the limits of deindustrialization; in others, interviewees make sense of boom, bust, and their place in it all. These stories are not just nostalgia—too many books about postindustrial places or other lost homes too easily gloss over local narratives about the past as backward-looking longing for something impossible to recreate. Rather, these narrative accounts emerge from the negotiation between everyday actions and stories speakers offer to explain those actions to themselves and other people.[49] In Southeast Chicago and Iron County, my interviewees talk about the past to name how the past still matters. Historic institutions created the geographies, communities, and economies of home and the disordering, and subsequent revaluing, of those three components of place limit and enable certain possibilities for the future. A close listen to these accounts also points to how interviewees are doing the work of sense-making to make home a more livable place today. Leveraging their long histories in place, residents diagnose problems and propose new ways of shaping their home communities into thriving places that ground individual and collective identities, inspire economic problem-solving, and cultivate new categories of community attachment.

Second, qualitative research produces its own questions. I began this study motivated to understand how collective identity collided with the long-term economic reverberations of deindustrialization. However, interacting with people in these two cases changed the tenor and range of questions I asked in the field. My first weeks in Iron County called forth puzzles of thriving and social well-being in a place that by all measures is one of the most economically bereft in the Midwest. And yet, while residents experience one of the highest poverty rates in Wisconsin, I watched them bid hundreds of dollars on the blue-ribbon peach pie at the annual County Fair 4-H fundraiser. As a beaming twelve-year-old walked her pie to her benefactor, the director of the county 4-H program leaned over to whisper in my ear, 'They have so little money but so much love.' Tight social networks signaled to me how community life might persist even without economic thriving. Locals' material generosity, in turn, highlighted the potential morality of money put into service for a larger purpose.

Economic crisis was likewise only part of the story in Southeast Chicago. Following up on an invitation from a former steelworker, I was stunned by the number of people attending the retired steelworkers' union meeting. Nearly sixty men and women warmly embraced each other before turning with a respectful hush as a tiny, elderly, and indomitable woman commandeered the stage to call for volunteers to protest at city hall on behalf of ununionized service workers at a local coffee shop. Someone across the table whispered the story of Bea Lumpkin, age one hundred—a force to be reckoned with during the steel mill days, in tandem with her husband Frank, a labor leader at Wisconsin Steel. Decades after steel mills disappeared, Bea still rallied her neighbors' spirits and called them toward a better future for all working-class folks in Chicago. These on-the-ground experiences challenged my presuppositions about the dominance of economic loss in collective stories and identities. I began asking new questions about what, precisely, was built during the industrial boom, what was lost during deindustrialization, and—most vitally—what remains at home today.

ORGANIZATION OF THE BOOK

This book chronologically and thematically explores the processes and people involved in constructing, questioning, and reimagining home in the long aftermath of macroeconomic crisis.

I organized the book into three parts—chapters 1 and 2 discuss the arc from boom to bust; chapters 3 and 4 analyze pragmatic strategies for employment and narratives of agency and attachment in the early years of residential persistence; and chapters 5 and 6 weigh the parallel options dominating debates about economic redevelopment in Iron County and Southeast Chicago. I structure comparison into my chapter organization. Chapters 1 through 4 contrast rural and urban cases across common questions and themes, while in chapters 5 and 6 I consider the two locations separately to pinpoint how geographic residues of the past define possible community and economic futures. Across all chapters, I trace how interviewees identify, reorganize, rationalize, and repair the triad of home—geography, community, and economy.

Chapter 1 discusses the formation of home under the control of late-nineteenth-century industrial capitalism. Interviewee accounts of the origins of their communities echoed what I read in local archives—their communities exist today because, over the course of a century, powerful institutions brought economic processes to specific geographic locations through the intentional organization of social and economic relations. Chapter 2 integrates economic history with interviewee lived experiences to demonstrate how residents interpreted the structural collapse of home-creating institutions and processes. Chapters 3 and 4 shift the timeline to the three decades following company closures. These chapters probe how and why people made the seemingly inexplicable decision to stay in places wracked by crisis. Chapter 3 traces three common strategies that residents used to make ends meet across both cases—informal labor, commuting, and retraining. These employment practices relied on social ties established during the height of iron and steel and ultimately resulted in residents' prioritizing their location at home over higher incomes elsewhere. Chapter 4 explores residents' stories of attachment to housing, neighborly and familial relationships, and familiar landscapes. When reflecting on why they resisted moving away from their postindustrial community, interviewees emphasized how their symbolic investments in place increased their tolerance for the topsy-turvy chaos of postindustrial geographies, communities, and economies.

The final two chapters bring the story up to date. These chapters unpack how and why political relationships, economic structures, and geographic contexts create similar opportunities for redevelopment across these two otherwise contrasting deindustrialized communities. In both locations, residents are seeking economic fixes rooted in local geographies that honor their relationships to place and community. In turn, this view of home shapes how both economic opportunities and environmental risks are perceived by residents. Iron County locals (see chapter 5) embrace the proposed return to an industrial past in part because it aligns with their collective environmental philosophy that nature is a resource to be *used*. At the same time, residents support well-established, nature-based tourism as a form of economic stimulation. In contrast, homegrown activists in Southeast Chicago (see chapter 6) fiercely resist reindustrialization due to the tight integration of millgate neighborhoods and the highly polluting new factories and waste depositories being sited on former steel mill properties. Some residents and policymakers offer park development as a means to create more environmental goods for residents. Ending with contemporary debates over land use demonstrates the tensions between the persistence of historical structures and the flexibility of home.

Home contains multitudes. It is the site of conflicting economic options, constraining physical vestiges of the past, and complex ideas of self and community. From opposite ends of a commodity chain and spanning more than a century, this book shows how people who have lived in hard places for a long time square the material realities of their postindustrial landscapes with the physical and cultural needs for a vibrant life together. To identify what possible futures might be regained, remade, or reimagined by those people who stay long after the ashfall of crisis has settled, we need to understand how—and by whom—home was originally constructed. As a capital-laden and physical process of domination, iron and steel shaped both landscapes and identities in Southeast Chicago and Iron County in lasting ways. The geography-shaping power of capital preserved otherwise unseen priorities: massive walls, brownfields, four miles of lakefront unused, houses, place names, and empty fields. Today, practical attempts to reimagine these places collide with legacies of industrial collapse—pollution, disinvestment, remoteness.

Yet the presence of the past is not merely a constraint. People who still call Iron County and Southeast Chicago home have spent decades making sense of their options and environments after their home's economic raison d'être moved on without them. Many admit that there's something about these places that both ties them down and enables them to thrive. Across the six chapters of this book, I speak to how collective and individual choices redefine home in the face of the ever-changing physicality of geographies, ebbs and flows of social relations, and experiences of economic experience.

1

CAPITALISM MAKES PLACE

Constructing an Industrial Home

Prophecy now involves a geographical rather than historical dimension; we should now talk of people making not their own history but their own geography.

—John Urry, "Social Relations, Space and Time, 1985"

"The only reason you have from Mellen, Wisconsin, to Wakefield, Michigan,"—Rupert punched the air at every word—"is what's below our feet."[1] His booming voice caught curious glances from passersby, who peered into the cavernous main room of the Iron County Historical Society, where we were meeting. Flushing with embarrassment, he silently gestured toward a large map on the wall. Rupert traced the diagonal line of the Gogebic Iron Range, which cuts through the dense forests of the northern half of the county, murmuring the names of a string of villages: Upson, Iron Belt, Hoyt, Pence, Montreal, Gile, and Hurley. Shallowly buried beneath these clusters of houses and into the Upper Peninsula of Michigan is eighty miles of high-quality iron ore.[2] In the nineteenth and twentieth centuries, this ore directly caused high wages, vibrant small businesses, and, for Rupert and many of his neighbors, a good life marked by few material wants. By 1950, the six iron ranges bordering Lake Superior, including the Gogebic, provided 80 percent of hematite iron ore bought in the United States.[3] Rupert tipped his chair back to lean against a shelf overflowing with scrapbooks of hand-clipped newspaper stories about the mining boom and bust, boxes of photographs organized by year, and bound monographs containing data about forests and iron ore. He smiled at me wryly. "Believe me, I'll brag the mines up to the end because I know how good they were for the area!"

Since every interview and historical narrative began with the construction of home by iron and steel companies, so thus begins this book. Over the course of a century of "boom," powerful representatives of industrial firms interconnected raw extractive geographies with metropolitan manufacturing hubs, built the physical infrastructures comprising laborers' communities, and linked local economic thriving to a single industry's continued success. Archival documents show how, from the organization of residential neighborhoods and the performance of wealth to the structure of family life and nature of social conflict, industrial firms in Southeast Chicago and Iron County literally created home through their management of local geographies, communal social life, and experiences of economic thriving. Such overlapping practices of capitalistic placemaking created not just workers but *worker-citizens*—laborers whose experiences of both home and employment were entangled in a landscape organized around the interests of capital.

This chapter centers on two themes—first, how powerful actors caused the calcification of durable meanings of home in the late nineteenth and twentieth centuries, and second, how those histories have been memorialized and interpreted by contemporary long-term residents. Home, for worker-citizens and their descendants, reflected industrial companies' power to integrate economic interests and control over workers into geographic landscapes. In the coming pages, I pull apart three intersecting and overlapping components of home—geography, community, and economy. Companies organized *geography* through managing infrastructures and narratives around late-nineteenth-century landscapes, housing, and experiences of place. They then built a tangled, dependent, and idealized *community* to protect capitalist interests. Within these contexts, residents experienced midcentury *economic* resources and statuses that would come to define their expectations for future possibilities long after the companies disappeared. Articulating how home was made in Iron County and Southeast Chicago is required to reveal what exactly was lost—and what remained—when companies began to close in the mid- twentieth century.

GEOGRAPHY: CAPITAL MAKES PLACE, LATE 1800S–EARLY 1900S

In the last decades of the nineteenth century, a group of capitalists exercised what urban planners and architects would today call *placemaking*: they practically and narratively transformed a remote fur-trading post in the forests near Lake Superior and a marshland on the edge of a new metropolis on Lake Michigan's shores into two nodes of a midwestern iron and steel commodity chain.[4] With intention and forethought, industrial entrepreneurs cleared forests, laid tracks, and dredged canals. But they framed this planned industrial boom as the inevitable ending to a predestined story. At the southern end of Lake Michigan, Chicago was the future "London of the west," ripe for rapid development and modern expansion, according to the *Chicago Tribune* in 1872.[5] In 1880, the newspaper editor William Bross declared that "nature . . . selected the site of this great city [Chicago]" because the rivers and Great Lakes allowed rapid settlement and ever-expanding trade with established East Coast cities.[6] Raw materials were needed to enable this growth. Boosters lauded the miraculous timing of the discovery of iron ore in the Ojibwe lands south of Lake Superior—some five hundred miles north of the city. Fortunately for industrial barons in Chicago, these lands were rich with high-quality iron ore, not far from water transportation, and lately and violently wrested from Indigenous peoples.[7] In 1886, the speculator and iron booster John E. Burton declared that ore from Iron County "is worth more to the people than to uncover the hidden gold of Capt. Kidd or to raise the sunken treasure of the Spanish Main."[8] To industrial entrepreneurs, these natural resources were there for the taking and the making of money.

This work of turning a generic "space" into distinctive, meaningful, and—most importantly for industrialists—profitable places created the physical and ideological basis for tens of thousands of peoples' sense of home.[9] In Southeast Chicago and Iron County, Wisconsin, industrial entrepreneurs coordinated with federal troops and local political machines to transform inconvenient topographies, overlay transportation infrastructures on well-established routes of trade historically established by Potawatomi and Ojibwe, and create housing for a new generation of workers.[10] Laborers hired by these powerful people set to work further transforming the land—they pulled ore from the earth, dredged silt from shallow rivers, and hammered spikes for new rail lines. The geographies of the American Upper Midwest evolved into a mutually reinforcing relationship between the physical substances of places and the meanings created to explain those places.

"A Million Tons a Year": Black Gold in Iron County

Walking along the ridge of one of the hills that the Ojibwe called Penokee, a fur trapper noticed his compass spinning.[11] Or maybe it was the logger hauling a chain through an old-growth forest who nonchalantly pocketed a reddish rock wedged in the roots of an uprooted tree. Or was it that geologist hired by the young state of Wisconsin in the 1870s, tasked with combing through the Upper Midwest for metals and mineral deposits to rival the newly discovered ores to the west and east of Lake Superior? Tales of how exactly white settler-colonists discovered iron ore in what would become Iron County vary, but they share a narrative of driven men exploiting the seemingly untapped minerals in the Penokee-Gogebic hills. Ore might have been a natural occurrence, but humans made it a "natural resource."

Steel entrepreneurs who flocked to the Northwoods of Wisconsin to seek their fortunes were, according to one nineteenth-century writer, "flung upon the golden thrones of an international empire of steel."[12] By the end of the 1880s, pursuit of iron ore metamorphosized the old growth forest into a hub for the Midwest's highest-earning railroad, Chicago and Northwestern. In coordination with three other railroad companies, Chicago and Northwestern laid tracks linking the shallow pit mines to the newest marvel of modern engineering—a mile-long extension of freight rail onto a dock into Lake Superior built exclusively for the transfer of iron ore from rail cars onto Great Lake shipping freighters.[13] Those ships brought iron to ports across the Midwest, including Southeast Chicago's industrial docks on the southeastern edge of the Calumet River.

For a mine in these remote woods to make money, capable and organized teams of laborers needed to dig and pack ore onto hundreds of railroad cars that ran routes to Lake Superior's docks nearly twenty-four hours a day, seven days a week. This endless churning of industry called for a rapid influx of laborers and a safe place for them to live. The first problem was relatively easy for companies to solve, as the lure of guaranteed work attracted able-bodied newcomers directly from immigration hubs. An enamored *Chicago Times* journalist observing the Wisconsin iron-ore boom in 1886 marveled, "Hundreds of people are arriving daily from all parts of the country and millionaires are being made by the dozens. The forests have given way to mining camps and towns, and a most bewildering transformation has taken place. . . . [Even in] the palmy days of gold mining . . . there is no record of anything so wonderful as the Gogebic."[14] In the forty years following ore's discovery, the population of the northern half of Iron County exploded from eighty individuals to more than ten thousand.[15]

But with these new arrivals came serious logistical problems. The Northwoods of Wisconsin lacked substantial, preexisting infrastructures and suffered brutally cold and snowy winters. Companies couldn't change the weather, but they could build better houses. Many of Iron County's largest mining companies established paternalistic, cradle-to-grave company towns—a popular nineteenth- and early-twentieth-century managerial approach that involved "providing employees with amenities not required by law or absolutely needed for operations."[16] Paternalistic mining companies in the Northwoods of Iron County typically paid for services like health care and policing and allocated their own land for the physical construction of schools, churches, and company houses. These houses in the northern Iron County region were, according to one late-nineteenth-century miner's reflection, "simple, but warm and dry, and . . . quite an improvement on the usual ones not owned by the company."[17] Supplying decent housing was a good business strategy that enabled companies to not only retain current employees but also poach workers away from other mines that only provided their employees with flimsy, "kindling-wood shacks."[18]

Nearly all rural interviewees directed my attention to the most notable company town in Iron County—the "sweet town of Montreal," as Dottie, eighty-two, put it.[19] In 1907, soon after purchasing the most productive mine in Iron County, Oglebay Norton Company imported fifty precut bungalows to a deforested field within a half mile of the mine shaft.[20] The little white houses were quaint and sturdy, with ample space for kitchen gardens and low rents that allowed workers to live there for generations (see figure 1.1). Over the next decade, an industrial landscape architect hired by the company designed everything a remote frontier town might need, "from the layout of the streets, to the shape and size of the houses, to the inclusion of a high-class recreation center."[21] By the 1930s, Montreal captured a village feel and function, with schools, markets, and one hundred clapboard houses.[22] In company towns like Montreal, there was no separation between work and home. Miners changed out of their dusty helmets and jackets in the dry house adjacent to the mine entrance, walked home down streets paved with tailings of iron ore, and entered their white frame homes that were repainted, landscaped, and redecorated at company expense every five years.[23] Tenants of company houses were instructed on the direction to plant their vegetable rows and when to let their cows out to graze. Even the company-provided bedsheets provided to miners emphasized the nature of their work: they were gray to minimize the unsightliness of the inevitable red stains from iron ore residue on the miners' skin.[24] Private and public spheres overlapped as miners and their families simultaneously experienced the social roles of employees and citizens of an industrial company.

FIGURE 1.1 Garden plot and typical company-owned bungalow in
Montreal, Wisconsin, c. 1920.

Courtesy of Iron County Historical Society Archives, Hurley, Wisconsin.

Company towns were built within walking distance of the
mines and quite literally on top of the natural resource that
enabled their existence. Worker-citizens and their families
organized everyday life around the routines, sights, and sounds
of their industrial home. In the Historical Society, Gary, fifty-
four, regaled me with stories of happy grade-school years spent
tracking the passage of time according to shift whistles and
train schedules. After school, he'd perch on the hill behind his
house with his little brother and count the hundreds of ore cars
trundling through toward the docks. "The trains ran and ran,
all through the night," he said with a smile. That same historical society is where I stumbled on a poem written by one of

Gary's classmates in 1964, two years after the largest mine closed. A newspaper clipping hand-pasted into a scrapbook preserved Holly Fellman's descriptions of the pulsing sounds, vibrations, and smells of geologic extraction:

> I heard th' thunderin' o' that rock in th'
> Ore cars poundin' down th' tracks,
> Shaking the very ground b'neath me,
> Car after car poundin' and a-poundin'.
>
> I heard th' crashin' o' ore tumblin' down
> Th' ore piles.
> Them big ore piles—like small red volcanoes.
> A million tons a year come out o' them
> Tall headframes
> Twen'y-four hours a day, five days a week,
> Fifty-two weeks a year,
> a hun'erd years.[25]

More than sixty years later, interviewees showed me how even the ghostly imprints of these capital-centric geographies continued to orient their routes across contemporary landscapes. Crossing the road in front of his house, a former miner, Mitchell, ninety-one, showed me the diminished "red volcano" piles of ore tailings, now covered with saplings. He then walked me to an old mine headframe that we could see from his front door—a forty-foot high, A-shaped scaffolding that used to hoist machinery, personnel, or materials into a mine shaft. A few doors down, Dottie pulled her grandson, twenty-eight, off his delivery route to drive me past that red volcano and further into the forest that had reclaimed former mine property. We peered into a cement shed that housed a massive fan that once pulled fresh air into the depths of the mine shafts and then drove up a mountain of mine tailings to visit a long-unrung fire bell perched at its summit.

In this former mining town, everyday life is and was a geographical experience. Because late-nineteenth-century industrial actors organized physical topographies—from transportation networks required to move "natural" resources across space and time to worker housing—to be "at home" meant to touch, hear, and rely on economic success of industrial capitalism. A version of Iron County lived—and would die—within the geographic constraints of the iron industry.

"We Lived the Mill": Southeast Chicago

Five hundred miles south of the crashing and pounding in the Gogebic Range, another group of industrial entrepreneurs transformed rural nineteenth-century geography. In the first of many parallels to the rurality of Iron County, white investors quickly designated the flat marshland newly and forcibly vacated by the Potawatomi for industry. In 1872, Colonel John H. Bowen, the founder of the Calumet and Chicago Canal and Dock Company and a significant landowner in the region, was eager to increase the young city of Chicago's profitability. On a sultry summer day, he took a boatload of local politicians and potential investors on a very slow ride down the winding, sluggish Calumet River, which for centuries had served as an efficient transportation connection between Lake Michigan and inland rivers. As their boat pushed through reeds and startled herons, Bowen offered his passengers a "glowing picture of the day, in the near future, when Lake Superior ore will be brought into the new harbor, and coal from Indiana, and limestone from Stony Island, a short distance away, would bring a large population to his new town to run blast furnaces."[26] Although the river was more than a dozen miles south of the city's downtown, Bowen predicted that the regional flow of materials and people would bring "Chicago . . . down toward Calumet, or Calumet up to Chicago."[27] With more investment, he declared, the Calumet River could play a central role in creating a modern Chicago.

Whether convinced by Bowen or merely reading the economic tides, politicians and private investors financed infrastructures for industrial development on the Southeast Side. In coordination with the Army Corps of Engineers, they widened the river, drained the surrounding marshlands, and constructed a few rudimentary streets.[28] Bowen offered industrial investors cheap plots of land—riverbank properties for mills that needed waterway access and inland lots for worker housing.[29] In 1875, Joseph H. Brown opened the first steel mill at 109th Street and the Calumet River. It eventually became Wisconsin Steel—a small but important mill central to many interviewee narratives. At its peak it employed close to five thousand workers. The North Chicago Rolling Mill was next to open in 1880 and, within fifty years, would be the largest in the region, occupying 576 acres and employing nearly twenty thousand as U.S. Steel's South Works.[30]

Although the new mills in Southeast Chicago were located closer to existing pools of labor than were the Wisconsin mines, the sheer number of laborers required to run the mass production operations in steel mills meant managers still had to import "practically all the laborers necessary to carry on the operations and to start new developments," according to a 1910 report on Chicago steel by the United States Immigration Commission.[31] In the late nineteenth century, company managers promised jobs to workers families and ethnic networks arriving from Italy, Croatia, and Eastern Europe through Ellis and Angel Islands.[32]

Mexican immigrants and African Americans arrived in Chicago in the second decade of the twentieth century, lured by the hope that demands for labor would outstrip any latent managerial resistance to their race or ethnicity. By 1925, the five mills scattered around the mouth of Calumet River and down the coast of Lake Michigan employed seventy-five thousand workers, nearly half of whom were foreign-born.[33]

Like in Iron County, housing all these new arrivals was a pressing problem. Even though the new steel mills were only a dozen miles south of a booming metropolis, when Southeast Chicago was first integrated into the city in 1880, its twenty-five square miles only claimed a few thousand people and a handful of roads and dwellings.[34] To house people working in this rural region's inaugural steel mill, Brown built boardinghouses for single men within walking distance of the mill. The next three mills to open in Southeast Chicago also either constructed cheap housing for rent or set aside land on which workers might build their own small houses. By the late 1880s, these settlements developed into four "millgate" communities, each with its own distinct character and all displaying variations of company beneficence and material provisions. Workers at Brown's mill not only rented his rooms but also bought food on credit at his company store, attended churches warmed by coal donated by his company, and walked on paved roads crisscrossing the neighborhood Brown dubbed "Irondale."[35] Over the next few decades, other steel managers funded Christmas parties; subsidized fuel for their employees and their growing numbers of ethnically distinctive churches, schools, and clubs; and established livestock grazing lands.[36] During the Great Depression, Brown's successor, Wisconsin Steel, provided two thousand employees with access to quarter-acre garden plots, seed kits, and fertilizer to supplement their dietary needs.[37]

While steel companies' paternalism was never as intensive as mining firms' management of housing and benefits in Iron County, the steel economy remained the regions' centripetal force.[38] In the 1950s, an advertisement for the Chicago steel industry declared that once "the spark of the steel industry was kindled, it magnified itself into the open-hearth furnaces and roaring Bessemer converters which at night set a torch to the skies for miles around—a symbol of the industrial center that the community's early founders had hoped and planned for."[39] Even as steelworkers purchased their own houses and relied less and less on their employers for food, fuel, and urban infrastructures, community life remained routinized around these geographies of steel—the roar of furnaces, bells signaling changes of shifts, booms from passing trains, and horns alerting foremen of the arrival of boats laden with ore, lime, coke, and coal. As a child, Jesús and his mother would time their walks to local shops around the flows of hundreds of cars in and out of the parking lot at U.S. Steel South Works, rotating based on shifts. He would wake at dawn with the clangs and bells of raw material deliveries arriving via Lake Michigan. To Jesús, these sounds represented the centrality of steel to their family's life. "I remember my father, when he would hear the ore boats in the [dock], he would always say, '*That's* the sound of money.' We lived the mill. I mean, everything that we did . . . was based around what happened to the steel mills."[40]

Home is first and foremost a geographic place—a landscape that produces physical boundaries, institutional connections, and collective identities. Environmental histories matter because they create paths of durable meaning for those who navigate those geographies today. William Cronon, in his chronology of early Chicago, argued, "By using the landscape, giving names to it, and calling it home people selected the features that mattered most to them, and drew their mental maps accordingly. Once they had labeled those maps in a particular way . . . natural and cultural landscapes began to shade into and reshape one another."[41] But not all people hold the same level of power to do this landscape naming. Geology might have directed the siting of mine communities in Wisconsin, and rivers cued the location of Chicago's steel mills, but companies in both cases exercised extreme control over the practices and stories that made these places *industrial.* Top-down management of geography organized economic relationships between places and solved practical problems such as worker housing in ways that structured daily life and persistent place meanings for worker-citizens. Bosses in Iron County leveraged their geographic remoteness to rationalize the expense of building totalizing company towns. Even in Chicago, steel companies widened rivers and built boardinghouses, setting the scene for future social relations between workers and employers. Through their efforts to organize the physical landscapes that contextualized and controlled workers' social interactions in the early decades of the twentieth century, firms in Southeast Chicago and Iron County claimed material and symbolic resources to coordinate community life.[42]

CAPITAL'S COMMUNITIES: INDUSTRIAL SOCIAL WORLDS

Commonsense conceptions of community assume that the politics, interpersonal conflicts, or mutual support systems are developed and maintained organically, reflecting the basic needs, collective interests, and biases of people living within a particular social milieu. But in the late nineteenth- and early twentieth centuries, iron and steel bosses in Iron County and Southeast Chicago exercised remarkable control over the social construction of community. These employers structured who lived where, and if and how their worker-citizens could easily interact with one another, engage in conflict, or access benefits of company beneficence. In part, such dominance derived from the top-down organization of the industrial boom in geographically isolated locations. Company-managed housing, for instance, meant that industrial managers could structure spaces of employment and nonemployment. Iron and steel companies central to this study intentionally pursued management strategies to cultivate a class of worker-citizens dependent on the firm for both economic stability and the material and social infrastructures of daily life.[43] As a result, interviewees' narratives of community were assessments of the wins and losses of the intrusion of economic interests into the private sphere.

"Everybody Knew Each Other": Iron County

Iron County's geographical remoteness limited the number of state-based social services, charitable organizations, or even private businesses located there in the early twentieth century. Mining companies filled that lacuna with their own social supports—company doctors vaccinated children and patched up injured miners; company police managed nightly curfews; company managers coordinated infrastructure repairs at the mine and in town. Such strict controls might be experienced as oppressive. But again and again, nearly all Wisconsin interviewees framed their company towns as an ideal type for a good, rural community.[44]

Living in company-controlled housing stock felt almost utopian. Rupert, whose story started this chapter, declared, "It was the best of times! Montreal was a mining town. They owned all the houses, [though] my dad built his own house there. But they sponsored our little leagues, they built our baseball fields. The mine did everything for us." Since miners and their bosses were next-door neighbors, living in comparably sized houses, sitting side-by-side on town councils, socializing in similar circles, and sending children to the same schools, differences between management and manual laborer felt minimal. Some interviewees and historical documents idealized this seemingly equitable structure for village life. Russ, who grew up in the company town of Montreal, mused, in an autobiographical essay, "My town . . . was a place where everyone lived with dignity and pride regardless of their occupations with the mining company and irrespective of living in a company house or one of their own. There was no such place as 'the other side of the tracks' or 'a bad part of town.' Everyone was 'somebody' in my town."[45]

Part and parcel to this good life were gender structures familiar to the midcentury middle-class. The majority of these "somebodies" were organized into traditional, male-headed households. In local mining culture, women were expected to stay at home caring for children, managing home gardens, and benefiting from men's high incomes. Families accessed healthcare and social services for free so long as their men were employed by the company. In an interview, Rupert offered warm praise of only "one person working" and, through that male breadwinner's efforts, enabling middle-class experiences for his family. "We all got an education; we had one-hundred-percent health care. They had a clinic [with] two doctors there." He held up his hand in preemptive argument against some expected criticism of these excesses of company benevolence. "We had to work, and do a lot of it! But they built a clubhouse for us, where we could play basketball, bowling . . . and Dad made a good living." Rupert's sense of what it meant to live a good life—to have a story of benefits that "we" experienced together—was wrapped up in how the company's presence enabled a certain kind of social relations.

Of course, there were exceptions to these glowing recollections of mine-centered community life. Beyond the household scale, the blurred lines between work and home created by industrial companies institutionalized their own forms of inequality in single-industry towns. Uneven household economic relations and land tenure arrangements in company towns like those in Iron County were used by those in power to perpetuate economic and social inequalities to their own benefit.[46] Even the physical layout of a company town meant the personalities and proclivities of workers could be regulated through sanctions at both work and home.[47] Michelle, a white woman in her mid-50s who grew up in an Iron County company town, was still skeptical of the motivations of the company decades later. She said with a cynical laugh, "The houses were company houses, doctor was a company doctor, the store was a company store. You got your money, but your money was wrapped up. . . . If you lived in a company home, I don't expect you'll be too good of a union man."

Michelle's cynicism about the totality of control over community life exerted by the mining company was well-founded. Even today, companies with outsized economic power can mute economic diversification, demographic heterogeneity, and even conflict with employers.[48] In the early twentieth century, mining companies were open about their rationales for such intensive control over the social contexts of everyday life. In 1923, a local Wisconsin newspaper profiling the company town of Montreal acknowledged that "managers are not giving the beautiful place in which to live entirely of a philanthropic motive, but consider the mutual benefits that will accrue inasmuch as a smaller turnover in labor makes for efficient operations and fewer mine accidents."[49] As late as the 1960s, company reports summarized that Oglebay Norton constructed their town in order to attract and maintain a "better class of workers"—sober men inclined to pursue steady paychecks rather than careless behavior in the mines, disorder after hours, or, most dangerously, union organizing.[50] The company town context created compliant workers more content with (or, less able to complain about) any injustices of wage labor. Because mining company executives were also town leaders, they could ensure that labor organizers instantly became both jobless and homeless.[51] Several interviewees recalled when managers banned "Red Finns"—Finnish émigrés with experience coordinating strikes—from renting company homes or building on mine-owned land. Donald, seventy-one, recalled that his Finnish uncle had been blacklisted for unionizing in the early 1930s. "That was a no-no. There was a rumor at that time of the union was going to try to come in. Needless to say, the mining company was Oglebay Norton, and as most big companies, they were not too friendly to our unions. But the problem in a one industry town [was that] the word got out. And then, you didn't work. I think that's what happened to my uncle. . . . He couldn't get a job [and] he and his family had to move to Detroit."

After federal protection of unionization was institutionalized in 1935, mining companies in the Upper Midwest started "taking a more friendly approach" to workers' concerns, according to a self-published autobiography by a former miner.[52] As employees with legal rights to collectively bargain with employers for better work conditions without risk of being fired or punished, most miners in the Lake Superior region organized with the United Steelworkers by the 1940s.[53] But even though historical records show that the local union in northern Iron County held monthly meetings, sponsored picnics, raised funds for the war effort, lobbied companies to upgrade equipment, and occasionally organized strikes, the union seemed to make very little impact on community life. While all of my sixty Iron County interviewees recalled the benefits of living in or near paternalistic mining company towns, only five mentioned unionization. One second-generation miner vaguely recalled that the local United Steelworkers Union organized perfunctory and routinized strikes "whenever new contracts came out—maybe every two years or something?" at a mine without a company town. Bill, another former miner in his late eighties, brushed aside union activities in general, arguing that walkouts were "short lived" because departed workers were easily replaced or rehired elsewhere due to "so many companies running at the same time." Some Iron County mine managers worked out an uneasy peace with rural miners and their unions in recognition that their employees were also neighbors and friends. Greg, now in his mid-fifties, recalled how "there was a conflict when you were on a long strike because these miners lived in company homes."[54] Similarly, Dave, in his late sixties, remembered how "Montreal had their little gimmick. They'd put on a picnic in Upson Park, they'd have it all set up so there was games for the kids, and there was anything the miners wanted to drink, they had music and stuff. They put on an all-day affair. You might have been on strike or what," he said, shrugging, "but they tried to keep harmony, anyway, on some level."

The geographies of community life enabled the company to easily constrain unions. At the same time, blurred boundaries between work and home created a curious mutual dependency between middle management and worker-citizens in Iron County's company towns. There, the tight overlap of work and home shaped the context for *all* residents' attachment to community. Some interviewees suggested that unions were unnecessary because the neighborly intimacy of company towns cut both ways. A former miner summarized aptly that managers knew that "in the small mining towns, everybody knew each other, [so] violence [against striking workers] would only serve to destroy valuable relationships."[55] Community life incentivized company managers to quickly negotiate with unhappy workers, arbitrate complaints directly, and expand their paternalistic offerings. Reflecting the basic human desire to retain supportive social networks, bosses needed their community just as their employees needed their jobs.

Millgate Neighborhoods: Southeast Chicago

Southeast Chicago's early-twentieth-century steel mills provided a much more diffuse form of company paternalism to their workers than did rural Iron County's. By the 1920s, the city's centralized transportation and utilities infrastructures had percolated to this far southeastern neighborhood, weaning steelworkers from reliance on their employers for fuel, food, or housing. Concurrently, steel companies exchanged any last remnants of traditional paternalism for a new model of worker management—welfare capitalism—which embedded non-income benefits, such as stock options, credit, or health insurance, into employee contracts to incentivize worker loyalty.[56] And yet, the centrality of steel to everyday life was never far from worker-citizens' minds. The output from their steel mills built not only trains and scaffolded skyscrapers but also funded hyperlocal economies that distinguished these communities from others. Each millgate neighborhood claimed a "workaday character," a 1985 city of Chicago report summarized, and was "highly sensitive to steel production and quite distinct from other portions of the Chicago area. . . . Many of the local small businesses—grocery stores, gas stations, hardware stores, bakeries, clinics, bars and so on—are totally local-serving, their livelihoods dependent upon the spending of people who live in the neighborhoods and work in the area."[57] Worker-citizens existed within social worlds constructed by their employer every time they shopped in stores fueled by their high wages, utilized company health insurance, or were in conflict with their manager through formalized arbitration or union processes.[58]

In contrast to iron miners' ambivalence toward their unionization, steelworkers in Southeast Chicago resented their bosses' strategic and occasionally violent resistance to labor organizing. In the first decades of the twentieth century, floor supervisors organized work teams across nationality and race to impede workers' capacity to communicate and organize. When strikes broke out in the 1920s and 1930s, steel bosses fanned the flames of racial resentment by hiring Mexican immigrants and African Americans as strikebreakers. Even after unions were legally protected by the federal government in 1935, managers racialized the work itself by offering entry-level workers who were Polish, Italian, Slovakian, as well as other "white ethnics," clean, safe, and skilled midlevel jobs, while giving Mexicans and African Americans brutal work tasks with few avenues for promotion.[59] Jerry experienced this shop-floor racism personally. An African American man who had moved from Tennessee to Chicago in 1965, he worked at Acme Steel for nearly thirty-five years. Seated in the former union office in Southeast Chicago, he explained how Blacks and Latinos were assigned to tough positions ("Hoo! Dirty and hot!" he explained, wiping his brow to emphasize the point), while white men were placed on jobs that were cleaner and easier, like carpenter or machinist.[60] He recalled that when he "first went to the mill in the '60s, on the ovens, there were no white guys working on the ovens, you know that?" The local union didn't seem capable of addressing this problem in the 1960s and 1970s, he mused. "The union don't do nothing for you, you know that? They collect your money, you know, they put you on hold." He wrinkled his nose in disappointment.

This racialization of workplaces shaped community life in two powerful ways. First, over decades, uneven earnings contributed to unequally resourced communities. Like many immigrant communities, Southeast Chicago neighborhoods reflected ethnic and racial clustering. When tens of thousands of new workers arrived in the earliest decades of the twentieth century, they funneled into neighborhoods with bars, churches, community baseball teams, and restaurants where they could speak their native tongues, socialize with kin, and, most pragmatically, find and retain safe housing. South Deering, near Wisconsin Steel, became a white ethnic community; the Bush, near U.S. Steel South Works, was Mexican; South Chicago grew into a Black community. At the same time, white neighborhoods were resisting racial integration across the city of Chicago. Housing discrimination, in the form of exclusionary language in deeds or landlord preferences, also played a role in sorting steel neighborhoods by race.[61] On the Southeast Side, steel companies' exploitation of racial and ethnic separations at work further exacerbated economic inequalities in racially segregated neighborhoods. White ethnics were among the first to be promoted to higher-paid work in the mills, meaning they were the first to purchase houses and cars, save money to send children to college, and benefit from interest gained on company stocks. Their neighborhoods were, then, the earliest to benefit from new small businesses. In turn, white millgate property values increased a little faster and drew more consistent city services.[62] And those neighborhoods were less physically proximate to the dirtiest steel mills or waste depositories—a pattern that would come to haunt communities in the century to come. While Jerry earned a promotion to foreman before his mill closed, he still felt the sluggishness of wealth distribution. He explained with a sigh that "no superintendents, no assistant superintendents were Black. They all were white. . . . [The] superintendent—he's the front man, and he calls the shots. You know they call the shots." He looked at me (a white researcher) with a mix of gentleness and resignation. "You all call the shots."

Second, even though in Jerry's view unions weren't effective in addressing the racialized workplaces in the 1960s, they did come to create sites of community building that were important outside the direct influence of company managers. In fact, I met Jerry at a meeting for retired union steelworkers. At these meetings, I heard proud monologues of how Southeast Chicago left a lasting mark in national labor history. Since the turn of the twentieth century, the region was home to early and well-recorded organized strikes, protests, and negotiations.[63] In one-on-one interviews, speakers often pointed to the importance of unions for building their sense of belonging. Against all managerial attempts to divide the working class along lines of race, the very process of achieving working class unity created a racially integrated and long-lasting community on the Southeast side (see figure 1.2). Callie, the adult daughter of a white Chicago steelworker, explained to me that 'union politics brought together racial tensions and coalitions; while the mills were all about racial divisions, [unions] were a place for interracial network building.' Oral histories and archival documents echoed her argument.[64] In an oral history conducted by Chicago-area high school students in 2005, Osborne, an African American worker laid off from Acme Steel, recalled how, "when we first started, it

FIGURE 1.2 Local 1033 Union election.

Courtesy of the Southeast Chicago Historical Society

Archive ID: 1981-077-079cc

was the Hispanics and the Blacks on the lower part of the peck-
ing order, you know. We had to band together to enforce some
kind of situation change, you know. . . . When we did that, it
was by the vote. When I started in '64, we had white leadership.
And after that, then the Blacks started getting involved in the
union."[65] By the late 1970s, local unions increasingly looked like
the working population. Flipping through company and union
newsletters from U.S. Steel Works and Wisconsin Steel shows
black-and-white photos of African American leadership standing

shoulder-to-shoulder with men from Mexico, Poland, Italy, and the Baltics. While company managers' racialized distribution of jobs and wealth troubled social relations on the ground, the best of the local unions reflected the racial diversity of Southeast side steelworkers and pursued wins that would benefit all laborers.[66]

The social worlds of midcentury Iron County and Southeast Chicago reflected the often-contradictory intersections of capital and home. Steel and iron companies simultaneously paid good wages and stifled racial integration, hosted family picnics and restrained unionization. Company managers were at once wilderness-defeaters and advertising men, landscape architects and immigration officers, social service providers and law enforcement, friendly neighbors and antagonistic bosses. Firms and their representatives crafted stories to explain these tensions. On the ground, industry's impact on community life was differently experienced in rural and urban contexts. Chicago's steel mills claimed less direct control over residential neighborhoods, but racialized shop-floor policies nonetheless impacted neighborhood structures and social interactions. Residents in Iron County rarely lost sight of how contingent their daily experiences were on the physical organization and social rules of mining companies. The mining company's ever-present infrastructural contributions to community life created a narrative of the "good company" that most contemporary interviewees welcomed in exchange for effective unionization. In contrast, Chicago's steel unions, as social organizations that existed beyond the reach of the direct authority of capital, more effectively countered steel companies' early attempts to undermine laborer resistance than did unions in Iron County. Industry might have set the tone for community through the infiltration of work into home, but unions enabled laborers to renegotiate the terms of conversation. For both, industrial power relations colored every-day social worlds.

ECONOMY: FEELING THE BLUE-COLLAR MIDDLE CLASS

The economy of iron and steel created not only houses and social networks but also fueled worker-citizens' expectations for upward mobility in midcentury America. In the postwar period, one out of three workers was employed in manufacturing. By 1950, processes of metals extraction and manufacturing that had been ramped up during World War II to build tanks, guns, and ships were redirected toward a ravenous demand for postwar buildings, agricultural machinery, airplanes, and automobiles. Half of these manufacturing jobs were in states and counties bordering the Great Lakes.[67] In both rural and urban communities, second and third generations of laborers entered the same mills and mines built by their fathers and grandfathers and, by the 1960s, their annual incomes were well within the middle-income bracket of $5,000–$10,000.[68]

But money is never merely material. As new generations of workers entered the mills and mines, interviewees fused their personal experiences of economic thriving into their concep-tions of what was plausible and possible to expect from work, company, and home. For these worker-citizens, home was tan-gled up not just with profits but also with promises of a middle-class lifestyle for blue-collar work. On landscapes organized by industrial entrepreneurs and in neighborhoods populated by both bosses and their fellow worker-citizens, midcentury iron miners and steelworkers delighted in financial stability, con-spicuous consumption, and middle-class status. Company credit unions and financial plans enabled them to buy houses, cars, and household appliances. Tailored clothes graced the bodies of wives and children. Vacation, travel, and education became possible for a generation of manual workers who had never dreamed that leisure time or upward social mobility might be theirs to experience.

Snug in these personalized versions of the American dream, worker-citizens phenomenologically embodied the premise of nineteenth-century steel companies: *this* place was *made* for iron and steel. Upward mobility and its associated wealth felt assured because entire geographies and communities were anchored by single industries with a voracious appetite for new workers. At home and at work, they experienced the sounds and smells of constantly churning, "giant machines bolted to the floors of brick-and-mortar factories" that cultivated "an aura of permanence," as the industrial historians Jefferson Cowie and Joseph Heathcott put it.[69] The work and the rewards of blue-collar labor in the steel furnaces or mines fueled residents' expectations about middle-class status and economic well-being that would come to outlast the steel industry.[70]

Bringing Boom Home: Iron County

"When we first talked about getting married," Sheila admitted, she and her high-school sweetheart, Paul, assumed he'd "be in the mine and we'd have it on easy street." The young couple's expectation had been well-founded. During and following World War II, military demand for steel had fueled mining in the Gogebic Range. One midcentury industrial report confidently projected that the rearmament program of the 1950s "made it clear that industry would necessarily depend on large tonnages of Lake

Superior ores for many years to come."[71] By the time Sheila and Paul got married in the early 1960s, the six iron ranges bordering Lake Superior supplied 81 percent of all domestic iron output. Of these mineral deposits, the Montreal Mine in Iron County was the most prolific in the state and one of the deepest iron mines in the world at 4,335 vertical feet.[72] Highly paid, consistent work in the mine was a well-proven career path for a young man. Base wages for entry-level workers in the Montreal Mine were $3.25 per hour—comparable to nearly $30 an hour in 2022. Ambitious miners could earn more through double-pay overtime and per-ton-mined bonuses.[73] These solidly middle-class wages combined with company-funded health care, pensions, and housing lured new generations to the mine shafts.

Secure with paychecks in hand and relishing company-sponsored amenities, such as Christmas parties at the neighborhood schools and free trolley service to and from the local train station, residents of Iron County experienced the best of boom years even in their very rural context. A third of my rural interviewees were too young to work in the mines but old enough to recall the "good old days." For this generation, these midcentury decades brimmed with opportunities to experience middle-class life as a promise fulfilled. While walking through the town of Hurley with me, Tom listed all the car dealers located just within the five-mile radius of the mining community. In the Historical Society kitchen, Cheryl and Patrick talked about their favorite Italian restaurants that were great date spots in the 1970s. Gary remembered slow Sunday drives through the town with his high-school friends, feeling rich with time, potential, and every hope that these dinners, cars, and houses were his promised future, too.

Even the mines themselves fueled expectations of a wealthy future. Jill, in her early sixties, leaned toward me, clutching her coffee mug. Eyes wide and curly white hair bouncing with every word, she recalled an era of economic boom that blurred the lines between paternalistic benefits of life in a company town and middle-class wages enabled by the mining work itself. "The mines kept everything so beautiful. The engine house was not far from where I lived and I'd go roller-skating down there—the floors in there were marble, and the big turbines were just clean, and they had big potted fern plants sitting on pedestals in different places. It's hard to imagine that a mine could be that way," Jill said, laughing, and shook her head in appreciation. "There was a little police building for the policemen who worked for the mine, and then in town, we also had our own doctor's office, and we had a beautiful school. The mine contributed to our school, our public library, and our public showers." She paused, rubbing her cheek thoughtfully. "They were nice communities—had just about everything! You didn't have to leave your community, you had everything right there." She sighed, delivering a summative line that echoed dozens of other Iron Countians' memories and would come to provide interviewees' reference point for all that was to come: "The mines were *so* good with the people."[74]

"Oh My God, I'm Loaded": Southeast Chicago

"You know how kids in high school have college fairs?" Louisa, a quick-witted woman of Polish descent, asked me as we rumbled through U.S. Steel's former neighborhood in her car. "We used to have Mill Fairs. I mean, all the mills would come to your high school to recruit for jobs." When Louisa graduated from high school in 1977, Chicago was the nation's preeminent center for fabricated metals employment and second only to Pittsburgh in total steel jobs. Chicago provided steel for markets stretching "from the Appalachians through the Rockies," according to a 1985 report by a panel of industrial and economic experts for the city of Chicago.[75] Steel from the Southeast Side was in such high demand by the nation's rapidly growing cities, U.S. military, and mechanized agriculture that the region's mills employed more than fifty thousand workers—nearly half of the neighborhood's workforce.[76]

Within this economic context, steelwork was competitive employment. Union organizing and steady market demand had increased the starting wage for entry-level laborers in Southeast Chicago to an average of $10 an hour in 1960—nearly double what workers in the industry made before 1940 and equivalent to nearly $100 an hour today. Louisa's father, a respected steel union leader, encouraged her to go "to the mill straight out of high school. Seventeen years old, and I went to work at Chicago Steel and Wire. The money was good. I'll never forget. I got my first paycheck—we'd get paid every week—and my first paycheck was, like, $270 bucks. This was 1977—I was like, oh my god, I'm loaded! Because it was good money!" Louisa laughed softly. Her first weekly paycheck was equivalent to $1,400 today. No wonder teenagers like Louisa were swept into the mills fresh out of high school. This manual labor was physically demanding, but it set young people on a proven path toward financial advancement through double-pay overtime, annual bonuses, wage raises, and pensions. After gaining seniority at fifteen years with one company, workers could take paid vacations, receive better rates from company credit unions, claim better shifts, and enter specialized training programs—all within walking distance of home.[77]

Workers and their families felt, tasted, and gazed upon the material evidence of their hard work. Richard and Penelope, an African American couple in their mid-sixties, remembered how steel employment raised the economic floor for their entire neighborhood of Black steelworkers from working poor to middle class. Penelope laughed in recollection of their neighbors' giddy delight in entering the consuming classes. In the 1970s, everyone on their block "had Lincoln Continentals, [and] they had their own houses. . . . I mean, young people with their own big houses!" In the 1970s and 1980s, homeownership rates in all millgate neighborhoods inched past 70 percent.[78] Her husband smiled appreciatively. "Oh man, them guys . . . they had some beautiful cars, big houses and stuff, you know!" In their twenties and newly married, Richard and Penelope bought cars and put down a mortgage on their first house a mile from the steel mill through low-cost loans through U.S. Steel Corporation's credit unions.[79] Penelope recalled, "We had a Volkswagen" "And a Cadillac!" Richard interjected enthusiastically. "They had a heater down there—you could turn the heater on when the car wasn't even moving!" Both sighed. "Yeah, that was nice, we had money," Richard murmured. "That was 1974. We had money. She had a mink hat with a mink coat, and a white Cadillac." The couple grinned with their recollections of their incredulity that this kind of economic well-being was available to them—so young, and so often excluded from the wins of American life as African Americans.

Capital investments by steel companies in the latest upgrades, technologies, and trainings also created an atmosphere of perpetual growth. In another oral history from the early 2000s, Victor said, "When something that was built that was new, you know, we felt that we were making progress and that jobs were secure." A few years before the mill began laying off workers, "they extended the 32, 36-inch mill, which involved . . . more employees. It was good. Then they put [in] the furnace, which was innovation in the steel industry, which was great. And they extend that, so everybody felt that that was . . . security. And people went out and bought cars and went out and bought houses." There's a pause in the transcript before Victor continued. "I experienced that we were making progress, that we felt everybody was going to have a job in the long run . . . [that] even after we retired, you know, there would be employment! But," he paused with a sigh, "it didn't work out that way and that's—that's sad."[80]

For midcentury iron and steelworkers, economic success felt inevitable. New generations of workers discovered that boundary markers around race and gender that once barred them from accessing benefits of homeownership, conspicuous consumption, or guaranteed work were now porous. Across the nation, wages were increasing and the middle class was expanding. Entire communities rose together in status and opportunity. For young people just entering the job market, all evidence suggested that work in the steel mills or mines was the most direct path to the newest houses, the best cars, and the biggest paychecks. In the Northwoods of Wisconsin and Southeast Chicago, economic thriving became central to people's conception of a "good home," and lived experiences of this economic thriving would come to set the tone for future narratives of loss, negotiation, and choice. Yet even as everyday people experienced economic thriving, they were never released from the conditioning forces of capitalism. The good home—and its good life—came at a cost: the totalizing control of a single industry over the local geography, community, and economy.

CONCLUSION: MAKING GEOGRAPHY, MAKING HOME, MAKING CONSTRAINTS

For the laborer communities constructed as stable nodes along an iron and steel commodity chain in the American Midwest, the processes of capitalism not only took place; they *made place*. Both the physical processes and intentional narratives of early industrial development rendered iron and steel the raison d'être of the northern half of a rural county and the southern edge of a large city. The social construction of home in Iron County and Southeast Chicago was explicitly managed by industry.

Powerful elites of nineteenth- and twentieth-century capital claimed the open country of northern Iron County and marshlands of Southeast Chicago for industrial development. Control over geographies, through the clearing of land and building of houses, enabled iron and steel entrepreneurs to foreground their priorities—laborer compliance and economic domination.[81] Within workers' communities, managerial hiring preferences (in Southeast Chicago) or access to company housing (in Iron County) unevenly shaped the accrual of wealth along lines of race, ethnicity, and gender. The people who became industrial worker-citizens experienced the wins of the blue-collar middle class even as they lived in a world fully contingent on the whim of the company. These place-based strategies of domination created material vestiges and durable meanings of home that would long outlast the companies themselves. Writing of an entirely different context, the sociologist John Urry accurately mused, "prophecy now involves a geographical rather than historical dimension; we should now talk of people making not their own history but their own geography."[82]

Understanding *how* home was made in Iron County and Southeast Chicago—and how contemporary residents interpret that past—matters when assessing *what* was lost when companies began to close in the mid-twentieth century. Interviewees pointed to how they experienced the capture of neighborhood structure, community relations, and economic well-being by industrial companies. Some voiced complicated feelings about how company involvement in community life scaffolded their perceptions of work and home, organized relationships, and circumscribed conflicts between laborers and capital. Others framed the practices and narratives of "good companies" as ideal models for future development. All agreed that because iron and steel companies quite literally constructed their homes, any discussion of boom and bust demanded an accounting of how worker-citizens experienced company closures as more than unemployment. In short: when work disappeared, worker-citizens lost their country.

2

HOME WITHOUT THE COMPANY

Deindustrializing the American Midwest

*Someone has to lose, said the stranger. That's economics. The
question is—who loses? That's progress.*
                    –Winifred Holtby, *South Riding*, 1936

"Closed all of them mills down at one time." Jerry's
voice cracked with emotion. "Chicago was run by all
of them steel mills, and they shut 'em all down! All
of them." He leaned back in his chair with moist eyes, palms
flat on the vast desk between us. Jerry's visible grief contrasted
with the muted laughter drifting through the open door. I had
pulled Jerry away from a catered lunch of fried chicken and
sheet cake that follows monthly meetings of the United Steelworkers Organization of Active Retirees. Now, as Jerry paused
to regain his composure, I gazed at the dusty photos hung on
the wood-paneled wall of the former United Steelworkers Local
1093 office—black and white images of union men standing arm
and arm, protective helmets jauntily askew. After a slow sip of
watery coffee, Jerry continued. "In '65, when I moved here, there
was [ten] thousand people working in that mill," he said with a
wave, referring to the U.S. Steel South Works. "And over there,"

he lifted his calloused hand to point out the high window to the former Republic Steel site, now an empty field with a few cement slabs interrupting prairie. Jerry frowned. "Nothing there now. Nobody making no money because what could they do?"

Fundamentally, deindustrialization was an economic problem. Starting in the late 1950s, international manufacturing plants outcompeted local minerals and metals markets, eating into profit margins that were already thin as technological changes and regulatory shifts caught up with factories. Companies in the United States involved in mining raw materials collapsed first. Between 1950 and 1970, employment in mining declined by 40 percent.[1] Iron County's five mines closed by the mid-1960s and the last stockpiled iron ore was shipped out by the early 1970s. Manufacturing was the next to go. Between 1967 and 1987, Chicago lost 60 percent of its manufacturing jobs; Philadelphia lost 64 percent, and New York City, 58 percent.[2] Across the country, metals manufacturing alone dropped by 40 percent between the 1960s and mid-1980s.[3] In Chicago alone, thirty thousand steelworkers lost their jobs in the second half of the twentieth century.[4] No matter how the data is parsed, the aggregate economic losses of late-twentieth-century deindustrialization are staggering.

And yet, people do not experience the economy only in the abstract. Jerry, along with tens of thousands of urban and rural industrial workers, experienced unemployment not only as wages lost but as crises of home. After decades of interventions by industry into the landscapes of working-class housing, on-the-ground social dynamics, and wealth creation, blue-collar workers, their families, and neighbors faced a tangled mess of silent factories and mines, defunct unions, and delayed or uncashable final paychecks. Closure severed commodity chains and disconnected geographies; boarded-up windows and empty houses replaced tightly knit company towns or millgate neighborhoods; family dynamics shifted as women and young people joined the workforce in a new crop of low-paid jobs. Without the "good company," employees were bereft—not just in economic terms but also as citizens of a community originally organized around industrial purposes.

How did people navigate and interpret the deconstruction of home? How did they sort through the disentangling of geography, thinning of community, and loss of upward economic mobility? This chapter explores how the newly unemployed and their family members diagnosed the causes and experienced the consequences of deindustrialization. In halting stories about crisis, culture, and class, interviewees identify the implications of company closures across scales—from macroeconomic movement of capital away from their geographies to company-level decisions that undermined community function, and, finally, to their own intimate experiences of financial loss and class collapse. Accounts of company closure capture the tension between the constraints created by such large-scale losses and the choices remaining for those left behind.

GEOGRAPHIES WITHOUT CAPITAL, 1960–1990

The first sign of trouble was silence. For decades, there had been movement and noise—laborer in-migration, expansions of equipment, new construction in neighborhoods, constant clanging and hazy air emanating from mine shafts and steel mills, and endlessly busy railroad spurs and docks. Then, steel and iron shop floors went quiet. There was a pause—a held breath. And then, as if reversing time, there was a flurry of movement again.

Within months and years, deindustrialization sucked away the animating economic processes that had made home for workers for three or four generations.

These reversals demanded interpretation from on-the-ground witnesses. Iron and steel companies did little to explain this regional collapse to their worker-citizens, so the newly unemployed wrestled with how to make sense of the unraveling of their industrial homes. They worked hard to locate the realities of locked factory gates and silenced mine pumps within the abstract forces that caused the rapid departure of mining and manufacturing. Astutely, residents linked other spatial changes and institutional actors to their hyperlocal problems—the displacement of mining and manufacturing to nonunionized states in the American south, the inundation of the U.S. steel market with raw iron ore and cheaper manufactured products from foreign sources, and the implications of changing regulatory and trade policy. Firm in the belief that capital flight was not due to some inherent flaw in their home's founding geology or mode of manufacturing, these witnesses of company closures sought to reconcile the disappearance of their founding industries with the unfolding transformations of the places they called home.

"Other Countries, Cheaper": Southeast Chicago

From the earliest reverberations of industrial collapse, steelworkers were attuned to the geographic movement of manufacturing away from home. José, a former steelworker, called out the role of international competition in an oral history project run by a local high school in the immediate wake of company closures. "They're killed, all. They told us, 'We cannot afford to pay you what you want.' We get this steel that we get in here from Japan and other countries, cheaper. So that's what killed us." His voice laced with grief, José named the institutional actor responsible for correcting this problem. "The country [the U.S], they shouldn't allow the imports and then we'll be okay. But this way, it's terrible." Even if the specific details were fuzzy to them, industrial workers like José quickly gained the vocabulary needed to diagnose the major processes and actors involved in the transformation of home. José's instinctive complaint about the role of the U.S. government in enabling the infiltration of foreign goods at significantly lower price points was accurate. Following World War II, the United States pursued a new approach to trade. In coordination with other postwar countries, it led the creation of the multilateral General Agreement on Tariffs and Trade (GATT) aimed at reducing tariffs and import caps in order to stimulate economies of war-torn, democratic countries.[5] Lower trade barriers greased the wheels of comparative advantage between countries—that is, when nations and their firms focus on producing fewer, more specialized commodities as cheaply as possible. As American tariff rates fell from an average of 60 percent in 1930 to 5.7 percent by 1980, domestic markets were flooded with cheaper goods—a boon to consumers but a threat to local producers unprepared for such fierce competition.[6]

In the 1970s, two more changes gutted manufacturing. The era of cheap energy that had fueled American manufacturing for decades was terminated when Middle Eastern countries decided to control oil prices.[7] Concurrently, the newly formed U.S. Environmental Protection Agency began issuing long-overdue regulations. For the first time since the industrial revolution, the government required the manufacturing sector to internalize costs of pollutant disposal, wastewater treatment, and release of unhealthy levels of airborne particulate matter. To avoid fines, companies needed to retrofit their factories and production systems with filters, catchment ponds, or chemical containment technologies. These upgrades required capital investments that some companies—particularly those that were nearly a century old, like those affiliated with the midwestern steel industry—were often unwilling or unable to make.[8]

Caught in this price-cost squeeze, many industrial companies chased cheaper production away from their midwestern origins. The American sunbelt, stretching from the Carolinas to Texas, offered cheaper land and less organized labor. Overseas, these benefits could be expanded, with very low wage expectations and nearly no regulations. In the abstract, the shift of capital from one place to another made economic sense—companies simply wanted to survive a changing economy. But, since those companies historically scaffolded everyday life in industrial communities like Southeast Chicago, home to Victor, a steelworker who was laid off from Republic Steel in the last decade of the twentieth century, abstractions were personal losses.[9] Victor conceptualized these geographic tradeoffs between distant gains and nearby losses in his oral history.[10] "You have laws that govern imports and exports and how industries are regulated over here. So, when you allow imports from other countries [that have] been subsidized by the government, you cannot compete. . . . So, you can come in and sell your products on low cost, you know. Just like when you go to the store, what you do? You look for a bargain. If they're nice, you don't care if they're from China or they're from Japan." Victor drove home his point with carefully chosen words: "But the thing is that they will affect the population of *this* country because if there's no jobs, like with the steel industry, then you have less buying power. So, I do definitely believe . . . they could have avoided the shutdown of all this industry. Not all of them, but a good majority of them. They could have been saved."

"Free Trade Is Not Fair Trade": Iron County

If companies' departures from Southeast Chicago disoriented manufacturing workers, mining firms' abandonment of Iron County gutted the remote villages straddling the iron ore deposit. Like most of the major mining operations along the Michigan-Wisconsin border in the mid-twentieth century, mine closures in Iron County were due to technological changes rather than to depletion of the founding natural resource.[11] Most residents were quick to point out that deep shaft mining became obsolete because of the development of a technique for mining and processing low-grade iron ore perfected in the late 1950s. Even before trade liberalization and globalization gutted prices for Iron County's hematite ore, this new method for pulling ore from waste rock—taconite mining—"was really death to the direct shipment lines," Travis told me in Wisconsin. Travis was a mechanical engineer of Italian descent who recently returned to the county to retire near family. Taconite mining, he explained to me, involves pulverizing and separating low-quality iron ore from rock in processing plants built adjacent to large-scale strip mines. Because taconite mining didn't require high-quality ore, this new technology opened up vast portions of the American Midwest for new iron ore exploration. Not only did Iron County's mines suffer from the sudden expansion of viable extractive sites beyond its geographic region, Travis reflected, but the downstream processes for refining low-grade iron ore left behind mines producing higher-quality ores. "The blast furnaces all of a sudden were designed to handle these uniform pellets which melted better and took less energy," he said with a wry smile. "And of course, the mines were getting deeper and deeper here." Today, at nearly a mile deep, the Montreal Mine remains one of the deepest iron mines in the world only because deep shaft technologies are now defunct.

Yet technological change was only one factor in drawing industrial capital away from home in Iron County. Locals echoed Southeast Chicagoans' argument that competition far from home—rather than a fundamental problem with their foundational industry—was to blame for company closures. Three years after the Montreal Mine laid off its final worker, a high school student, Holly Fellman, published a poem in the local newspaper that captured this causal interpretation.

> Thirteen million tons lost forever, buried an' a-rustin'
> "Why," we asked, "this waste o' sweat an ore?"
> "Your ways are old and costly," said them
> Big city boys with th' trim coats an' shiny shoes.
> "There are new cheaper mines far away in
> Southern lands—we cannot buy from you!"[12]

Similarly, a local Iron County newspaper reported in 1962 that the region's largest mine closed "because it could find no market for its ore, a non-magnetic variety that tests between 51 and 52 percent iron content." The newspaper article summarized the losses incurred by comparative advantage that I came to hear again and again: "Foreign ores are glutting the market."[13]

Also mirroring Chicagoans' concerns, rural interviewees posited that the distant economic threats that were upending their local geographies were enabled by government policy. Free trade—the loosening of economic restraints and displacement of industries to new geographic locations—incurred much direct criticism in Iron County. As tariff reductions were integrated into federal policies following World War II, midcentury economists such as Milton Friedman, N. Gregory Mankiw, and their fellow New Keynesians suggested that this freeing of trade would increase wealth for all Americans as U.S. sellers reached new buyers across the globe.[14] Companies could increase profit margins by relocating to places with fewer environmental or labor regulations, cheaper wages, and better access to raw materials. Sure, there would be some losses as the economy expanded across borders, agreed most politicians. But the political and economic consensus in the second half of the twentieth century was that economic efficiency would increase, prices would decrease, and general standards of living would rise for more people through open trade policies.[15]

Yet as interviewees in Iron County pointed out again and again, the disappearance of mining wasn't a distant, macroeconomic process; it was the loss of the single institution that had, for generations, quite literally organized landscapes around the single goal of making the most money from place-based natural resources. Rupert grimaced knowingly at me. "We're in a worldwide market now. A lot of these trade agreements, they talked about free trade. Well, free trade is not fair trade. They talk it up, and they do [the deals], and more people lose their jobs. They [the miners] were working for $25 with pensions and health care. Now if they want the job, it's $14 with no benefits." He concluded with a shrug, "What are you going to do? All the big players moved."

Not only was free trade to blame for capital's flight, in Rupert's diagnosis, but so was the global unevenness of environmental regulation. He continued, "Why [would] you want to fight your local area when you can go to South America or somewhere else?" His wife, Nan, agreed. "China!" Rupert nodded. "And you have that cheap labor and don't have to worry about the environment." I heard a similar complaint in a conversation with Dottie and her friend Lola, both in their late eighties. The friends quickly argued that the permeation of local markets by "outside" ore was due to "these other countries." But

Dottie continued that these places "don't have rules and regulations, and they're destroying their country, and you can get it so cheap there. China, especially. It's just a battle," Dottie sighed.[16] Economists often argue that when taken as a whole, the spatial impacts of deindustrialization, free trade, and capital mobility are merely symbolic.[17] Certainly, when considered in aggregate, employment levels in the second half of the twentieth century remained steady and economic well-being increased as the American economy reallocated jobs away from industries that were facing high levels of import competition and comparative advantage to more profitable sectors. Manufacturing and mining jobs were, job for job, replaced by new positions in the service sector, ranging from retail sales to office receptionists.[18]

But "aggregate" presupposes that the economy is out there, unmoored in geography. Interviewees in both cases balked at this characterization. The disappearance of iron and steel was not geographically abstract; it was the loss of the single largest job-creating industry in Iron County and Southeast Chicago. At the heart of interviewees' diagnoses of trade liberalization, deregulation, and outsourcing was a common complaint that these economic transformations—and the invisible "big actors" who controlled them—failed the places left behind by capital mobility.[19] Free trade might have meant to raise all boats, but like many in the shrinking American industrial corridor, Iron Countians and Southeast Chicagoans were instead swept away in the flood.

COMMUNITIES WITHOUT COMPANIES

For generations, companies were the contexts for community life. Steel and iron employers exercised remarkable control over the norms of collective behavior and avenues for social conflict.

Managers and foremen played contradictory roles of conflict mediators, landlords, realtors, city planners, and social coordinators. Daily life revolved around the sounds, sights, and routines of industrial shiftwork, transportation, union meetings, company picnics, and paydays. Such place-making created worker-citizens—laborers whose experiences of both home and employment were inherently embedded in a landscape organized around the interests of capital. Because work and home were one and the same, company closure was a threat to community function.

Since companies were social safety nets and place-makers, *how* they responded to the macroeconomic abstractions of free trade or comparative advantage directly impacted localized employees' experience of deindustrialization. Employees' losses were exacerbated or mitigated by whether companies gradually laid off workers or suddenly locked the doors, maintained institutional function or went completely bankrupt, or abandoned one location in favor of new investments elsewhere. Companies' varied approaches to breaking social, and at times, legal contracts with employees not only left their worker communities bereft of the benefits of living in a region entangled with a single industry but threw doubt on the origin stories of the beneficence of capital. Without themselves moving away, workers transformed into citizens of a disappeared country.

"Everybody Lost Out Big": Southeast Chicago

Half of Chicago's steel mills declared bankruptcy between 1980 and 2001. Bankruptcy meant that companies were sheltered from individual lawsuits. Employees were often left without paychecks, access to their pensions, health insurance, or other accrued benefits. Even federally backed bankruptcy processes or pension guarantees left former employees bereft due to the mismatched timelines between when people need to pay their bills and when funds are made available to them.[20] In an oral history, Victor explained, "If a company shuts and they're not a [bankrupt] company, they could pay the benefits. They might offer you a package. But the company went bankrupt, which most of the companies around here other than U.S. Steel [did]. Wisconsin Steel went bankrupt. Acme Steel went bankrupt. Republic Steel went bankrupt. There was no money there available for a package, so you lost your insurance and [a portion of] your pension." Victor concluded, "Everybody lost out big."[21]

The first—and most dramatic—company bankruptcy was the first on Victor's list: Wisconsin Steel. In an ironic bookend, the first mill to open back in 1875 as Brown's Mill was also the first to close a century later. Brown's Mill was purchased in the early twentieth century by an agricultural implement company that would, over the course of several mergers, become International Harvester.[22] By 1980, the latest owner of Wisconsin Steel found itself facing a new wave of regulatory and trade constraints and financially underwater. By way of announcing their pending bankruptcy to their employees, the owners locked the mill's gates behind the last shift of workers without warning and turned away the ore boat preparing to deliver the next day's raw materials.[23]

As more than a century of multigenerational work for laborers living in Wisconsin Steel's millgate neighborhood dramatically disappeared overnight, steel laborers across Southeast Chicago began questioning what their companies actually owed them as worker-citizens. In an interview, Richard recalled, "When Wisconsin went out, they went out bankrupt and didn't nobody know. They paid 'em that morning, that afternoon wasn't no money in the bank for them to cash their checks. So, you know how they felt. When they tried to go cash their checks they said, 'We don't have no money for you to cash your check!'" Richard captured the outrage of betrayal that I heard from other interviewees and archival records. In the months following closure, Wisconsin Steel failed to issue final paychecks to some of its 3,330 newly unemployed workers, and those that had been issued right before company declared bankruptcy were not honored by local bankers. Until "bankruptcy hearings decide[d] the deposition of the mill assets[,] they would not value the checks," reported the local newspaper, the *Daily Calumet*.[24] While the company owners scrambled to manage the uproar, promising that the closure was temporary, the local newspaper reported that "the jobless" were feeling "bitterness over the eight-month deception of announcements made practically every month that Wisconsin Steel would reopen by the following month."[25] By the end of the year, however, it was clear to all observers that closure would be permanent.

More gradual company closures incurred less bitterness. In contrast to the locked gates of unexpected bankruptcy, the largest mill—U.S. Steel South Works—very slowly reduced its output and its workforce over a decade. Ed Sadlowski, a Chicago union leader, recalled in an oral history that the mill "started to actually phase . . . out beginning in the mid-80s . . . and probably shut the last light bulb off in the mid-90s or so." At first, managers laid off a few thousand workers from departments across the mill based on seniority and skill level. By the time it closed in 1992, employment at the mill had already shifted from eleven thousand workers to fewer than seven hundred.[26] Jesús and Marcos were some of the youngest in the mill in the 1980s and among the first to get laid off. Their fathers and uncles soon followed them home, however, as the gradual dimming of the mill caught up with their seniority. They admitted that staggered layoffs from a company that still exists today was certainly better than bankruptcy. Unlike at International Harvester's Wisconsin Steel, workers could cash their final paychecks, their pensions were kept intact, and, at least in theory, they could emotionally and socially prepare for unemployment. But regardless of how companies closed, closures eroded the social fabric of community life.

Unions, once central to Chicago steelworkers' social engagement in Southeast Chicago, came to play a different role in postindustrial community life. Without companies with which to collectively bargain, steelworker unions lost their purpose.[27] Between 1979 to 1983, more than one thousand United Steelworkers Union branches disbanded across iron and steel locations in the United States.[28] And yet, the social networks created by these defunct local organizations remained vital to community function even without a company. When Wisconsin Steel shuttered, its independent union offered mutual aid to newly unemployed workers. Headed by Frank Lumpkin, an African American with decades of experience at the mill, this group created an ad hoc food bank, aided their fellow jobless in looking for work and applying for government aid, and coordinated communication with—and eventual lawsuits against—their delinquent company.[29] When mills closed more gradually, union representatives could support their members' transitions to unemployment in the months before and after company closure. Oliver was a union representative at a smaller mill that slowly laid off teams of employees until its last day in the 1990s. Oliver told me in a clipped, Italian accent that he saw his role as helping to prepare his members for the big loss. "Being in the union," he said, "I knew for long time this was going to happen and I was trying to prepare the members. 'It's a matter of time and we are going to be shut down.' But they did not believe [me], so I said, 'Okay. You know, when time comes, we'll witness this together.'" On the final day of work, Oliver joined his coworkers in tearfully cleaning out lockers, returning steel-toed boots, and walking out into their millgate neighborhoods to face whatever came next.

"They're Just, 'You're Done'": Iron County

In Iron County, mining company closures were gradual, but the loss of the "good company" nonetheless left a gaping hole in the local social fabric. Charles, eighty-four and a sharp-witted veteran of the Montreal Mine, exclaimed, "We were the first ones that got laid off, and then the mine went until 1962, and then everybody [got laid off]." Leaning forward over the massive plank of a table in the Iron County Historical Society, he snapped his fingers and said, "They're just, 'You're done.'" Oglebay Norton's Montreal Mine was one of the last to close in Iron County and the Upper Peninsula of Michigan. Managers slowly laid off six hundred workers over a period of months. But even still, the final day of work still unnerved Charles. Voice thick with feeling, he told me that receiving his notice of termination "was the first time ever . . . you know something's going on."

Mining companies in the upper Midwest typically did not go bankrupt. Rather, they closed in response to market pressures that undercut their profits. Yet so dominant was the narrative of the "good company" that workers seemed unprepared to perceive their employer as a player in capitalist competition. Nonetheless, mining firms like Oglebay Norton Company, the owner of Iron County's most prolific mine and manager of the company town of Montreal, responded to the economic stressors of the mid-twentieth century like the profit-seeking company that it was, rather than the paternalistic caregiver role that it had historically performed. Beginning in the 1930s, Oglebay had poured funding into research and development of new mining technologies related to taconite mining.[30] In 1960—two years before it fired its last employee at the Montreal Mine—Oglebay opened a large taconite mine in Eveleth, Minnesota. In company documents, the firm rationalized this technological pivot as inevitable—"the high costs (and unpredictable payoff) of domestic underground exploration" forced "iron and steel producers . . . to seek alternative sources of high-grade ore through overseas exploration and research into converting low-grade ores like taconite . . . into more useful materials."[31]

In the years immediately prior to their disinvestment in the Montreal Mine, Oglebay pursued a second maneuver that threw doubt on its identity as a "good company." Company executives offered to retain segments of the workforce if the union would agree to a collective wage decrease. When union organizers resisted, senior management sent a strongly worded letter to all Montreal Mine employees demanding that if laborers, as the "most costly" component of production, wanted to retain their jobs for a few months longer, they must ignore the union's efforts to organize a strike.[32] In 1961, dispirited workers quickly agreed to reductions in fringe benefits, pay, and hours for the last months of their employment.

While unions in Chicago attempted to smooth transitions of closure, in Iron County, the union was as ineffective in death as it had been in life. None of my interviewees discussed unions after closure. What they did call attention to, however, was the loss of the company town itself. The same year that they closed the Montreal Mine in Iron County, Oglebay sold their matching white company houses to private residents, removed their company doctors, and shuttered their community center.[33] By 1963, most evidence of the "good company" had simply disappeared. In Montreal and its adjacent villages, unemployment meant more than just job losses.

The nearly complete collapse of the American steel and iron industry during the second half of the twentieth century reveals the fundamental presupposition of company-fueled community construction. No matter how strategically brokered by unions or voluntarily offered by managers, the ingredients of a good work life—pensions, health care, company towns, and final paychecks—were always conditioned on the perpetuity of a specific company. In lockstep, access to the best of community life was also contingent on employment, so much so that even the nature of company closure altered the on-the-ground experiences of social life.

In theory, rights of living in a place should not be attached to what a person can offer the rights-granting institution. In practice, "full citizenship rights" are merely "conditional privileges only available to those who have something to exchange that the market deems of equivalent value, usually money or labor," as the sociologists Fred Block and Margaret Somers explain.[34] While Block and Somers speak of citizenship in terms of national politics, similar contingency applied to capital-centric residential contexts like industrial communities. As one mill or mine after the other shuttered, worker-citizens found themselves with neither work *nor* the rights and benefits of citizenship in a home historically organized around capital. Whether companies closed through bankruptcy, phased layoffs, or dramatic disinvestments informed if and how worker-citizens could access benefits that might soften the transition to unemployment.

FEELING ECONOMIC DISPLACEMENT

As the economic floor disappeared, entire communities tumbled from blue-collar and middle-class to poverty. Nearly overnight, interviewees shifted from buying houses, paying off car loans, and contributing to food banks to accessing charity originally reserved for those unlucky enough to not work in the mines or mills. Mid-twentieth-century trends of income equalization and economic prosperity were replaced with growing income inequality. Against the promises of free trade economists, between 1973 and 1982, across the United States, the percentage of families earning enough income to be categorized as middle-class stopped growing for the first time in decades.[35] Specifically in the American industrial corridor, good jobs lost combined with poor jobs gained caused a "great U-turn" in both wealth and subjective experiences of class.[36] Without employment and citizenship to steel mills and iron mines, workers and their families lost the dignity, purpose, and sense of belonging that they had, for generations, derived from their high-wage jobs, social safety nets, and social relations embedded in their millgate neighborhoods and company towns. The suddenly unemployed found themselves emotionally upended, unmoored from their place at home.

What Does a Lost Job Feel Like?
Southeast Chicago

Back at Richard and Penelope's kitchen table in Chicago, the couple compared life before and after Richard lost his job in the steel mill to illustrate the gut-wrenching inversion of industrial closure. Richard's eyes grew wide as he exclaimed, "We went from $70,000 a year to $7,000—what a shock![37] Our block was one of the richest blocks in the whole neighborhood. Because we were steel mill workers, you know, we made the money. We got dirty, but when we put our clothes on, we were . . ." He shrugged and made eye contact with his wife. "I stayed at that mill because I made big money. I mean, we went to church in nice clothes, I mean . . . my kids, they [were] in handmade clothes, every day. I had my children's clothes *made*."

That was 1974. A decade later, Richard was laid off from U.S. Steel South Works. Within a matter of months, he and Penelope tumbled from wearing tailored clothes and driving new cars to filling out forms to get unemployment benefits, food stamps, and temporary medical insurance. He grimaced as he recalled how they began frequenting the same church food bank to which they, in better times, had donated. "The church saved us, really," Richard said with a sigh. But unemployment checks and weekly charity boxes couldn't keep the steel mill's credit union from reclaiming the cars they had purchased through their loan program. Penelope recalled, "They came and took those, and we were back to riding the bus and the train everywhere we went. And we were cutting back for what we had to get for the kids and you know, how to make a meal out of nothing, and all of that stuff." Most of their neighbors were "in the same predicament," she continued. "Because most of them were [from U.S. Steel]," they had purchased cars and houses and had "maybe two or three kids, maybe more." Penelope threw up her hands. "It just went"—she snapped her fingers—"just like that."

Even though the whole community was facing the same problem, Richard was haunted by a personal sense of failure. He rubbed his eyes wearily as he continued, "I had to sit out there in my backyard with my son on my lap, just looking at the sky for long periods of time. Just looking at that sky, wondering what happened to all that money and all that stuff I did." Richard frowned at memories vivid even after thirty-five years. "I think my way out of things. And, to think my way out of the U.S. Steel thing was hard. . . . It drove me to drinking." Penelope's face froze. She avoided eye contact with me and looked stonily at the table as Richard's story brushed against still-raw scars. Their family of five lived well below the federal poverty line for years as Richard found his way out of the bottle and back into a full-time job.[38]

Poverty is not merely about income; it's entangled with basic material, social, and emotional resources required for people to live in a state of dignity.[39] On the Southeast Side, steelwork enabled workers to feel middle-class by serving as their families' primary breadwinners, paying mortgages, and contributing to charities. This work also provided the foundation for individuals' sense of self, meaning, pride, and purpose. When Richard lost his job, he lost both his capacity to support his family and his sense of self-respect.

Richard was not alone in his struggles for dignity. In the years following closure, many former steelworkers struggled with poor physical and mental health. In an oral history, Victor recalled that, on the last day of his mill's operation, "it was very sad because they felt like they lost like a member of the family. Some of them were crying, you know. It's very sad and personal because if you feel you can't get another job, then you say, 'What am I going to do to support my family?' It's a very sad situation." Always, some workers "couldn't cope," he quietly admitted. "A lot of the people that I know were in really bad situations, two or three of them committed suicide. They said, 'That's it!' you know. The one guy, I talked to him the day before he hanged himself. That was a very bad experience." Dozens of studies on the aftermath of company closures note escalated rates of suicide and depression following job loss.[40] In her semi-autobiographical book, Christine Walley recorded that 800 of Wisconsin Steel's 3,400 former workers died within ten years of the mill closing, many after battling alcoholism and depression.[41] Contemporary studies reaffirm the interlocking relationship between economic and physical well-being. In 2012, the economists Justin Pierce and Peter Schott observed that U.S. counties most impacted by trade liberalization and import competition consistently experienced higher unemployment, lower labor force participation, lower income, and a notable spike in alcohol-related liver disease.[42]

Finding new work might have softened the blow of losing steel jobs. But steel's collapse was so widespread, the location of the steel neighborhoods so peripheral, and new jobs available so poor in quality that new employment was not a simple path out of poverty. Richard looked for a full-time job to replace what he had in the mill for four years. "There weren't no jobs. Wasn't nobody working for a long time." Richard's memory holds true: according to a survey conducted by the Chicago Mayor's Office the year after Richard lost his job, in 1985, laid-off steelworkers reported "an average drop in family income of around 50 percent. Unemployment has tripled. As many as one in three local labor force participants is unemployed."[43]

This was a region fifteen miles south of downtown, an industrial zone distinct from the rest of the city with a majority of employment historically anchored in one industry. When mills began to phase out in 1970, and fully shutter in 1980, what jobs were available tended to be short-term gigs, part-time work, or temp jobs located miles from the Southeast Side and arranged through labor brokers who took a cut of each paycheck.[44] For some workers, the contrast between lost blue-collar jobs and available work dissuaded them from even trying to reenter the workforce. Ed Sadlowski, the former union leader, summarized in an oral history how steel's collapse "had a terrible impact on the community. You went from—these were all high-paying jobs I'm talking about—union jobs that were paying a decent living wage and, you know, benefits, what have you—down to pushing a broom in a hospital somewhere at four dollars, five dollars an hour or so. I don't mean that in a demeaning way, that people that push brooms in hospitals . . ." He paused, selecting his words carefully. "But it's a hell of cut from twenty-five dollars an hour to five dollars an hour, pushing a broom, you know? Terrible, terrible impact."

For older workers, the hunt for new employment was littered with even more hurdles. In the old union office in Chicago, Oliver's voice cracked as he told me, "I felt so bad that I could not help them. I could not find a job for them. When you are used to working in the steel industry, it's kind of hard to go out and get a job elsewhere. Especially if you are [in your] fifties or older and if you are not a go-getter, your life is going to be miserable because nobody is going to offer you a job. Making decent wages, having insurance for your family . . ." His voice trailed off and he shrugged to indicate the hopelessness that such a situation might cultivate. Oliver's observation reflected a broader trend. While two-thirds of displaced workers under the age of fifty find a new job, for displaced workers between the ages of fifty-five and sixty-four, the likelihood of finding a job drops below 50 percent.[45] Typically lacking high school or college degrees and often discarded by bankrupt companies that were, at least initially, unable to fulfill pension responsibilities to their unemployed, workers over age fifty indeed faced a harsh future.

Without good work options, the model of the single-income, middle-class family reliant solely on the male breadwinner came up empty. Interviewees—some with pride, others with shame—admitted that soon after losing their jobs, their wives found work to support the family. In fact, in part due to the mass exodus of men from blue-collar manufacturing and mining, between 1950 and 2016 women's participation in the formal U.S. labor market nearly doubled from 34 percent to almost 57 percent in 2016.[46] Women's wages not only paid the bills but also bolstered a failing social and economic safety net. For instance, after losing his job in the 1980s, Peter found himself without company-subsidized insurance but too ashamed to enroll in Medicaid. To avoid the financial cost of a potential health crisis, his wife became his family's provider. Still squirming at the memory decades later, he explained, "The most unnerving part is when they took all our health insurance away. And so, if my wife wasn't working, I would have had no insurance."[47] Richard felt more positively about his wife's role in supporting their family. During his four years of unemployment, Penelope filled the gap by landing a job in the service sector. "My wife, she went to work and helped me. She made some good money," he explained, looking fondly at her. "She made more money than me!"

"I Don't Want to Seem as Poor": Iron County

All the components that made the experience of economic collapse challenging in Southeast Chicago were exacerbated by geographic remoteness and natural resource dependency in Iron County. In this rural region, most employed people worked in the mines or for industries serving the mines, like trucking, rail, or timber. The local economy of the northern half of Iron County overspecialized iron ore extraction at the expense of more diversified employment and economic development options.[48] Dottie described how her husband, in his twenties in the early 1960s, didn't think twice about following his father and her uncles into the mine. "Mining jobs were good jobs, so when you had them you just hung on to them and didn't look any further."

Mine closure meant nearly instant community collapse. Without mining companies, no market existed for timber braces for headframe openings supplied by loggers or mine building maintenance provided by construction teams. Without incomes from the mines, residents couldn't buy cars from the half-dozen car dealers that interviewees described to me with relish or purchase fresh pasta from their favorite Italian restaurant. Businesses shuttered one by one, not only erasing the economic framework for community life but also significantly reducing the possibilities for local people to experience a middle-class life together. Company benefits beyond wages—free health care, office buildings with polished marble floors, entertainment centers, and infrastructural upkeep—disappeared within a year of the last mine closing. Within a few years of the final mine closing in Iron County, the state of Wisconsin declared it one of twenty "economically distressed" counties. "This means," a local newspaper editorial observed in 1985, "there is little or nothing in the line of other work available."[49]

Residents' internal orientation to their economic position changed much more slowly than did the realities of their daily expenses. Interviewees experienced dissonance between their internalized class identity and their inability to maintain a middle-class lifestyle. Without the presence of the company that historically assisted them, locals were loath to seek assistance from charity or government sources. When Rupert's father and grandfather lost their jobs in the mine, their families expressed hesitancy to depend on government aid—even though dependency on the company had been so vital to everyday life for generations. "My grandma said they're not taking welfare— they'll eat the bark off a tree first," he recalled with a frown. But double-digit unemployment rates in their single-industry town quickly trumped any political or cultural resistance to accepting food aid. Rupert looked visibly uncomfortable as his wife, Nan, explained to me how their family ultimately decided to accept federal food aid distributed in the months after company closure. "Our kids still remember, every time we all get together, 'Remember when we had to drink that dried milk? They hated that." Even today, she explained, their adult children bring up the food aid as a symbol of their family history. Rupert and Nan supplemented this despised food aid with weekly baskets from the local church-based food bank, their own garden produce, and winter hunting and trapping. "Of all the things we had to cut back on, that was the thing that sticks with them, having to drink powdered milk," Nan said, staring at her clasped hands. Their kids were fed and they made it through. But, even decades after closure, they both felt like they failed their family somehow—that reliance on charity or federal food aid was an acceptance of poverty as status and reality.

Sociologists refer to these sentiments of incongruity between a person's expectations of what wealth should feel, taste, or look like and the objective realities of lost income as class ambiguity.[50] Temporal contrasts between one's anticipated identification as middle-class and one's actual experience within an altered, material reality can produce sentiments of anger, disappointment, or guilt. Sudden changes in economic fates can make individuals feel social stress and a sense of being in the out-group—even if most of a locale is experiencing the same thing. In Iron County, like in Southeast Chicago and other postindustrial contexts, expectations of upward mobility and steady wealth that were taken-for-granted one month were suddenly void and empty the next.

In response to the dissonance between expectations of continued economic well-being and disappointing post closure realities, interviewees across generations expressed bitterness about the failures of both defunct companies and other institutions, like the federal government, to fulfill perceived promises of social care and upward class mobility. Some in the younger generation—those who would've been the age of Nan and Rupert's kids—expressed shame for having experienced such dire poverty. Melanie, a woman in her fifties, modulated her voice to be barely audible over the chatter of the local coffee shop where we sat. Her dad had worked in the mine most of his life, but what she wanted to talk about was the food they had to eat when he lost his job. "I mean, I don't want to seem as poor, but you know . . ." she began to almost whisper. "[I remember] going to get the commodities of cheese, and that Spam." She groaned. "I mean Spam almost every meal. Mom did her best to do with it what she could and what we had."

This younger generation also recalled the struggle of their parents or grandparents to find work and make sense of lives that, for the first time, would exist without iron mining. Rupert was visibly angry when recalling how a copper mine that hired newly unemployed iron miners proceeded to close. "We seen guys that got kicked in the face one time, get kicked in the face . . . [and] now they're older. Now they're in their late fifties or sixties. Now, where do you get a job?" Likewise, Carl's lip curled in disgust as he recounted that his sixty-year-old father "was working at the mine when it closed, and he wasn't eligible for social security, or anything else." His eyes glinted with anger. Missing the cutoff for higher pension rates by a year, Carl's father knew he would receive a mere pittance of $25 per month from the company's pension fund when it began issuing checks a year later. Unemployment insurance was insufficient for Carl's large family, he explained. Too financially strapped to go back to school and too old to begin an entry-level position in a completely new career, Carl's father left his family and the impossible job search in rural Wisconsin and moved to Grants, New Mexico, "to work in the uranium mines down there, and he worked down there for a couple of years," Carl explained. "But then my grandmother, his mother, was ill, and he moved back in '64. After that, he just got minimal jobs around here. He was too old to get a good job. So, towards the end of their life was . . ." He sighed heavily. "So much less income than they had. They were hurting that way. My mother had to go to work, and she worked until she was 87." Carl's eyes closed as he added bitterly, "*That* was the result of the mine."

The structural displacement of industrial work not only caused crises of objective wealth but also changed workers' subjective experiences of class. In Chicago, Iron County, and countless other communities built around one industry, newly unemployed industrial workers and their neighbors found themselves confused about where they belonged in the class hierarchies of the United States.[51] The jobless were stupefied by their overdue bills, repossessed cars, and welfare offices. Women and young people entered the wage-labor workforce only to earn paltry incomes. Stress-related diseases increased in deindustrialized communities, as did suicides and depression.[52] Entire communities internalized the contrast between their present poverty and their just-out-of-reach wealth and middle-class status. "How far," one steelworker's daughter quipped, "we have fallen."

These collective sentiments of disorientation and trauma echo other research on communities upended by a large-scale disaster. In his study of a flash flood that destroyed a coal mining town, the sociologist Kai Erikson noted how survivors of this flood exhibited "the classic symptoms of mourning and bereavement. People are grieving for their lost friends and lost home, but they are grieving too for their lost cultural surround; and they feel dazed at least in part because they are not sure what to do in the absence of that familiar setting." Much like these survivors, worker-citizens in Iron County and Southeast Chicago found themselves grieving and dazed, lacking external structures of regular wages and familiar shops, schedules, and means of feeding their families. The newly unemployed found themselves at odds with their environment, confused at their class status, and lost at home.[53]

CONCLUSION

In the years immediately following company closure, how home looked, sounded, and functioned fundamentally changed. Foremen switched off the water pumps that had run for decades to push back the flow of groundwater seeping through rock and into the underground mine shafts. Trains fell silent, barren of ore cars. Company offices were boarded up and sold. Steel mill factory gates were chained shut. Union leaders shifted from organizing protests to coordinating food banks. Deindustrialization created what the cultural sociologist Ann Swidler referred to as an "unsettled" episode of social breakdown, where people had to navigate the loss of "taken-for-granted externalized cultural scaffolding."[54] In crisis situations, people who cannot rely on past general rules about how their world works must reconsider their cultural and material resources and intentionally make their way.[55] Closure forced residents of Iron County and Southeast Chicago to reconceive home without the resources that iron and steel companies had offered in earlier decades—geographic integration into core economic systems, social supports for community function, and upward economic mobility. With the wisdom of hindsight, interviewees worked hard to make sense of the lacuna of cultural scaffolding. They offered accounts of the perceived causes and lasting effects of company closure, and contrasted the emerging limitations of deindustrialization with their own struggles to maintain social safety nets without formerly taken-for-granted rights as worker-citizens and renegotiate their sense of class, purpose, and self.

But crisis wasn't the end of the story; it was the creation of a new kind of home. Hidden in interviewee accounts comparing departure and competition, fairness and loss, and personal griefs is another quiet contrast—one between macroeconomic mobility and residential stability. Interviewees' diagnoses of geographic shifts and local economic problems would set up their explanation for why they stayed in place even after all the jobs left. Back in Iron County, in an apparent non sequitur to diagnoses of fair trade and international regulation, Dottie concluded, "We're not gonna quit and we're not moving." Her friend Lola chuckled and added, "Move where?"

For some, the way forward was the way out through migration to new locations. But for others, managing economic disaster required a different form of movement. As the next chapters will show, the newly unemployed pursued multiple forms of mobility that kept them within their home regions; they worked to maintain community by leveraging material resources in their physical landscapes and shifting their expectations for economic well-being. As time passed, these practical strategies to stay reflected and consolidated their individual and collective definitions of home. Iron and steel might have fled the places people called home, but many of its worker-citizens did not.

3

HOW TO STAY IN THE RUST BELT

Work, Choice, and Home in the Decade

After Company Closure

We're all tougher than we think we are. We're fixed so that almost anything heals.

—Wallace Stegner, *Crossing to Safety*, 1987

Charles, ninety-three, ran his fingers along the top of the dusty mining helmet that he set before me on the table. Drumming his fingers across its crown, he explained how in 1967, as the last load of stockpiled iron ore was ceremoniously placed on the final train out of town, he and his fellow unemployed miners were wrestling with a fundamental question: What now? He sighed, remembering. "Nothing was any good [here]. What are they going to do? You go to the city and look for work, or pick up something here or there. . . . It was tough, real tough." Nearly one century after the discovery of iron ore in the hills of northern Iron County, working-age men no longer had high-wage employment in the mines to tie them to their rural homes. For many, moving forward meant moving away. Once the last and largest iron mine closed, one in seven newly unemployed miners and their families migrated to locations that promised better wages and a possible return to economic stability. "A lot of them went to the Texas mines and all over," Charles explained.

Charles's fleeing neighbors intuitively understood a pattern that rural and urban sociologists have tracked for decades: industrial job losses were not just a problem of markets; they were a crisis of geography. These were communities built in the image of capital that no longer existed, where localized economic thriving had been gloriously, if precariously, contingent a single employer. Now, without iron and steel and lacking a more diversified economy, worker-citizens moved away in search of jobs. To earn competitive wages, workers need to escape the place that was undergoing large-scale, economic upheaval.[1] In both Iron County and in Southeast Chicago, everyone knew someone who sold their house, pulled their kids from school, and permanently relocated elsewhere—some to the mines in Missouri or North Dakota, others to a Maytag factory in the Chicago suburbs. Between 1970 and 2000, the net population of Iron County declined by 24 percent and Southeast Chicago's population shrank by 21 percent.[2]

Even though Charles lived in a region with many more unemployed workers than available jobs, he refused to move. Jutting out his stubbly chin, he recalled that after losing the only work that he, his father, and his grandfather had ever known, "I says, 'I am not going to leave here.' There's only one place in the world! That's when [I got] my antiques store going, and I took a job roofing." Charles paused his work narrative as Cheryl, seventy-five, and the widow of another former miner, peered into the room. She leaned on the doorjamb and listened for a moment before entering to top up our coffee mugs from a fresh pot. Smiling at Charles, she interjected, "But we're here because we want to be here, and that's the bottom line. We're a hidden secret. A well-hidden secret! People don't live here unless they want to. We've made the choice," Cheryl concluded, "to stick it out."

Charles and Cheryl are part of a larger cohort of long-term residents who experienced the arc from boom to bust, and yet stayed through decades of economic depression, depopulation, and disinvestment. Based on demographic, employment, and homeownership data, at least 30 percent of former ironworkers and steelworkers, their families, and their neighbors still live in Iron County and Southeast Chicago.[3] How and why do people make the decision to stay in places wracked by crisis?

Study after study describes deindustrialized communities as hard places to live. Industrial closures trigger the collapse of smaller companies that fueled industrial work—hardware stores, trucking outfits, and even restaurants. In turn, these closures lead to the dissolution of social institutions once linked to a company town or neighborhood. Schools and churches consolidate and housing values plummet. Staying put, particularly in those first few years after company closure, meant attempting to manage complex social and geographical problems with a shrinking set of economic resources. Weakened social structures and disintegrated infrastructures smacked up against values, priorities, and visions for the future, constraining locals' choices. Those who study people living in hard places—and often, people who themselves affected by economic crisis—question how much agency actually exists in places made topsy-turvy by structural change.[4] Yet through pragmatic decisions made within hard contexts, people assess what parts of their homes— and themselves—are rooted in place, worth saving, and, quite often, sources of joy.[5]

Because this book focuses on the residentially persistent like Charles and Cheryl, nearly every interview contained stories about employment decisions made in spite of—and, at times, because of—the post-industrial transformations of geography, community, and economy that make their place home. In this chapter, I concentrate on the parts of interviewee stories focused on those first few years after company closure, when former miners and millworkers addressed their most immediate problem: how to make ends meet in the wake of deindustrialization. Across cases, long-term residents negotiated what was lost—and what was left behind in Iron County and Southeast Chicago—to pursue three categories of work. Interviewees waited out the first years of unemployment by hustling for *informal work*—gigs available only because of their familiarity with local people and places. Then, as the permanence of deindustrialization sunk in, interviewees began *commuting* to higher-paid work located outside the geographic stranglehold of economic depression. These workers did not permanently depart, however—left-behind family members remained to maintain household function and preserve some social stability. Eventually, many long-term residents traded higher incomes for locational preference, securing lower-paid employment in their much-altered local economy. *Returning* required workers to revise their skills, certifications, and perhaps, most importantly, their own expectations of class and wealth. While interviewees often explained their hustles and strategies as reasonable responses to economic crisis, they also spoke positively of these years of change—delighting in their own cleverness, persistence, and commitment to the places and people they loved. Over time, these choices rebalanced the relative weight that interviewees placed on the components of home, increasing their value of certain vestiges of community and geographical resources while expanding their economic strategies for survival.

LOCAL HUSTLE: INFORMAL WORK IN AN EMPTY ECONOMY

Most newly unemployed interviewees first worked in the informal sector—making money "by doing whatever is necessary to survive or simply make ends meet," as the urban sociologist William Julius Wilson defined. Informal work involves short-term gigs paid under the table. While such "hustling" characterizes many segments of society, it becomes widespread when formal employment is geographically scarce or available jobs have less social status within a person's value system.[6] When more than half of the jobs in Iron County and Southeast Chicago disappeared within a few years, the newly unemployed leveraged two characteristics of home that remained without industry: residues of industrial-era community relationships and physical elements inherent to their geographies.[7] Informal labor only works when someone local wants to buy what you're selling. What people were selling was their relationship to place.

Forest Work: Iron County

Living in a sparsely populated rural community that had been, for nearly a century, controlled by one major industry meant that when Iron County's mines let their workers go, other formal employment was scarce. To solve economic problems, interviewees plugged holes in income flows through work found through place-based social networks, performed close to home, and paid cash or in kind. Notably, informal work was possible only because of their deep knowledge of localized nature and close-knit social ties—two resources that extended far beyond the scope of iron mining or the companies that had controlled the original construction of home. Again and again, I heard stories of newly unemployed miners turning to piecemeal work that leveraged their knowledge of nature and their relationships with neighbors. Charles patched people's roofs; Cheryl tutored kids in math after school; Julian plowed snow; Paul drove a logging truck and maintained his village's roads in the summer; Mitchell sold his time as a day laborer and carpenter to a local construction company. While interviewees framed this work as necessary, they also were proud of their cleverness in this season of hustle.

In her living room, Dottie told me how her husband Henry was laid off in 1962. With a growing family at home, federal unemployment and a tiny pension couldn't pay their bills. As soon as he came home with his pink slip, Henry started knocking on neighbors' doors to see if they'd pay him for labor. He "got some odd jobs delivering . . . coal and different things. Or he would help somebody who is hanging [sheet rock] or anything like that." In between Henry's handyman jobs, Dottie sold eggs, milk, and cheese from their small homestead farm and picked up extra shifts in the ticket booth at the local ski hill, at a glove factory, or as a part-time wreath-maker. She smiled brightly as she recalled how the wreath-making company would transform an old mine equipment storage building into a seasonal Christmas wreath assembly line. Blurring the lines between informal work and regularized wages, the company would buy truckloads of greenery from residents who walked their forests, cutting down boughs to wreath-making specifications, and then hire locals to twist the branches into wreaths for one month each fall. Dottie said, "I learned how to do it and I made candy canes and I made crosses for churches, and I would go through a pair of those heavy garden gloves—leather!—a day." Dottie laughed as she wiggled her fingers dramatically in front of her face. "And then I'd be taping [them] with duct tape on the cracks so I wouldn't cut my fingers on the wires." The work was hard but Dottie was proud that, between the efforts of the two of them, she and Henry "never missed a house payment. Even after he ran out of unemployment."

Similarly, Dave described his reliance on the gig economy booming in the dense forest near his house. After losing his mining job, he said, "We had some lean years. I had a wife and four children, and we just about bottomed out." But, he explained, he did okay because "I worked in the woods off and on with my dad and, of course, with my children. We peeled pulp, that is. We peeled aspen." Dave was one of half a dozen interviewees who described "working in the woods"—local shorthand for under-the-table work with the timber industry. Locals would congregate at timber camps, armed with their own C-shaped metal tool—"it's about a foot and a half long with a sharp edge on it," Dave patiently explained to me. With this tool, they'd pry the bark off aspen trees before the trees were processed for paper making.[8] Modeling the technique of bark-peeling with his hands, Dave described to me how central this work was to his transition period between unemployment and his new job as an entry-level construction worker a year after mine closure. By working in the woods, "the kids made some extra money, and of course I did too, on weekends and evenings," he explained. "And then we came out of it pretty good, see," he added with a contented smile. Dave's "work in the woods" was only one type of natural resource use that interviewees described to me— others dug and pulverized rocks for gravel, built trails, cleared snow, or hunted deer both on- and off-season to feed their families. Each form of labor reflected their unique relationships with each other and their geography.

Eggs and Beer: Chicago

In Chicago, the unemployed didn't "work in the woods," as they did in Iron County, but they did find odd jobs that leveraged their own physical and social contexts. Because steel mill closures were staggered over two decades, some interviewees benefited from under-the-table work that relied on remnants of the formal economy. Richard, who lost his steel job in the mid-1980s, turned to selling street food to his fellow steelworkers in his first few months of unemployment. Sipping hot tea in their quiet dining room, his wife Penelope explained that he always "stayed going—always doing something. I remember one time he was just selling eggs. He'd do anything rather than stay home. I was like 'What are you doing now?' 'I'm selling eggs.'" She shook her head and gazed at her husband. His mouth twisted with a complicated blend of sadness and merriment. He stared at his mug of tea as he explained how, in the late 80s, he had an insider contact at a nearby bulk food store. "I'd get crates of eggs and sell them—an egg and a beer, an egg and a beer." He'd hawk hard-boiled eggs and single cans of beer outside his old steel mill around shift-change time, selling the snacks to the few hundred remaining steelworkers. He concluded, "They bought all those eggs and beers, oh boy!"

But when his former mill finally closed its doors, Richard lost his meager customer base. The fresh influx of unemployed workers made competing for the few formal jobs in the neighborhood an even more daunting task, so Richard forewent legal employment for several years. "I did work everywhere," he continued. "People's houses, all kinds of stuff just to make a meal for my . . ." his voice faded as a specific memory caught him. "One time I worked for two hot dogs and a box of rice. Yeah, that's how bad it was. Two hot dogs and a box of rice! This guy had his basement flooded up to the top." He raised his hands above his head. "I unflooded it with tubes, and he gave me two hot dogs and a box of rice." He snorted, still annoyed that he agreed to such a poor barter. But after that meager meal was gone, he explained to me with a shrug, "I went somewhere else and made some more money somewhere else."

Richard had no illusions that selling eggs or working as a handyman would do anything more than put food on his family's table for a day or a week. But the small money made through these haphazard jobs was a form of active waiting, a finger stuck in the crumbling dam holding back financial crisis. Working odd jobs allowed people like Richard to simply wait: to wait for the immediate crisis of unemployment to ebb; to wait for unemployment checks to come through; or to wait for hung-up pensions or uncashable paychecks to be cleared by a slow-moving judicial system. Maybe Penelope's garden would produce more vegetables, the bank would hold off on calling in their loans, and Richard's luck would change. Richard and a half dozen other Chicago interviewees shyly admitted that they'd held out hope that their companies would call them back to work. It had happened before—temporary closures, furloughs, and slowdowns implemented by steel companies during brief, economic downturns.[9] Given a few months or even a year, they expected to be lining back up at the mill gates to get their old jobs back. Until then, informal work would continue to be a core source of cash and food.

But the waiting didn't pay off, and job loss—no matter how collective or dramatic—didn't stop the bills from piling up. At some point, as many of my Chicago interviewees admitted to me, they finally internalized the permanence of closure. For some, that moment of clarity came when they witnessed bulldozers crushing industrial buildings (see figure 3.1). For others, it was when they touched the rusted clasp of the chain wrapped around the gate to their darkened mill or watched their next-door neighbors put up for-sale signs in their front yards. For Richard, it was when he burned out on the ceaseless activity of those little jobs—refinishing floors, cleaning buildings, bartering labor for food, or selling snacks in the street. At the end of four months of hustling to make ends meet, Richard was exhausted, scared, and depressed. Informal work in their millgate neighborhood was never meant to replace full-time employment.

Looking back at that season of their lives today, Penelope laughed at how his efforts to win them time and pay their bills were at once necessary and fruitless. "You have to have laughter

FIGURE 3.1 Former steelworkers walking over the rubble of U.S. Steel South Works.

Photograph by the author.

with that, because, you know," she said, her voice thick with emotion, "you have to laugh about it sometimes." Richard forced a chuckle as he concluded, "We just, you know, tried to make ends meet and do it anyway. It could have been so much worse. You know, but you never say never. Because you can do it, anybody can do it if they really, really try." He placed his hand on his wife's shoulder reassuringly. "If you love your family you going to do it."

So much of daily life was unrecognizable in those first years after company closure. No wages, no work routines, no shift whistles. But the practical needs remained the same. Informal labor enabled job seekers to walk out their front doors and look for aspects of everyday life that, in fact, remained the same: a neighbor who needed a handyman, forests offering their bounty, or cash exchanged for unlicensed street food. This informal labor was possible only *because* workers stayed in their communities and geographies with which they were intimately familiar. Hustling rewards deep familiarity with the human and nonhuman landscapes of everyday life—resources that would've been lost to Southeast Chicagoans and Iron Countians if they had immediately migrated to a new place in search of work. Yet while cash in hand kept bills paid and food on the table, most interviewees continued their search for full-time, formal jobs—employment that paid regularized wages, offered benefits, and guaranteed work through a legally binding contract. Informal work was merely the home base in an exhausting project of trying to survive in a hard place.

TETHERED DEPARTURES: COMMUTING

If unemployment in Southeast Chicago and Wisconsin had been due to a series of firm-specific redundancies or mergers, residents would have had more options for reentering local, full-time employment. But because deindustrialization undermined the economy of entire geographic regions, to find a full-time job most interviewees had to leave the local community—at least temporarily. Economists consistently show that distance from the epicenter of an economic crisis correlates with increased wages for blue-collar work.[10] Former steelworkers in Chicago described their ten- or twenty-mile commutes to the suburbs for jobs similar to those they held in steel. Only an hour of commute time, on average, but still a significant shift from the millgate model of walking to work. Commuting in Wisconsin involved much more distance—often workers traveled hundreds of miles each week to blue-collar work in far-flung cities.[11]

Why did job seekers previously unfamiliar to significant commutes choose this employment option? Because a bread-winner hit the road, the rationale went, kids could stay at their schools, dwindling friendship networks could be maintained, and houses could be paid off. Interviewees hoped that commuting might offer the best of both worlds—higher wages and stability of home.

Megacommutes: Iron County

With only two, two-lane highways linking small villages to large cities, like Duluth, Green Bay, or Milwaukee, hundreds of miles away, Iron County is geographically remote by all definitions of the term. Only through megacommuting—traveling ninety minutes or more to work—could breadwinners escape the centripetal force of this economically depressed zone and find much higher wages in trades in which they were already trained. Nearly every interviewee in Wisconsin shared a story of a megacommute pursued by someone in their family in order to allow life back home to continue on as if the iron mines had never closed.

At Dottie's dining room table, she brought me into family lore about her husband's megacommutes. It was 1963, and Dottie found out she was pregnant with their second child. Desperate for a regular paycheck to support his growing family, Henry and six other out-of-work miners drove from the northernmost corner of Wisconsin to Louisiana and then west and north again through Missouri, Iowa, and the Dakotas, applying for jobs at mines and manufacturing plants along the way. At night, Dottie told me, "when places were closed, they'd go to do laundry— six pairs of jeans went into wash, six pair underwear, six socks. That's the way they did it." The men would pause their multimonth road trip when someone got work; after a few weeks, they'd roll on with the remaining job seekers. Laura, Dottie and Henry's eldest, said, "They would just buy a loaf of bread and a pack of baloney . . . and whoever could get a job, they would pool their money and send it back home." Henry finally found work six hours and 350 miles south of his hometown at a car manufacturing plant in Milwaukee, Wisconsin. When Henry returned to Iron County after his first shift, he met his newborn daughter and then promptly packed his bag and left again. For the next three years, he would bunk with coworkers and drive home, paycheck in hand, every two months.

Commuting from Iron County was more akin to short-term migration than the national average of a twenty-minute commute. Like migration, megacommutes relied on the stability of women at home to maintain the social bearings and kinship networks for traveling men. This weekly or monthly familial separation created relational losses not unlike those experienced by migrants crossing national borders.[12] Dottie grieved that Henry missed key moments in his family's life while she faced the trials of solo parenthood. "One time when he was [away]," Dottie began, "Maria was a baby and we got the flu, all of us. I had the cows and I had the kids." Their house on a little homestead bordering the former company town "had a wood fireplace—a furnace—downstairs. Maria was throwing up so hard I was afraid she was going to choke, but I didn't dare leave her alone long enough to go into the basement to start the fire." Dottie bit her lip as she relived her fear. "I usually walked to my dad's every day, just for exercising and to get the kids out of the house. My folks, the second day when I didn't show up, they think something's wrong. So, they came up. My dad heard the cows mooing in the barn 'cause I hadn't been able to take care of them. So, he ran into the barn, and my mother ran into the cold house and made the fire up as she hollered to make sure somebody was alive." Dottie sat deathly still, her eyes inward and her face grim. "That was one of the worst times. I didn't have time to be scared." She pulled herself back to the present, studying her hands before making eye contact with me. "But I wasn't the only one going through that. There's a lot of them."[13]

For the younger generation of interviewees, a father's short-term migration might've avoided the upheaval of moving to a new school in the middle of the year, but it brought its own childhood griefs. Laura told me, "That's something I distinctly remember—my dad being gone because he was looking for work. A lot of families were split that way. The wife stayed here, but then the husband, the miner, was out looking for work." She recalled that her aunt lived alone while her husband worked in an automobile manufacturing plant eight hours away. Across the street, Mitchell's wife struggled alone with early onset Alzheimer's once their boys went off to college. Joan, a neighbor of Dottie's, recalled how her dad got a management position with a mine ten hours away in Minnesota. Joan was finishing high school at the time and her parents wanted to keep her close to friends and family. "He'd come home on weekends," she said, "with the guys he stayed there with at the boardinghouse. It was hard. It was hard for him to be away too." Gray-haired and a grandmother herself now, Joan's eyes still glimmered with tears for her father's absence from her high school graduation. "We graduated on Friday night, and he was in transit."

Breadwinner absences were crushing for those at home. So when women and children themselves hit the road, the constancy of home life degraded even more.[14] When Joan left for college a few hours away, in Michigan, hers was a family of full-time commuters based in their mortgage-free house that was too undervalued to sell and traveling to places that were too expensive to resettle in. "My dad would have to go up to Northern Minnesota and my mother had to be at work in Bowler Junction or Mercer, depending on which job she went to. . . . We were all in transit. We'd have maybe a day or a day and a half together, and I'd have to go back to school." Her family might have not moved out of her childhood home, but Joan was homesick for her constantly commuting family. Better wages might have been available out there, but life was being lived—and missed—at home.

Suburbs and City: Chicago

Commuting in Chicago was more comparable to national averages than were the dramatic distances of Iron County's megacommutes. As steel mills shuttered through the 1980s and 1990s, workers seeking formal employment frequently found new work within the metropolitan region. Recall from chapter 2 how, in aggregate, jobs lost due to industrial collapse were nearly simultaneously replaced by new service jobs located elsewhere in the country. This national pattern appeared in the Chicago metropolitan region, as the total number of metals and manufacturing positions lost on the Southeast Side reappeared in the form of white-collar work and small factory jobs in downtown Chicago or the suburbs. Between 1976 and 1996, 60 percent of the new jobs created in the Chicago metropolitan area were sited in its northwest suburbs—some thirty to fifty miles away from the former steel mill neighborhoods.[15] While the proximity of these new jobs promised a less socially disruptive path out of economic depression when compared to Iron County's mega-commutes, this spatial shift of employment still troubled the millgate neighborhoods. Neighborhoods shifted from walkable clusters of houses centered on a common employer to merely resting places during the workweek. For former steelworkers following manufacturing jobs beyond the reach of public transportation to the suburbs an hour away, rising gas prices in the 1980s and costs of vehicle maintenance ate into wages. Job seekers who wanted to still live in Southeast Chicago paid financial and social costs for their residential stability.

But for many interviewees, the economic costs of commuting were balanced by the increasing weight they placed on other values of remaining at home. For instance, Alberto told me how when he and his brothers lost their jobs in the steel mills, "our goal was to find a job that would last us a lifetime, get us a pension and whatnot." Unhappy with the local options and unwilling to waste their twenties waiting for the right job to appear in their shrinking neighborhood, most of his siblings immediately moved away. Alberto frowned in disappointment. "My oldest brother, he moved to Florida. I have two younger sisters who, after everything collapsed, they went to Mexico to live with family, to go to school. Ended up marrying and staying there," he concluded with a disapproving shrug. In contrast, Alberto wanted to stay close to his parents and make the most of their father's hard migration from Mexico to Chicago in the 1950s. He decided that he was willing to wade through several years of underemployment. "My father found work at the scrap yard. . . . My older brother, who lost his job in a mill, like me, he floated around from small job to small job. I went to Solo Cup"—a plasticware factory located along the Calumet River on the Southeast Side. These jobs didn't provide that sought-after pension or good wage, but they paid the bills. His younger brother also remained in the neighborhood, finding steady employment with a utilities company located south of the city. "That was good," Alberto nodded with a smile. And his own luck changed soon after. A few years after he lost his mill job, Alberto finally got a position with the Chicago Transit Authority at their headquarters located forty-five minutes away. The commute was annoying, but the job came with his hoped-for pension and enabled Alberto to live around the corner from his aging parents. He started in that job as a single twenty-something young man and, when he spoke with me, had recently retired, happy with his past choices.

As a young and single man, Alberto could wait until he found that pension-bearing position in a troubled local economy. But with a growing family, Richard did not feel so free. He and Penelope were lucky to own their house outright, but they hated that they were defaulting on their car payments, relying on food banks, and praying health scares away while he searched for permanent employment for four long years. His anxiety increased when Penelope found out she was pregnant with their fifth child. For four years, Richard had been applying for jobs throughout the city, but "every time we'd fill out an application, they'd say we were overqualified!" Perhaps he was truly overqualified— he had fifteen years' experience as an industrial machinist. The

Chicago historians David Bensman and Roberta Lynch suggest an additional interpretation: "overqualified" was coded language by businesses concerned that the once-unionized steelworkers would grow dissatisfied with low wages and rabble-rouse.[16]

Serendipitously, a friend told him that the U.S. Postal Service was prioritizing hiring unemployed steelworkers and military veterans, two categories Richard fulfilled. In the late 1980s, an entry-level job opened at the headquarters of the city's U.S. postal service some sixteen miles, and forty-five minutes via bus, north of Southeast Chicago. He interviewed and was hired on the spot. With visible relief, he recalled, "I went to the post office, started working there. [That was] the only thing that saved me." Although he was initially hired as a janitor, his skills as a machine operator combined with a charismatic personality and clear leadership potential earned him a rapid promotion to a management position. Penelope was proud of how quickly he came to oversee the service of the air conditioners and heating machines that kept the largest post-office building in the city comfortable. Richard was pleased that he was able to keep his kids in their house and school, provide a steady income, and benefit from a pension and health insurance reminiscent of his steel mill days.

As time passed, Richard's commute via bus became more difficult to manage as the city, on an austerity budget, disinvested in public transportation. Even though any job, anywhere, was welcome to Richard and his fellow former steelworkers, the residues of absent steel continued to haunt their daily routines. Gone were the days when work was within easy walking distance of home, where blue-collar work could accrue middle-class wealth. In fact, after twenty years of faithful work, Richard earned from the post office barely half of what he had earned at the steel mill in the 1980s. Every day he rode his long bus route, he was reminded that his home—once central to the region's economy due to the mills—was now on the periphery. The city had moved on, and he was still here.

Commuters adopted onerous drives or lengthy absences in hopes of maintaining some ember of familial stability, social duty, or financial security that would have been lost through a permanent move away. Almost-paid-off mortgages could be brought to maturation, kids could keep going to their familiar schools, and women and extended families could continue care-giving routines in what had become an otherwise disordered landscaped. The mobility of the breadwinner beyond Southeast Chicago, and to a much greater extent, rural Iron County, both required and enabled a deepening of material and social ties back home. Just as the movement of iron and steel required the establishment of stable nodes along the commodity chain, so too did the mobility of bodies in search of work *out there* require the stability of *here*.[17]

But some commuters found that in practice, their repeated departures threatened the values that far-flung work was initially intended to preserve.[18] The stressors of commuting revealed taken-for-granted conceptions of what type of postindustrial home was desirable, or even possible, to preserve.[19] Work is not merely about wages, and home is not simply a resting place for repeated departures. For many interviewees, actually being at home was the only way to maintain its core meanings.

PURPOSIVE TRADE-OFFS: RETURNING HOME FOR LOCAL JOBS

While not always chronological, work narratives often con-cluded with *returning* home through an intentional retooling of skills, certifications, and, ultimately, internal expectations of work and home. Revision was a strategy to return home, typically after multiple years of commuting—one that demanded acceptance of the limitations of living long-term in a deindustrialized context. After a decade of deindustrialization, both Iron County and Southeast Chicago experienced a slow-down in outmigration and an equilibration of economic changes. Many people who became long-term residents sought out lower-wage work back home in fields that, typically, had little to do with their past work experience. To qualify for jobs as clerks and front-desk receptionists, in-home nurses, restaurant waitstaff, or technicians in smaller-scale mines and factories, many enrolled in the local community college, took advantage of government-subsidized retraining programs, or apprenticed in the trades.[20] Because these jobs were located within economically struggling regions, most new positions paid around half of historic mining or millwork wages. Yet long-term residents often framed choices about new educational and employment trajectories as intentional resistance to the insecurities of informal labor and the trials of commuting. Many interviewees argued that lower pay was a worthwhile trade-off for the privilege of living in a geography and community where they wished to stay.

Retraining and Reentry: Iron County

After years of informal work, Mitchell wanted a steady paycheck. He hadn't gone to college and didn't give a straight answer when I asked whether or not he'd finished high school before starting work at the iron mine in his teens. So, in 1962, when he learned that he could enroll for free in a welding training program funded in part by the federal government, he was delighted.

"You see," he told me, "in the mine I welded some." He had a steady hand but there were significant gaps in his knowledge. "I didn't know one rod from the other. They just gave you rods and you welded."

In 1962, a state-based commission for retraining arrived in northern Wisconsin to aid newly unemployed miners in identifying skills for reemployment. This "industrial commission task force has been working in Hurley, interviewing and testing miners to find talents that can be put to use in other industry," a local newspaper optimistically reported. Over several weeks, the report continued, "over 300 men have taken aptitude tests and the results indicate little trouble in retraining, with the majority showing a lot of potential."[21] One of those men tested was Mitchell. Funded by the Area Development Act, one of the Kennedy administration's multiple, interlocking job training programs, he enrolled in a welding program at a local vocational college because, he recalled with a little smile, "I've got to find out what rods to use on certain things!"[22]

His timing was fortuitous. Just as he completed his welding certification in 1963, the training program was defunded and discontinued. But because federal job training focused on skill development without accounting for local employer demand, Mitchell could only find a job in central Illinois.[23] The job was steady and the pay was satisfactory, but the commute was massive—a seven-hour drive one way. Echoing a pattern that labor historians have repeatedly observed, Mitchell only lasted in his new career for a few months. Like many megacommuters, Mitchell lived near work during the week and returned home on weekends. Driving across beige prairie each week, he grew dissatisfied with the trade-offs of time and pay. His two boys were applying for colleges that year—a point of pride for Mitchell and his wife—and if he was going to be away from his family anyway, he wanted to make it count for more. On his commute north in April 1964, Mitchell stopped by a long-haul trucking company that he'd heard was offering better pay for less time than his current welding position. He started the new job the following week. What was one more job pivot?

Mitchell's brief tenure with his retrained field reflects a problematic presupposition of larger debates and policies supporting education, retraining, or retooling for the American unemployed: that once workers have gained their certifications in welding or auto mechanics, or earned their GEDs or college degrees, they will be willing and able to travel—or permanently move—beyond their economically depressed community to match with suitable jobs. Driven by concerns for upward mobility, enabling people to leave home for good is an economically sound strategy. According to the sociologists Peter Blau and Otis Duncan, chasing employment far afield is good for workers and good for the nation because "geographic movement is associated with superior occupational achievement, regardless of place of birth or destination."[24] But this fails to account for how geographical location of the job contradicts people's own geographical ties.[25] By the time that many of my interviewees—and eventual "long-term residents"—would have completed retraining, they had already doubled down on their commitment to stay in Iron County. Like Mitchell, many had children in school, a mortgage nearly paid off, and even other family members employed locally that made the pull to stay outweigh any impulse to follow work away from home.

In lieu of formal retraining that might take them far afield, most of my interviewees in Wisconsin returned to school, apprenticed in new trades, or explored on-the-job training and certifications in new fields that might enable them to return, or stay, at home. Interviewees often pursued multiple iterations of these less formal repositioning attempts. For instance, Dottie entered the workforce to supplement lost income, as did tens of thousands of women across the United States in the 1970s. She worked during the day as a town clerk and took night classes toward her associate degree in early childhood education. Her work paid the last years of her family's mortgage. Keen to rejoin his wife and kids back home, Henry, her husband, quit his mega-commuting job to take a position as the manager of a grocery store in Iron County. Although he had no prior experience in the service industry, and the pay was much lower than he was used to, Henry found that he valued time at home over the higher wage far away.

Mitchell also exchanged higher wages for a lower-wage job in another mine two hours away from Iron County. "I had twenty-two years at White Pine. Thirty-seven years altogether, with fifteen in the ore mine," he explained to me. We were speaking in the kitchen of the house that he and his wife, Gina, built together sixty years ago. Gina's Alzheimer's meant her attention to our conversation wavered, but she briefly returned to our discussion at this point, smiling sweetly at the fleeting memory. "I had to call him!" she exclaimed. It was the early 1970s. A copper mine in Michigan a few hours east of their house in Wisconsin was hiring and Mitchell's application was the next on the wait-list. The White Pine employment office told Gina to "'tell him to come in to get a physical,'" Mitchell recalled. "She said, 'He's in Salt Lake City right now.' 'What's he doing there?' 'Working!' she says. 'Well does he still want to come to White Pine?' She says, 'Yeah, I guess he does.'" And indeed, Mitchell did want to come work in a mine again. The pay was less and the work was dirtier than in the iron mines, with large-scale machinery and massive trucks kicking up red dust and asbestos. But he'd get to use his welding training and live life with his wife, in his own house, and near his old neighbors. He returned a month later and began daily commutes across a time zone and fifty-five miles of back roads to the Keweenaw Peninsula of northern Michigan. He worked this job until retirement. A decade of informal gigs, commuting, and retraining might have been tough, but he always had work to do. He shrugged self-deprecatingly. "Like I say, I always had to work. No trouble finding work." This last job, however, was the one he wanted—a job that allowed him to stay at home.

Of all work strategies, accepting lower-paid work required interviewees to make intentional decisions about their work location. Hardly following the path of least resistance, interviewees needed to explicitly connect their locational, cultural, and personal priorities with their employment decisions. Commitment to remaining *here* meant that employment decisions were tangled up with ideological priorities in addition to practical concerns. A life-long Iron Countian, Patrick intentionally linked his intention to stay at home with his job choices. After being laid off from the White Pine copper mine in the early 1990s, Patrick retrained as an auto mechanic through another federally funded program. He explained that even though he could've worked anywhere, he got a job in an Iron County auto shop. But it was "for exactly one-half of what I was making [at the mine]! When raising a family! It was a shock to the system." He gave a short bark of a laugh. Only in his last year of work, some thirty years after losing his mining job, were his annual earnings comparable to his starting salary at the copper mine in the 1980s. But, he clarified, this economic choice was in service to a greater value. "Growing up, a lot of people right out of high school moved to the cities. I thought to myself, well, I want my kids to grow up like I did, small town, quiet. So, I had my mind made up to stay in the area. If I went to the cities, I probably could've retired a lot earlier." He waved his hand dismissively. "In the end, I'm glad I did."

College and New Careers: Chicago

In the steel mill community, educational credentials were, for many, the first step in postindustrial retraining.[26] A high school diploma had not been required for steel workers to make good money in Southeast Chicago, David explained in an oral history. "When I was coming up, there was the mills—out of grade school, you go into the steel mills. You never bother going to school. Now, you have to have your schooling and you begin to see other fields to go into. But for us old-timers there was no other way." With few employers accepting minimal education, David observed that "a lot of them did go to school" after they lost their jobs.[27] High school graduates entering the labor market in the years after midwestern mills and mines closed faced less earning potential than did their parents' generation.[28] Chicago's exploding service sector demanded technical or college degrees for entry-level jobs in offices, entertainment, hospitals, and schools. Even remnant industrial work required specialized training. Twenty miles east in Gary, Indiana, a sparse but highly trained staff operated an increasingly automated U.S. Steel plant.[29]

Since walking straight from junior high or high school into a highly paid steel job was no longer an option, many former workers found their way to retraining programs. Like in Iron County, few interviewees in Chicago took advantage of the federally funded programs available during the height of mill closure. Similar to Iron County, the topics of training offered were misaligned with the local job market. By the time Chicago-area steelworkers needed new options in the 1980s, the two federally-funded job retraining programs available — welding and machining—did not reflect actual employment needs in the Chicago region. To make up for this mismatch, the South Chicago Development Commission applied federal funding to their own suite of training for areas that they observed were hiring, like building maintenance, auto parts sales, and electronics. But in the end, as Bensman and Lynch report, even this highly localized program helped only half of its participants find local jobs in their new skill area.[30] Most of my interviewees repositioned through GED programs, community college courses, apprenticeships, or on-the-job training. Oliver exchanged his seat in his mill's union office for computer science classes at the local community college. Louisa transitioned from the mill to college. Jesús went to art school. Marcos joined the fire department. Richard learned about HVAC systems on the job.

For families and married couples, revising work trajectories through education or repositioning was a two-person process. Simonetta echoed Dottie's experience in Wisconsin. She was still finishing her bachelor's degree at Chicago State University one course at a time when Christopher lost his job at U.S. Steel. She explained, "When we got married, it was always one of us worked, one of us was going to school. Once he got the job at U.S. Steel [in the 1980s], I started going to school full time. Then I had a baby, and so then it took me 10 years." After closure, Simonetta paused her coursework to take care of their two young children as Christopher searched for job openings at factories in the suburbs, where manufacturing companies were opening a new generation of smaller factories on cheaper land. These factories paid well and were often hiring certified machinists— formal training that Christopher had secured through the steel mill union as soon as he heard rumors that he would be laid off. Certificate in one hand and car keys in the other, he was much better positioned than the general laborers in the mill to manage the displacement of industrial jobs to Chicago's suburbs.[31] While Christopher drove an hour and a half to work, Simonetta finished her last degree requirements and entered the workforce as an administrator in her local alderman's office—work that would set her up for activism later in her life (discussed in chapter 6).[32]

Revising skill sets enabled some interviewees to patchwork together multiple jobs over decades. Rebecca, one of Richard's former coworkers at U.S. Steel South Works, shared a work story rife with reinventions of her skills that cobbled together both informal work and contract employment to meet her family's needs. Sitting with me in the Southeast Chicago Historical Society, she was clearly proud of her decade working as a skilled machine operator in the steel mill—one of the only women in her division. With waving hands and a broad smile, she explained how she strategically took on overtime hours and put aside bonus pay to buy a house for her and her son that was located a block from her mother. After she lost her steel job in the 1980s, she still had a mortgage to pay. She supplemented a part-time waitressing job with an under-the-table gig as a custodian at her church. When her employer learned that Rebecca was a skilled heavy-machine operator, the pastor paid her to run a front-end loader for a landscaping project in front of the sanctuary. Through word of mouth, she developed a reputation as a capable, freelance operator who, for a fee, would operate rented front-end loaders and backhoes. She hung up her waitressing apron and happily returned to the cabs of large machines.

Retraining and clever reinvention of her skills enabled her to meet her financial and social obligations at home; and staying at home offered her opportunities that wouldn't have necessarily been available in a new location. Energetically tapping her foot on the floor, she explained how, rather than sit still in the winters when machine digging was impossible, she brought in a little cash as a home health aid and, improbably, as a clown for children's parties. A decade ago, she began to serve as her elderly mother's caregiver. She realized that, with some formal training, she could get paid by the state as a home care nurse for other elderly neighbors—steady work that she enjoyed and that kept her close to home. She completed the paperwork, training, and trial period and, to this day, continues to care for aging neighbors as a paid home health care worker. Rebecca liked her job as a part-time party clown best of all, she told me with a grin. She slid a Polaroid photo toward me. Blurry children in the foreground seemed to dance around this unemployed steelworker. Her petite frame is elongated by giant shoes and a huge hat, her arms thrown wide and a huge smile on her face. Unemployment from the steel mills certainly brought hardship, but Rebecca emphasized that this was a problem she solved with creativity and persistence.

Former miners and millworkers didn't lose their jobs because they were stumped by the latest technology—it was the dearth of good jobs in the right places, rather than lack of skills, that kept them underemployed.[33] When those who became long-term residents found their skill sets mismatched with their geographies, they not only revised their skills but also reevaluated their expectations of economic thriving. For Mitchell, Rebecca, Simonetta, and many other men and women, getting a GED or certification, going to college, or simply accepting underwhelming or unexpected job offers enabled them to raise their kids where they wanted, keep their houses, care for their aging parents, and live with beloved family members. Absent from these narratives of revision and return was any expectation that these local jobs would return them to their middle-class status of the industrial era. Within the economic wasteland of postindustrial Iron County or Southeast Chicago, interviewees tacitly accepted that there was no longer a blue-collar, middle class to be put back together—at least not in the form and content that was familiar in the mid-twentieth century.[34] In their pursuit of making ends meet, residents reweighted the importance of economic well-being to decision-making processes. Clear-eyed about the trade-offs, they prioritized location over economic gain.

CONCLUSION: TRADING INCOME FOR A PLACE CALLED HOME

Company closure undermined many of the geographic, social, and economic resources of these two locations. The people who became long-term residents leveraged what resources remained to make ends meet. They accepted the challenges of under-the-table wages, exceptionally long commutes, and lower-paid work to avoid possible material and social losses of moving away. Informal work leveraged familiar social and physical characteristics and bought the newly unemployed time to make decisions about their next steps. Commuting offered job seekers access to higher-paid, skilled work outside of the geographic reach of economic depression. Reemployment in entirely new sectors brought workplaces closer to home. Each work strategy prioritized two characteristics of home that remained without industry: residues of industrial-era community relationships and physical elements inherent to their geographies. This is *how* people stayed.

But work narratives are more than just records of economic strategies. In the process of making decisions about work and economic survival, long-term residents refined and reinterpreted what home meant to them. They didn't stay because it was easy; they stayed because keeping their kids in school, staying close to family, or paying off their mortgage mattered to them. Wanting to stay closed off some options, such as chasing a better job to a new location. But staying also made other options more valuable, such as informal work and gaining training or education that would make them more employable in their economically depressed region. Stories about *how* they stayed brought forth deeper reflections about choice, motivation, and the layered actions required to navigate within—rather than move away from—an inhospitable economic landscape. Every work decision made by long-term residents required a clear articulation of a dichotomous trade-off—money versus home, stability versus opportunity, relationships with people or places versus losses of the same. And every trade-off demanded a rationalization—to themselves and to observers like me—of why they were going out of their way to stay at home in a place where it was so hard to make ends meet. While interviewees didn't always explicitly rationalize their residential stability through their work narratives, their practices demonstrated how their preferences to live in a particular location drove their employment choices. Through the small and quiet strategies of getting cash in hand, postindustrial residents recentered their home away from their defunct industry and toward the people and places who remained.

Deindustrialization was not the end of the line for these places and their people; it was the beginning of the rest of their lives. By the ten-year anniversary of company closures, remaining residents were developing shared stories to explain *why* they were still there. Through the practical processes of curating, creating, and selecting localized employment options, remnant populations faced the task of reimagining what their home region, and their lives together, could and should mean in the years to come. In landscapes laid waste by widescale economic depression, denuded of company support, and stripped bare of employment opportunities that would enable upward mobility, former ironworkers and steelworkers who resisted out-migrating created new maps to guide their paths forward.

4

STORIES OF HOUSE, LANDSCAPE, COMMUNITY

Narrating the Declining Action of Deindustrialization

People are attached to places as they are attached to families and friends. When these loyalties come together, one then has the most tenacious cement possible for human society.

—Lewis Mumford, *The City in History*, 1961

I t was midday on a Saturday. Simonetta led me from the open front door to her sitting room and settled next to her husband, Christopher, on the couch. For the first decade of their marriage, Christopher had worked a few blocks away at U.S. Steel South Works. With just a high school diploma, he was earning three times the minimum wage—more than enough to buy a house near Simonetta's parents before their first baby arrived in the mid-1980s. Like their neighbors, steel set Simonetta and Christopher's expectations for work and home in midcentury Southeast Chicago. So it's collapse "was devastating" to people living in this neighborhood, Simonetta told me. As mill after mill shuttered in the last two decades of the twentieth century, people began to outmigrate to find new work— mostly service jobs—far from the reach of unemployment and economic depression. The couple mourned as neighbor after neighbor permanently moved away. Brimming with emotion, Simonetta pointed to the boarded-up houses visible through the living room windows and cried, "Why couldn't they just stay? It wasn't like they went out for real jobs or something, you know what I mean."

Staring with them at the silent street for a heavy moment, I asked, "Why did *you* stay?" Simonetta's eyes widened and she nervously wrung her hands. Perhaps unsure if I would find their reasoning sound, Christopher, a nearly-silent man in his sixties, spoke up for the first time in our interview. With a noticeably defensive tremor to his words, he said: "I can go anywhere in the country if I wanted to, but we stay here," he said, gesturing to his steel-toed boots and slate-gray jumpsuit. He'd just completed a week of overnight shifts an hour away in the suburbs at an electrical plant. With a specialized machine maintenance certification earned in the waning years of steel in hand, he'd had more success than most in finding well-paid work beyond the limits of Southeast Chicago. Even still, he had a shaky work history—he'd lost his job a half-dozen times as one suburban employer after another was hit by the ripple effects of deindustrialization. Earlier in our interview, Simonetta had admitted how they financially struggled every time his latest employer downsized, the unemployment checks stopped, their kids had a health scare, or tuition for Simonetta's classes at Chicago State University was due.

Nonetheless, they resisted moving closer to the suburbs an hour away where Christopher typically found work. So why did they stay? After a pause, Christopher continued, "We had the building, for one." The couple owned their three-story row home outright after decades of paying off the mortgage. Sure, it had some crumbling corners and the roof sagged, but it was *theirs*. These four walls remained solid during and after the topsy-turvy years of economic collapse. Leaning forward in her recliner, Simonetta spoke up. "We survived, and that's why we didn't leave. The community has changed, but where else are we going to go? I mean, we've been here for fifty-something years," she sputtered. "This is *my* neighborhood. . . . That's [how] you destroy neighborhoods—" Christopher interjected, "By leaving!"

To live in a landscape characterized by crisis required residents to not only navigate the trade-offs inherent to certain employment choices, as discussed in chapter 3, but to create coherent stories explaining their residential persistence. *Why* people said they stay tangled individual priorities with irreplaceable material and symbolic resources that would be lost if they moved away. In Iron County and Chicago alike, interviewees' staying stories echoed Christopher and Simonetta's rationale that, even without the economy of industry, there was something valuable about the geography and community that embedded long-term residents in place in the long decades following company closure: this was *their* house, *their* landscapes, *their* neighbors, and *their* identities.

This chapter focuses on three stories of staying consistently offered by interviewees—stories that account for the shifting economic realities, cultural values, and disconnected landscapes characterizing their deindustrialized regions. Many interviewees began their stories of residential stability with a practical—and economic—concern: the finances and freedoms of homeownership. For long-term residents, out-migration was economically impossible due to depressed housing values and costs of moving. Yet many of the same interviewees argued that owning their house offered them a little piece of stability in those early, tenuous years of unemployment. Second, speakers emphasized how, even as years became decades, their individual identities intersected with the places, landscapes, and neighborhoods that delineated their sense of home. They drove me to their favorite lakes, parks, and forests, sketched out maps to their beloved shops or hiking paths, and pointed out historical markers of industrial pasts that they deemed important. Finally, interviewees celebrated the social networks, past and present, that anchored their identities in place. They mapped their attachment to home onto familiar neighborhoods, annual parades, and regular reunions. Within the fractured scaffolding of postindustrial social life, a generation of long-term residents has doggedly sought new ways to still belong to one another.[1]

Interviewees were quick to admit that the sprawling crisis of deindustrialization constrained choices and limited their options. For some, owning a house felt like both a refuge and a shackle to an economically struggling locale; their physical landscape both animated their identities and restricted future possibilities; and dense social networks simultaneously rooted and smothered individual choices. But to call a place home is to experience both grief and love. Interviewees stitched together stories that held the losses caused by deindustrialization in tension with their repeated recommitments to place and community. Through narratives of attachment and belonging, they imbued remnant landscapes, social connections, and economic resources with new value and meaning. In short, for the people who became long-term residents, who they are today is grounded where they call home.

CHEAP HOUSES AND HOME BASES: HOMEOWNERSHIP IN RESIDENTIAL STABILITY

When asked why they stayed in communities drained of economic resources, interviewees across both cases often began their stories with the most material requirement for staying: houses. In the mid-twentieth century, good wages combined with federally backed home loans opened avenues of homeownership for blue-collar iron and steelworkers. Beginning in the 1960s, Southeast Chicago transitioned from a majority rental community to one where between 60 and 70 percent of houses were owner-occupied. This contrasts with 30 to 40 percent of housing being owner-occupied across the city of Chicago during the same time. Northern Iron County's homeownership rate also increased in the waning years of mining, as company towns began relinquishing housing stock to private owners. By the 1970s, approximately 80 percent of locals owned their primary residence.[2]

In the second half of the twentieth century, high wages and seemingly guaranteed work meant that, for most of my interviewees, buying a home was a sound financial decision and a path toward achieving the American middle-class goal of wealth-building through private property ownership. While brick-and-mortar buildings are expected to appreciate over time, houses are more than simply material investments. Houses are meant, in most cases, to be *home:* a place of "familiarity, order, permanency, comfort and place-bound culture," as the sociologist Jan Duyvendak put it, and a source of stability from which one can venture into the world.[3] In Iron County and Southeast Chicago, homeownership offered an opportunity to buy into the idea, culture, and financial future of the iron and steel economy.

But as crisis hit northern Wisconsin and Southeast Chicago, house and home took new meanings. Mass unemployment turned sound financial investments into nearly unsaleable commitments to troubled places. Whereas before deindustrialization, home values in both locations were comparable to those in adjacent Wisconsin counties or Chicago neighborhoods, in the more than five decades since company closures, houses in both communities have consistently sold for 40 percent less than their former competition.[4] Across the American Midwest, the U.S. Census Bureau recorded spikes in the housing vacancy rate—that is, the proportion of houses vacant for sale—during the double peaks of deindustrialization in the late 1960s and the mid-1980s.[5] Homeowners in newly deindustrialized regions could not sell houses for a profit, if they succeeded in selling them at all.

Homeownership summoned narratives of ambivalence from my interviewees. For some, homeownership was a burden—looming foreclosures or the likelihood of financial losses due to selling in a rapidly depreciating context suffocated any hope of leaving town with money in their pockets. For others, owning property was their saving grace—a place not only to wait and see what opportunities might be on the horizon but also a haven of choice to protect vulnerable stability when everything else was in turmoil.

Familiarity and Four Walls: Chicago

Christopher and Simonetta's house was an old steelworkers' boarding house. "It's 100 years old!" Simonetta proudly stated. "Upstairs in the attic there were bathrooms, and they were used as apartments. Probably a family or a group of men lived in these two rooms. It was more like two, four, six, maybe eight apartments instead of a three-flat." They bought the house in the early 1980s, right after they got married. In between the birth of their two kids and Christopher's long shifts at U.S. Steel, the young couple gradually converted the multi-unit house into a spacious single-family home. As they discussed their episodic renovations, they elaborated on Christopher's earlier argument that they stayed because they owned the deed to the building. Christopher admitted that, when they made the down payment in 1980, they benefited from already-plummeting house prices. Wisconsin Steel had just closed, and housing prices in South Deering had already dropped by 9 percent.[6] But they hadn't expected the whole region's housing bubble to pop. Home values in the Bush millgate neighborhood began to fall as U.S. Steel slowly laid off workers through the 1980s and 1990s. Even today, the median price of homes listed in Southeast Chicago ranges from $80,000–100,000, less than a third of Chicago's median of $330,000.[7]

But buying a home is never purely a financial decision. Simonetta and Christopher's house was their family story. In the first half of the twentieth century, Simonetta's parents had immigrated from Mexico, near the Rio Grande. Christopher's grandparents were also from Mexico, but they'd arrived back at the turn of the twentieth century. Simonetta explained that since they had grown up in the same neighborhood, when they got married, they wanted to buy a place within walking distance of both sets of parents and their webs of aunts, uncles, and cousins. When they bought their place as the first mills closed, they never doubted their extended families' intentions to stay. She recalled, "My father, my parents still lived [in the neighborhood]. They weren't going anywhere. Where were they going to go?" Their entire familial network was located within a few short blocks of Southeast Chicago. Simonetta frowned, placing herself back in the late 1980s. She continued, "It's not like we're rich. I mean, the mill's closed. We were unemployed!" Even if their parents wanted to sell their house and start a new life in a more promising location, selling in the economic freefall of deindustrialization would have cost them too much. In this place of need and within reach of family networks, having "the building," as Christopher called their house, made their path forward simple: pay their mortgages, put food on the table, and look out for each other.

Richard and Penelope also felt they could better look for work, navigate school closures, and mitigate other limitations of postclosure life if they stayed in their South Chicago house. They bought their house in the 1970s. When Richard's position at the steel mill disappeared in the late 1980s, they decided to stay to "pay off our house, you know. And raise our children," Richard stated. They didn't want to move because, Penelope explained, they were friendly with their neighbors and their kids were happy at the local elementary school. In addition, it was only because Richard knew his neighbors that he was able to find informal work and odd jobs during his four years of unemployment.[8] Moving out of a mortgaged house posed much more than just a financial risk. It would erase the few remaining, if tenuous, components of home—those dense social networks and familiar landscapes built in the era of industrial thriving that helped workers bridge jobs, feed and watch their kids, and make ends meet.

During this era of depreciation, owning a house could feel like trap to be escaped—the physical embodiment of the powerless immobility experienced by workers made newly unemployed. But at the same time, the familiar walls of a house offered an island of security in a sea of change. I heard echoes of this tension while talking with Marcellus, a former steelworker now in his seventies. Hardly pausing from his work sweeping a park building, he mused how right after the steel mills closed, "there was nowhere for me to go. I had the house paid, I couldn't go, at the time, anywhere. So, we just stayed, waiting for, you know . . ." He grimaced in my direction with a look of amused embarrassment. Even a brief drive through his East Side neighborhood today showed that his waiting—for steel companies to reopen, for property values to go up, for some economic boom to uplift the region once again—was a miscalculation. A young man when the mills closed, he could have found a new career elsewhere. But the idea of moving was inconceivable to him. "I didn't want to leave the neighborhood because I *knew* the neighborhood," he murmured, gazing at Lake Michigan glittering in the summer sun, broom in hand. With a shrug, he returned to sweeping. His house was, to him, a place of security and familiarity. The declining but known *here* would always be a more valuable home than a hypothetically better *there*.

Deep Roots and an Unsellable House: Wisconsin

Five hundred miles north, Iron Countians also faced the double-edged sword of homeownership: the joy of owning a piece of the American dream colliding with the financial impossibilities of recouping that investment. Again and again, interviewees pointed out how complicated decisions to sell their houses could be. Between 1965 and 1975, housing values dropped by 10 percent. Low prices didn't mean an easy sale, however. It was tough to find a buyer in a quickly depopulating and geographically remote region that was designated by the state of Wisconsin as part of an economically depressed, twenty-county zone of concern. Ron, a retiree of Finnish descent, recalled with some bitterness the faulty assumptions of a politician visiting Iron County in the mid-1960s. "The governor at the time [of the mine closure] said, 'Well, the people would just have to move and re-establish themselves, sell their homes.' The problem is, who are you going to sell your home to? Your neighbor had one for sale!"

The challenge of selling a house was compounded by the costs of moving to another location. Moving is expensive—from renting the truck, to writing that check for first and last month's rent or paying the down payment for a new house, with all its associated taxes, fees, and insurance requirements, to navigating the costly learning curve of finding cheap groceries and gas in a new place. Tony was in high school when his dad lost his job of twenty-five years at the Montreal Mine. He glumly recalled, "My folks were talking about moving. Now, looking back, we didn't have the money to pick up roots and move." Owning a depreciating house was less financially risky for Tony's family than moving to a more economically thriving—and thus, more expensive—location.[9] Weighing the economic calculations of moving versus staying, Tony's dad opted for commuting four and a half hours to work in the maintenance department of a boarding school rather than uprooting his family and selling their house at a loss. The trade-off, however, was a cap on future economic thriving for him and his family. Tony shared how his dad, who was in his late fifties when the mine closed, "worked until he was sixty-two and then he retired. Of course, he didn't have much pension from the Montreal Mine—he had around $50 a month. And then, social security. And they lived off that— as a lot of people do up here. They lived on very little."

Even today, homeownership complicates the economic decision-making in Iron County. In Montreal and Hurley, the two incorporated towns most impacted by mine closure, the median price of homes listed on Zillow between 2010 and 2020 was $50,000 and $90,000, respectively. In that same time frame, the median price of houses listed for sale across the state of Wisconsin was four times higher.[10] Leah, a local community leader, told me, "People say, 'why don't you move?' Well, like most families, most of our wealth is tied up in our primary residences." Making that wealth liquid by selling a house not only displaces the people who call that house a home, but it risks realizing the extremely low market value for the building and property. Because of the remoteness of Iron County's "location, location,

location"—as the famous realtor's principle goes—staying put continues to make economic sense for many residents.[11]

But in addition to the economic rationales of staying in place, interviewees frequently argued that their house was *both* economic fate and a choice. Nan described how "our families *chose* to stay here." Her father "made decisions. . . . He traveled to White Pine. He had to get up at 3 a.m., get on the bus, to keep that house in Montreal. That's what he chose to do." Mitchell similarly explained why they stayed in the bungalow that he and Gina remodeled and updated for fifty years with a thump of his fist against the doorframe of his house. "We built this," he said flatly. Likewise, Dottie was proud of the role she personally played in maintaining her family's residential stability. It was her paycheck from her job as a town clerk that covered the mortgage, she stated. "I made 31 dollars and 90 some cents and our house payment was 28 dollars. So, we had a few dollars and 70 some cents that we could spend." And even though Tony missed his father as he worked far from home, he acknowledged that staying in their childhood house meant that he and his brothers could finish high school with friends and family.

Nearly all homeowners I spoke with in Iron County considered their houses more than just poor economic investments. Buildings of brick and wood might've been undervalued on the market, but to interviewees, they served as symbols of stability in the face of change. New parents carried their babies across thresholds; adult children tended to their elders in back rooms; porches and yards hosted parties, card games, or playdates. The industrial foundations of home might've been long dispersed, but these houses were still home.

Stories about houses blur the lines between material context and meaningful choice. In both Southeast Chicago and Iron

County, homeownership illuminated the tenuous relationship between agentive attachment to a physical location and the contradictions of socioeconomic change. While interviewees in Iron County more frequently pointed to the financial challenges of homeownership than did those in Chicago, they also spoke more forcefully of their affection and commitment to their long-time homes. In both cases, interviewee narratives moved fluidly between stories of decisions forced by circumstance and those prioritizing less economic rationales, like familial connection, affection for neighborhood or village, or commitment to stability maintenance for vulnerable family members. This constant weighing of pros and cons bred in my interviewees a peculiar kind of ambivalence about homeownership—not an individualized, psychological malaise but rather a matter-of-fact assessment of the challenges of being quite literally tied to a place that had changed so much. The material realities of homeownership were so beyond individual control that they required interviewees to not only solve practical problems of paying the mortgage but to also manage their "mixed feelings and compromised behavior," as the social theorist Robert Merton defined ambivalence.[12]

At the same time, however, narratives of homeownership often referenced meanings of home that talk about houses, as economic resources, failed to capture. Staying in a house was metaphorically overlaid with staying at *home*. Home is where material embeddedness, socially constructed identities, and familiar, embodied experiences coalesce in a concrete, physical location. Even as a material object of indisputably declining economic value, houses are a center of significance and a shelter from the chaos of financial loss and instability. For better or worse, houses are not transferable to another location.

"IT'S WHO WE ARE!": AFFECTION FOR LANDSCAPES OF CHANGE

In their stories of staying, many interviewees managed their ambivalence about homeownership by embedding their buildings—and themselves—in landscapes that they viewed as worthy of their affection. While I was conducting interviews in Southeast Chicago and Iron County, long-term residents frequently walked and drove me to places they loved—to a high view of endless forest, across a marshland rippling with waterfowl, or past monuments at long-disappeared iron or steel company buildings. These natural and human-made objects seemed to allow people to, as the environmental psychologist Theodore Sarbin argued, "emplot" their personal and collective experiences in both local geographies and bigger stories of change and crisis.[13] Whereas homeownership brought with it wins and losses, local places beyond the front door seemed to ground positive sentiments, slow down social relationships, and emplace changing meanings of home and self over time.[14] In Wisconsin and Chicago, interviewees' articulations of place attachment—as this line of geographically-located emotional sentiment is called—illuminated how, when deindustrialization stripped away the dominant purpose of home it offered space for reinterpretations of what remained. Like geological formations, stories of affection for natural and human landscapes layered new meanings on geographies of industrial pasts.

Nature in the City: Chicago

The physical geography of Southeast Chicago has an unexpected feeling of rurality. The Calumet River slices through twenty-five square miles of sparsely-populated residential blocks. Four miles of nearly undeveloped lakefront with secretive inlets and marshlands lure boaters and birdwatchers. Fishermen slip through gaps in chain link fences and silently cast lines off industrial docks (see figure 4.1). Thousands of acres of former steel mill properties lie vacant of buildings and carpeted with low reeds. Either by design, in the form of new public parks, or due to abandonment, hundreds of acres of unused prairie are now reclaimed by grasses and young trees.

With only a few exceptions, the wildest natural landscapes in this former steel mill neighborhood were also historically the

FIGURE 4.1 Chicago fishermen at the mouth of the Calumet River, Southeast Chicago.

Photograph by the author.

most industrial—a tension that seemed to thrill many of my interviewees. Louisa bundled me into her son's car to drive us to her favorite view of Lake Michigan at an old steel mill site. Paul took me on a walk along a path circumscribing a newly established bike park built on a capped landfill, scooping up shotgun shells from illegal hunting with one hand and pointing out a small herd of white-tailed deer sprinting across the sparse forest with the other. Jesús and Marcos drove me to their favorite view of the city—the glittering Chicago skyline starkly juxtaposed against the moody beauty of Lake Michigan and the gray, cement remnants of the region's largest steel mill. The line on the horizon where this land and water met was "sacred," Marcos explained.

Place attachment is not only about what is "out there"; it also reflects how people understand their own identities and priorities. Take, for instance, Ted's story. His grandparents migrated to Southeast Chicago from Yugoslavia at the turn of the twentieth century. His dad worked at Wisconsin Steel, retiring just before it closed. In his sixties now, he reflected on his growing-up years in a millgate neighborhood adjacent to Wisconsin Steel. "I just thought it was the greatest place in the world to live. Yes, we did have pollution from the steel mills and from the electrical station, but we could walk to Lake Michigan. We had the forest preserves, we had Wolf Lake that separates Hegewisch and East Side. So, it was like a small town, and it was separated by the [Calumet] River and then we had Indiana on the Southeast Side. Most of the people that I grew up with, there's always that, 'I'm going to move to a better place.' Although geographically, this is the best place in the world because of the lake in the forest preserve and Wolf Lake and that. But people always want to move up." He shook his head in disapproval. Ted resisted "moving up" not only because he valued the woods and the lake as sites of wild nature but also because his childhood neighborhood grounded his personal identity. Home was not a physical building for Ted but rather a cluster of meaningful objects and relationships that grounded his identity in his perception of landscape, geography, and memory. The philosopher and sociologist Henri Lefebvre termed this "existential insideness," a state of feeling so at ease in a place that its importance to a person is taken for granted until some crisis threatens the status quo.

When the mills started to close some forty years ago, Ted and his wife decided to buy a house in a neighborhood a few miles west from his childhood home on the East Side. But this was a lateral move—a geographical shift rather than a "move up," he quickly added. His center of identity remained grounded in his old home. "I have lived in Beverly since 1980. I still consider myself an East Sider and I always will. I don't have any allegiance or closeness to Beverly, although that's where I live." As much as he could, he sought to maintain that feeling of "existential insideness" by revisiting his old haunts. He routinely drove to those marshlands he loved as a child every week for a walk, and I first met him a stone's throw from his childhood neighborhood rather than at his "new" house, as he still referred to it. At the Southeast Chicago Historical Museum, located in a Chicago Park District building in a sprawling green field abutting Lake Michigan, Ted flipped through meticulously curated photo collections of industrial history. "I've lived in Beverly longer than I lived on [the] East Side but my *home* is the East Side." He waved at the historical objects in the room. "The roots just build here, and they won't go away. They won't go away."

Free to Roam: Wisconsin

While long-term residents in Southeast Chicago love their region's surprising collision of industry and nature, residents in Iron County double-down on their landscape's utter remoteness.

Walter, sixty-nine, told me, "If you want to come up here and wander around in the woods, it's the best place to do that, by far. Look at this map up here!" He pointed to a map of the county that was nearly covered with shades of green. "It's national forests, state forests, national parks, state parks, county parks—it just covered the whole . . ." He ran his open palm across the county map. "So, you're free to roam where you want to." He began laughing. "If you're not into that, I don't know what else you'll do!" Walter's right—96 percent of land in Iron County is classified as "woodlands," and nearly all of it is publicly accessible.[15] Thousands of miles of once-industrial railroad rights-of-way cutting through these forests are now hiking, snowmobiling, skiing, and hunting paths. Residents and visitors access those lands first via two unlit, two-lane highways and then by dirt roads that connect small villages scattered dozens of miles apart. The county's population density is eight people per square mile and the nearest regional airport is across the state border in Michigan. This is an outdoor paradise.

Walter's delight in the wilderness echoed a sentiment I heard across Iron County interviews. Repeatedly, affection for nature and the lifestyle it afforded summoned effusive declarations of residential commitment. Over coffee and sandwiches in the kitchen of the Iron County Historical Society, Cheryl told me, "My husband's a hunter and a fisherman—just loves it. And it's hard to take Hurley out of the boy." She explained that after the mines closed, she and her husband moved away for a short period of time. "We lived in [a southern Wisconsin city] for five or six years while he finished school." Pursing her lips in a silent laugh, she concluded, "The minute he was done, we were back!" This place—with its long, snowy winters punctuated by lush summers and jewel-toned Octobers—has worked its way into the identities of long-term residents.

And yet, the tie people have to this landscape is not just a love for wilderness. To explain the best parts of their home county,

many interviewees directed my attention to sites of industry hidden in the wilds. Industrial buildings, old rail cars, and
rusted mining equipment—carefully preserved and narrated
by historical markers—are tucked into wooded groves. Tree-
covered mountains of iron ore tailings skirt the central roadway.
An unusually flat field of trees marks the site of the Montreal
Mine's beloved company-sponsored recreation center. Unnatu-
rally straight roads remind drivers of long-defunct trolley and
train services that linked company towns to other mining villages (figure 4.2). Interviewees' articulated how these industrial
remnants continue to ground their identities. In Mitchell and
Gina's house, Gina's laughed as she described how she used to
ski down hills of mining waste, known as tailings. She would
wait to launch herself from the thirty-foot drop of rocks and
rubble until the mine shift changed so she could show off her
skills to gape-mouthed men—Mitchell included. At Dottie's
insistence, her grandson drove me to the top of one of those tail-
ing hills, now covered with trees and brush, and pointed towards
the best boating launch into Lake Superior. And Ian walked me
through a cross-country ski trail marked with historical mining
information. While nature has overtaken these vestiges of iron
mining, they still provide residents "navigational equipment"
for making sense of themselves in place and in time—both the
"inner compasses" and "outer maps," as the sociologist Kai Erikson mused.[16]

Sheila and Paul provided the most direct account of how
indistinguishable their personal identities were from their geographic contexts. Born and raised in the same northern Wisconsin village, they decided to get married when Sheila was finishing
college in Milwaukee. "He's from Iron Belt also, so, we decided
we didn't want to raise our children in the city and moved back.
And that's when the mine closed." She groaned and shook her
head. With lighthearted wonderment of people who've survived

FIGURE 4.2 Northern Iron County dirt road.

Photograph by the author.

a near miss, the couple recounted that somehow, even though Paul only worked in the mine for a few months, they still managed to buy their house and begin their family. He earned money by working on the county maintenance team and plowing snow. Nearly six decades later, they sipped coffee with me only a few miles from where they were born.

"I guess we've lived here all of our lives," Sheila mused. She is seventy-seven and Paul is eighty-two. "Even after the kids started moving, I thought, 'Oh good! Now we've got someplace to *visit*.' But it never entered our heads, even in the winter, to move somewhere else." She continued, "A lot of our friends now go to Florida or Arizona for the winter, three or four months. I don't know . . ." She paused. "We wouldn't even think of it," Paul interjected with the look of someone who has resisted this suggestion on many occasions in the past. "I wouldn't mind going for, like, a few weeks," Sheila objected with a wave to the light flurries already falling in October. The winters in northern Wisconsin begin early and often last until April, with cold winds from Lake Superior accumulating several hundred inches of snow over six months of frigid temperatures. Sheila continued, "We did travel extensively when we were younger—Europe, and islands, and Alaska. But to go anyplace for any length of time . . ." Her words faded and she joined her husband's resolutely shaking head with a grin. "I guess it's never entered our heads; we stick it out. We just like it around here," Paul agreed, softening. "I would never move; no, I would never leave here. Snow or more snow, I still won't leave." Sheila closed the subject with a brief summary: "It's just *who* we are."

Questions of "who we are" are always intimately related to questions of "where we are." *Why* Sheila and Paul continue to live in their snow-covered community or Ted regularly returns "home" to his old East Side neighborhood reflect how external circumstances intersect with the internally orienting effects of natural and industrial landscapes. On one hand, claims to identity are grounded in places that are meaningful both *in spite of* and *because of* being marked by deindustrialization. Without the constant rumbles of freight trains and whir of industrial-strength water pumps, the wilds of the dark forests and clear lakes lured locals back into the woods and prairies—first, to peel bark or sell food, and, in the later decades, to find new meaning and identity without industry. On the other hand, the changing circumstances of place itself provided interviewees attuned to its transformation a more grounded sense of self. The geographer Edward Relph famously said that core to what it means to be alive is "to live in a world that is filled with significant places: to be human is to have and know *your* place."[17] For all the griefs of iron and steel closures, the unknown territory of deindustrialization itself demanded residents' clarification of what about their home's geography they would claim as beautiful, valuable, and core to their identities.

PEOPLE WHO MAKE US: COLLECTIVE MEMORY AND COMMUNITY ATTACHMENT

In 1961—the same year that the first pink slips were handed out to Iron County miners—the historian Lewis Mumford wrote, "People are attached to places as they are attached to families and friends. When these loyalties come together, one then has the most tenacious cement possible for human society."[18] Even as thousands of their neighbors fled Iron County and Southeast Chicago, interviewees' rationales for residential stability often circled back to *who* remained in their urban neighborhoods and rural forests. Just as houses are located in specific geographies, an individual's stories of residential stability are oriented within social histories. When framed as collective memories or familial histories, some social stories seemed to limit options for some interviewees. For others, a pervasive sense of place-based community motivated their decisions.[19] Frequently, interviewee stories revealed that even without iron and steel, their home regions still offered such an attractive way of living, raising kids, and being neighborly that they chose, over the course of decades, to ignore repeated opportunities to out-migrate.

Families Past and Present: Chicago

In Southeast Chicago, people and places tightly overlapped. Alfred, who started working at Republic Steel when he was eighteen because "I could see it from my front window," said in an oral history, "It was a good place to work. I can say that there were bad days, but as a whole, it was a good place to work. And the people [I] worked with . . . even those that weren't friends when we worked, when we'd come across each other at our picnic or something like that, we'd hug. And it's like it was a family, really, and I always tell my wife, I said, 'You know what?' I said, 'This is my second family at home. *That* was my first one.'"[20]

Today, many former steelworkers still act like family. Every month for decades, nearly sixty former steelworkers gather together to eat a catered lunch and organize protests for labor rights in the city and state capital as part of the United Steelworkers Organization for Active Retirees. While I was attending one of these monthly meetings, Jerry walked into the old union hall on Avenue O and was greeted with a chorus of happy shouts and warm handshakes. Several fellow attendees nudged my arm to point him out, explaining that he was a beloved foreman who trained up a younger generation in his mill right before it closed. In our interview, he told me that he's owned his house in South Chicago, a historically Black neighborhood in the northernmost part of the steel mill area, for decades. He continued in his gravelly voice, "I know a lot of people over there. It's where I came from. . . . Most of them [are] still there, you know. They didn't move out." Perhaps Jerry's neighbors didn't move out because of circumstances, or perhaps it was their intentional choice. But as Jerry turned his wide smile from me to his roomful of friends, I realized that that tension between fate and decision might not matter in the day-to-day work of recreating community. Maintaining emotional currency in a much-changed social context requires active engagement, effortful sociality, and intentional work. The regular attendance of Jerry and his steelworking neighbors at union meetings recreated collective stories of identity and mutual belonging.

For long-term residents like Jamie, fifty-two, who grew up in the area but didn't work in the mills, community attachment was grounded in the millgate neighborhoods themselves. Jamie articulated how the physical structure of his neighborhood helped him feel connected to his family and friends. "It's a good place because—as smelly as it can be, as awful as the mills were—it's the people. And in my case, it's a lot of memories, having been here for a long time." Since childhood, Jamie has lived in Chicago's Southeast Side. His grandparents immigrated from Poland, his parents served in World War II, and upon their return, his father worked for nearly thirty years as an electrician for one of the largest steel mills.

Smoothing the white tablecloth with rough hands, he drew an imaginary map of his street with his finger. He tapped on the corner of the table to indicate his childhood home and then traced the route to his grandmother's house. "My Buscha lived at 89th and Escanaba. I never knew my grandfathers, but I knew both of my grandmothers. But they're all here; they're all retained." He tapped his forehead. Returning to his map, he pointed out the Polish church where he was baptized—one of half a dozen churches that, while perhaps warmed by company-funded coal in the past, were by Jamie's youth fully independent of the steel mill's shadow. And at this corner still stands the tavern where he and his father got dinner every Sunday for decades until the week before his dad passed away. Erasing his imaginary map with a swipe of his hand, he grinned. "We had really great neighbors, we did. We had the Kings on one side, we had the Browns across the street, we had the Washingtons next to them, we had the Ducrees on this side. All Black families, really great people who I won't forget." He smiled warmly. "I was there long enough to know them. They came to my dad's funeral, my mom's funeral. *That's* a community." As his family aged and neighbors died, Jamie's ties to his community could've weakened. But actively returning to familiar streets, houses, and, on occasion, reconnecting with friends and family maintained his sense of belonging.

Even in the face of tremendous change, daily life is populated with "ghosts of place" who haunt houses and neighborhoods, union halls and empty fields.[21] Some ghostly social relations were worth forgetting—those that propped up racist housing practices or steamrolled organized labor or activism, for instance, rarely emerged in interviews. However, most interviewees echoed Jamie's desire to lean into the life-giving bonds of community. Guided by carefully curated ghostly presences, a choice to remain residentially stable was a choice to accomplish the work of pursuing social connection. If Jamie—or Jerry or Alfred—had moved away, they would have lost webs of relational capital that informed their personal identity.

Through these processes of returning to familiar haunts, the lines between residential stability being a choice or a forced hand blurred even further. When I asked Jamie why he stayed in light of his changing neighborhood, he said, "I mean, Polish people and other ethnics, we're stubborn people. We don't move. We die." He mused, "These were stubborn people who walked to work, their fathers walked to work. It's an odd thing. . . . They built their churches and they wanted to die in their churches." Within the same breath as this declaration of choosing home, belonging, and community, Jamie grounded himself back in geography in the most ultimate form: "And where would I go? I'm a lifer. I got the plot paid in full at Holy Cross Cemetery."

Small Town Neighbors: Wisconsin

Iron County's geographical remoteness not only motivated attachment to its wild nature but also spurred stories of affection for a particular kind of social life. Immediately after explaining her husband's eagerness to return to the forests of Iron County after finishing school, Cheryl mentioned that his entire family remained in the county. And as for their kids—well, Cheryl argued, Iron County is "a wonderful place to live. A great place to raise kids." Patrick, whose story of retraining as an auto mechanic was in chapter 3, similarly linked his residential stability to both his affection for the county's four seasons and his expectations of a kind of family life that would only be possible in a rural community. Although his lifetime of work in Iron County paid a fraction of what he could have made in a larger city, he was committed to remaining in Iron County because he wanted his kids to "grow up like I did. Small town. Quiet." Patrick viewed certain components of the good life as so inherent to his rural setting that geographical location was more important than any economic gains of moving away.

This idealized vision of the rural quietude of the Northwoods echoes a cultural narrative which scholars dub the "rural idyll"— a view of rurality that portrays these geographies as healthier, happier, and with fewer social problems than urban areas. From ancient Greek poems to Victorian morality tales to National Parks advertisements, the clean air and wholesome social surrounds of rural life have been billed as a desirable alternative to the environmental pollution and social noise of the city.[22] In Iron County, both interviewee narratives and formal marketing strategies reflect the rural idyll. County tourism pamphlets and websites declaim acres of forests and small-town contexts as the perfect escape from the chaos of everyday life. Residents wax poetic about the pleasures of four seasons, open forests, and social intimacies of tiny villages.

Particularly for long-term residents, the rural idyll trades not only in nature but also in the social legacies of industry. When alerted to my interest in mining, nearly all interviewees suggested a drive through the preserved company town of Montreal to see the still-matching white houses sitting side by side along the two-lane road. Today, more than sixty years after closure, the town looks like a colorized version of early-twentieth-century photographs—identical white bungalows neatly trimmed with shrubbery and divided by gravel roads. After the Montreal Mining Company sold the company homes in the 1960s, private owners maintained their houses' white exteriors voluntarily until the town was formalized in the National Register of Historic Places in 1980 through the efforts of the newly formed Iron County Historical Society.[23] Taverns are still not allowed in Montreal, and the 9 p.m. curfew whistle still blows every night. Even decades after these industrial villages lost their mines, their residents still reproduce components of rural life that they clearly deem valuable.

Contemporary Iron Countians intentionally pursue social activities to keep relationships dense and overlapping in a community characterized by low population levels.[24] Maintaining these networks takes intentional symbolic and practical work. Today, long-term residents still describe themselves by high school graduating class ("Tom graduated one year above me, in '58"), kinship lines ("Did you know that Bill's wife's cousin is related to me through my husband?"), and childhood village (Iron Belt, Oma, Montreal, Gile, and more). Eighty-year-old Bob coordinates his fellow veterans' funerals. Laura helps to plan the annual, county-wide Heritage Festival while also managing a regular Meals on Wheels delivery route. Dottie gets weekly meals from the senior's center, served by the children she taught in preschool thirty years ago. Each Tuesday and Thursday, she also volunteers at the local historical society making Finnish handicrafts to sell for building maintenance funds. Ninety-three-year-old Charles arrived at our interview in this building dressed in his Montreal Mining uniform. (He would wear the same overalls and helmet to attend public meetings about the proposed mine, which is discussed in chapter 5). Beyond individual efforts, Iron County's collective experience is remarkably vibrant. Clubs and social associations thrive—a local carpentry shop organizes a woodworking after-school program, a snowmobiling club maintains trails on abandoned railroad rights-of-ways, and the 4-H program is buoyed by donations from citizens of one of the poorest counties in the state. Even in the ever-changing contexts of a deindustrialized rural community, long-term residents have found new ways to pursue their ideal of rural neighborliness.

Long-term residents make sense of who and where they are by "taking soundings" off each other, Kai Erikson writes. "As if employing a subtle form of radar they probe other people in their immediate surround with looks and words and gestures, hoping to learn something about themselves from the return signals."[25] In Southeast Chicago and Iron County, long-term residents take soundings off collective memories of community life and the geographical locations where they took place—union buildings, street corners, and company towns. Much like houses and physical landscapes of nature, industrial remnants, and wilderness, these community relations cannot be carried into a new setting. Community only holds if the community member stays in place.

CONCLUSION: STORIES FOR THE FUTURE

Long-term resident accounts of why they stayed emphasize again and again that the wins outweighed the losses of remaining within a geography of economic depression. Homeownership provided interviewees a consistent site from which to "venture forth" into a troubled economic context, to riff on the geographer Yi-Fu Tuan.[26] Natural and industrial geographies rooted their sense of self in the stability of field, forest, and monument. Social connections past and present provided a map of belonging and purpose in communities marked by depopulation. Certainly, some interviewees experienced ambivalence about their residential persistence—a nagging concern about being tied to a place characterized by so many decades of economic struggle. But most interviewees told stories of staying that highlighted the gains of their decisions. Remaining at home outweighed the financial and personal costs of selling houses, leaving familiar landscapes, and abandoning place-based kinship and friendship networks. In lieu of departure, interviewees re-evaluated who they were in light of where they were. Through stories of choice, resilience, and attachment that both acknowledge and leverage the very real, material constraints of Iron County and Southeast Chicago, long-term residents rewrote the meanings and purposes of their deindustrialized geographies, communities, and economies.

Narratives are powerful tools of identity and belonging, but good stories don't erase the challenges of economic development in deindustrialized regions. Truly reconstructing home requires institutional revisions of industrial vestiges. Even though long-term residents have, for decades, strategized their own employment, homeownership, and avenues of attachment to stay in place, the place they call home still suffers from disconnected geographies, depopulation, and nearly fifty years of economic depression. Chapters 5 and 6 bring Iron County and Southeast Chicago up to date, articulating interviewees' diagnoses of two contemporary options for economic revitalization: nature-based tourism and new mining or manufacturing. Long-term residents and their policymakers attempt to reimagine home through pragmatic problem-solving. But making a new home together requires shared ideas of collective problems and how to correct them.

5

NATURAL RESOURCE FUTURES

Iron County

We are born and have our being in a place of memory
—bell hooks, *Belonging: A Culture of Place*, 2009

Economies are built around resources, and so that's what we're trying to do.
—Pete, head of Iron County Economic Development

W rapped in flannel and sitting side by side, Nan and Rupert were nearing the end of their story. In a chronology mirroring the arc of this book, we'd talked first about their histories. Their parents and grandparents worked in the mines, and after closure, the young couple stayed put, found work, and raised their kids. They had their hard years—all fifty years of their employment history occurred during Iron County's ongoing economic depression. The couple managed seasons of unemployment with Nan picking up tutoring gigs and Rupert working as a handyman. Now, Nan had only recently retired from her career as a high school math teacher. Rupert was still working off and on as the manager of a construction company. Rupert said with breathy laugh, "There *are* opportunities here. I've done very well, and my wife has too. I'm self-employed. That's the only way I'll ever be, but there's no guaranteed check on Friday." Gesturing toward the sounds of happy chatter in the next room at the historical society, he continued, "There's some people who stay here." Nan added with a wry smile, "But they've got to think a little out of the box."

It's a tight box. Interviewees agreed with five decades of fiscal data that the dominant problem in Iron County had been, and remains, the lack of economic opportunities—a problem perpetuated by the county's geographic remoteness. Since 1965, the unemployment rate in Iron County has hovered around 12 percent, more than double the state's average.[1] This lack of work has created a peculiar loop of demographic and economic problems. Since the 1990s, only 43 percent of young people born in Iron County stay to adulthood.[2] In turn, a scarcity of both employers and employees means a small tax base for the county and its unincorporated municipalities, which undermines funding for public services and further dissuades young people from staying. Today, only one-third of the public schools open during the mining era remain functional, and each year, more population-based social services, such as post offices and hospitals, permanently close.[3] For decades, policymakers, nonprofit organizers, and long-term residents have attempted to solve these interlinked problems with coordinated economic development strategies. But a third problem—geographic remoteness—seems to stand in the way.

Since the nearest major metropolitan area is hundreds of miles away, Rupert argued, "We're not going to get a GM plant here. We're not going to get any big manufacturers. We're on the end of the road." He pointed to the vast blue and green portions of the map signifying water and forest: "[There] you've got Lake Superior and Canada." Rupert pointed to another map of iron ore deposits in Wisconsin hanging on the wall above our heads.

"*That's* why I was for the new mine," he declared. Every Iron County interviewee mentioned the recent hope of a new iron mine—an ill-fated proposal to open a four-mile-long strip mine that drew controversy across the state. As a small businessowner and member of the Chamber of Commerce, Rupert quickly became an advocate for the proposed mine. He spent months attending public meetings in favor of the mine. "And [here's] what I testified," he explained, "I said, we're only going to have more people up here, and more jobs, as we develop our natural resources. We have our timber, lumber, our ski hills, and tourists, the lakes and the streams. The only thing we have here is what God gave us: our natural resources." He acknowledged the voices of environmental activists questioning the apparent contradiction between the proposed mine and the county's economic dependence on outdoor recreation. But Rupert declared that Iron County has "got to keep on building tourism, and then look at your natural resources, and try and develop those, all within a safe way that you save the environment." He sighed and concluded, "If we're looking to grow our population, it's going to have to be something around natural resources."

One hundred and fifty years ago, Iron County's economy was organized around natural resources. This chapter brings the story and structure of this natural resource legacy—and Iron County residents' expectations of it—up to date. For decades, the people who have become long-term residents, like Rupert and Nan, have been individually strategic in the face of deindustrialization and collectively committed to rebuilding a coherent community. However, there are structural challenges that undermine macroeconomic, spatial, and social revitalization for the whole of Iron County.

Interviewees in both Iron County and Southeast Chicago communities took significant time in our conversations to discuss large-scale challenges facing their home community. These last two chapters dive deeply—and separately—into debates between long-term residents and policymakers in Iron County (chapter 5) and Southeast Chicago (chapter 6) about the best possible future for their home regions. In Iron County, interviewees repeatedly drew my attention to three dominant problems facing their post-industrial region—geographic remoteness, demographic declines, and underemployment. Echoing Rupert's reflections, other residents and local leaders repeatedly weighed the pros and cons of two natural resource–based solutions to these problems: a new generation of iron ore extraction (what I call *reindustrialization*) and the expansion of a nature-based tourism industry that already draws thousands of visitors to Iron County's forests, lakes, and industrial heritage sites (*tourism*). Proponents of a new generation of industrial jobs promise a more employed—and potentially, more populated—community that mimics familiar versions of industrial communities past, while supporters of nature- and heritage-based tourism appreciate the commodification of landscapes that locals already value. Whether supportive of reindustrialization or tourism, rural interviewees consistently voiced hopes that leveraging their natural resources (their geography) would mitigate deindustrialization-fueled economic depression and population decline.

Separating city from country in these final two chapters directs our attention to differences—to internal debates, conflicts, and concerns; to contrasting political priorities; and to the different economic, infrastructural, and spatial contexts that distinguish rural Iron County from urban Southeast Chicago. Yet for all these differences, the menu of options for economic redevelopment is remarkably similar across the region.[4] In both the forests of Wisconsin and the marshlands of the Second

City, locals weigh the capacity of reindustrialization and outdoor recreation to provide jobs, manage spatial and transportation disconnections, and rebuild a sense of community. Iron Countians and Southeast Siders disagree on the desirability of each option, and spent significant time in interviews wrestling with how these solutions may or may not solve deindustrialization problems effectively. But in both settings, their dreams for the future are grounded in ideas about the past—beliefs about what is possible, practical, and familiar given the geographically-specific remnants of the building blocks of home—geography, community, and economy.

DEINDUSTRIALIZATION PROBLEMS: DIAGNOSING THE CONSTRAINTS OF PLACE WITHOUT INDUSTRY

Like Rupert, many long-term residents of Iron County worked hard to communicate the context for their collective, economic struggles. With memories of the past colliding with lived realities of the present, long-term residents are particularly well suited to diagnosing the causes of contemporary problems in their communities. In fact, on average, rural interviewees spent half of their narratives identifying why, even decades after mine closures, industrial collapse caused significant problems for everyday life.

Take, for instance, Sheila and Paul's experiences. Sheila described the declines that she and Paul witnessed in their community. "When we got married, 55 years ago . . . we still had several churches, three grocery stores, and we had five or six taverns. Now, we've got two taverns and no grocery stores." Paul added, "At one time, Iron Belt"—their home village—"was three thousand people!" Sheila supplied, "Now, it's three hundred." With Sheila nodding along, Paul continued, "First the school goes, then the church goes." Today, Iron Belt no longer has its own schools or churches. In fact, the five hundred children who live in remote villages in the northern half of the county are all bused to one of two schools in the largest town of Hurley. The couple drives ten miles each way on back roads to the nearest grocery store—a Walmart, across the border in the Upper Peninsula of Michigan—and thirty-five miles south to the hospital for regular appointments. Paul concluded, "We got nothing. You either work in the woods or do odd jobs here and there, where with the mine, when you got in there, you got it made."

Sheila—the same person who earlier in our conversation (and discussed in chapter 4) said with affection that Iron County is "just *who* we are"—leaned back in her chair looking pensive. "I am sad because of how things are now, but nobody seems to know how to turn it around. And for a while, there seemed like there were small industries that were looking to come this way, but the powers that be, just . . . I don't know. They didn't know how to go about it?" Considering such significant economic declines, geographic marginalization, and community depopulation, Sheila and Paul advocated for a more coordinated, institutional approach to solve big, structural problems— postindustrial problems that are certainly beyond the capacity of individual actors to address. Even in the politically conservative context of Iron County, many interviewees expressed the conviction that local government should play a larger role in rescuing community life and rebuilding a collective sense of home.[5]

In part, these expectations of top-down solutions emerged from past actions by Iron County's local government. In 1961—a year before the Montreal Mine closed—a committee of citizens and elected officials wrote a report proposing policies for building a more resilient economy in the wake of the impending collapse of the mining industry.[6] Inspired in part by this planning, in 1963, this same group formalized a nonprofit (the Iron County Resource Development Association, Inc., or ICRDA) to establish an industrial park and attract new employers. Over the next decade, the ICRDA reclaimed a former iron mine property, directed utility development and, in 1979, broke ground on the construction of several acres of corrugated metal buildings to house a dozen small manufacturers, construction companies, and machinists. Today, this industrial park employs between 200 and 250 people—around one tenth of the working-age population in the county.[7]

Every new job reduces the problem of unemployment in Iron County. But contemporary work is rife with other limitations. At the industrial park and beyond, jobs in Iron County pay some of the lowest wages in the state—between a third to half of the state average annual income for comparable work.[8] Henry, an older man whose dad worked in the mines, grumbled to me that at the industrial park, "you get a little bit here, a little bit there. Then they'll close, or they stay open . . . for the cheap labor, [paying] $8, 9, 10 an hour." And there are not that many jobs to choose from. In the two incorporated towns in the northern half of the county, small businesses and government sectors only employ several hundred full-time workers. Service industries employ more than seven hundred people, though many on part-time schedules.

It should not be surprising, then, that in this county built *for* natural resource exploitation, the most stable and highest-wage jobs are linked with the environment. Pete, who works in economic development, optimistically summarized this perspective: "We like to say, T and T—timber and tourism! Recreation's important to us . . . [and] timber's really important. Those are our resources." Cutting and managing forests on county-owned land pays the highest wages in the state and employs five hundred full-time workers—a significant proportion of employment in a county with only three thousand working-aged people.[9] The majority of part-time service jobs in the county are linked to recreational tourism. Echoing Rupert, Pete concluded, "Economies are built around resources, and so that's what we're trying to do."

The potential of a new generation of natural resource jobs is impeded by spatial disconnection from markets, however. Again and again, residents—both those involved directly in developing new job opportunities and those who have experienced their region's economy change—pointed to geographical remoteness as a core driver of their county's six decades of underemployment. Sheila explained with a sigh, "Everybody says, 'Oh, you can't have anything there because it's too far from anyplace, how are you going to get anything in and out.' " Similarly, Rupert argued, "If we could get some people interested in entrepreneurship, maybe they could come back here and start something . . . [but] we're too far away from where they sell the products." Rebuilding infrastructural connections would bridge the physical gaps between the remote Northwoods and the city centers far afield, interviewees suggested. Sheila argued that trains were the best hope for restoring transportation. Not only did freight trains run regularly on the iron range when she was younger, but passenger trains from Chicago regularly passed through. Now, no tracks remain and it's financially untenable for freight rail to continue without regular output. She grimaced and said, "If somehow they could manage to find somebody with the money"—she paused and smiled mirthlessly—"to get that kind of transportation back."

This is one problem with living on the rural side of a defunct commodity chain. When producers, transportation companies, or local governments decide that connective links are no longer profitable, those nodes are quite literally disconnected. Companies with the capital and capacity to rebuild rail, reinstate shipping, or improve roads have little economic motivation to invest in locations far from commercial centers if more geographically adjacent locations can serve similar purposes. These intertwined geographic, economic, and social problems are not unique to Iron County. Across the United States, rural sociologists have tracked how distance from commercial centers, a small labor pool, and lower average education levels tend to discourage small or midsize companies from seeking out rural communities as new hubs for investment.[10] Like in Iron County, fewer companies mean fewer jobs, a stunted economy, and a community where younger people seeking upward mobility feel forced to leave.

To try to mitigate such disadvantageous cycles, long-term Iron Countians who are in positions of political power have for decades tried to lure new employers to the region. For instance, Darrell, a long-time member of the Iron County Resource Development Association, called me while driving across gravel roads in a forest near Lake Superior. "I've been screwing around with this industrial development for 50 years, and it hasn't been easy." Shouting over the rumbling background noise, he explained how he measured his lifetime of residency in Iron County in terms of the grants his board applied to, the businesses they've tried to attract, and the customers he's met at his hardware store. "We sure haven't had any help from the state, I'll tell you straight out. And we didn't get help when they pulled the rail out." He swore under his breath. He declared that economic problems are more than joblessness; it's an issue of visibility and the dearth of components that make Iron County a stable place to call home. With fewer than six thousand residents, the county government is allocating decreasing amounts of state funding for day-to-day operations with every budgeting cycle. And, echoing Sheila and Rupert's concerns, without transportation networks, potential employers and new residents alike cannot access the Northwoods. Darrell correlated continued economic loss with this geographic invisibility. He hollered into the phone, "If you're down in Green Bay, they call themselves northeastern Wisconsin. Now we're 220 miles north of Green Bay. . . . If *they're* northeastern Wisconsin, are we in the state? They think the north ends at Green Bay. They call themselves northern Wisconsin from Wausau down, that don't leave us much to be in the state! Do I sound paranoid?"

Likewise, Leah, who sits on the county board, declared that the regions' depopulation and poverty was entangled in infrastructural marginalization. "We don't have a four-lane highway here. We're 100 miles from the nearest freeway. Like I said, we don't even have a stoplight!" With a loud sigh, she continued her diagnosis of her county's problems. "In Iron County we have 5,900 people. We don't have any political clout up here. We don't. We're old, we're poor, we're few in numbers. We have the lowest workforce participation rate in the state . . . [and] the highest unemployment. Our statistics aren't good at all. And the youth leave in droves." Those who remain face underpaid jobs and often string together multiple jobs to make ends meet, just as they did in the 1960s. "We have people who will do lawn care in the summer; in the fall they'll go work at the cranberry bogs; when that season is over then they go to work at the ski hills; when that is over, they'll go on to Michigan and they'll plant trees out there at the tree farm. And that's how they make their living: they just go from seasonal job to seasonal job."

Geographic remoteness and economic struggles clearly impact the third component of home—community life. Without jobs, population levels are precarious and paying the bills can be a struggle. Without roads and rail, new jobs are rare. With all of these issues combined, the future of this county has grown murkier with every passing year. With bitterness, Sheila mourned these intractable problems that she, her neighbors, and her local government face every day. "We have good people . . . I would like to see some industry. Not necessarily mining, but people here are very loyal, and they are very intelligent, and for some reason, it just seems like . . ." She threw up her hands with a huff of despair.

Long-term residents and policymakers alike offered these critical diagnoses not in dour cynicism, but in hope for resolutions to such tangled problems. Since repairs to these infrastructural, locational, and economic problems were far beyond the scope of individuals and, at times, impossible for even local governmental actors to solve, interviewees longed for something big and transformative. The best future, they concurred, would circumvent the institutional and economic constraints of the region, leverage immutable characteristics of geography, and in the process, repopulate and enliven community life.

IRON ORE 2.0: DREAMING OF RECONNECTION AND EMPLOYMENT IN A NEW GENERATION OF MINING

The return of a large-scale iron mine was just the kind of future that many in Iron County were hoping for. In 2010, a mining company, Gogebic Taconite (GTac), proposed to invest $1.5 billion in a strip mine that would stretch four miles across two counties and a watershed and border an Ojibwe reservation. GTac promised to employ seven hundred people, pay the county land-leasing fees, and create an additional 1,500 jobs in supporting industries like trucking, security, housing, and food.[11] The majority of my interviewees hoped that this massive mining project would not only reinsert the county into a functional and familiar commodity chain but would also guarantee direct investment of capital into the county. Taxes and land-lease fees might empower the defunded county government to repair degrading infrastructures. Expanded transportation or housing options might encourage other businesses to return to northern Iron County. These businesses would employ local people, possibly drawing younger generations back home. This rising sea of economic benefits would come to aid everyone in the county, according to Lewis, a gruff Finnish man in his sixties. "I was kind of excited about the mine situation . . . between Upson and Mellen. I thought, huh, that'd be pretty good . . . [to] get things moving again. More stores, more things to do, more family-type things, property values may move up."

Nearly all Iron County residents that I interviewed voiced support for this proposed mine, and many explicitly called attention to the need for good industrial jobs for the youngest generation. Echoing trends familiar to most postindustrial and rural communities in the United States, most graduating high school seniors leave Iron County for college or vocational school and then stay away for better jobs. As of the 2020 census, 30 percent of the permanent population is older than sixty-five, and only half of the population is within the federal category of "working age" of fifteen to sixty-five. Retired residents rely on fixed incomes, like pensions and social security, while twenty-somethings piece together part-time gigs until they finally decide to leave.[12]

Population loss is not due to lack of desire to stay, interviewees argued. Cheryl told me that her "children would love to come back. My sons are skiers, and they'd give anything to come back. But they can't—they have jobs, and there's nothing here for them." With the new mine proposal making headlines, locals hoped that better work would staunch the flow of young people from the community. Particularly in the early days of this mine proposal, locals dreamed of a new generation of employees recreating some echo of a multigenerational community. Laura told me that two of her cousins were "hoping that mining would open back up in Iron County" so they can "come home" from Alaskan oil fields, Missouri mines, or cross-country trucking routes. Charles, a former miner himself, hoped that the ripple effect of the new mine would fuel a new generation of work. "It's just like that mine that they'd talked about that'd go through, now. It [only] employs so many people, and last[s] so many years, but the shops outside the mine, like different trucking outfits and railroad people, that's all extra people who'd go to work!" He nodded confidently. "It would employ a lot more local people."

The mining company itself intentionally encouraged local narratives of return to the "good" days of mining employment. In 2013, GTac constructed a parade float for the county's annual Heritage Festival and asked local children to march alongside a flatbed of modern mining equipment carrying a banner that read "Jobs for the Next Generation."[13] It opened a local office, hosted public forums, and proposed transportation infrastructure development, in the form of road construction and funds for highway maintenance, in order to directly address locals' concerns about geographic remoteness.[14] In interviews and statements, GTac's communications team consistently argued that this new mine would replicate the tight-knit, well-employed company town of the past.[15]

These hopeful visions were amplified through Iron County media discourse and political machinations. Town chambers of commerce and board members initiated meetings with company representatives to offer land access, office space, and airwaves.[16] County board members quickly moved to lease county land to the company for sample drilling at a reduced rate.[17] According to some calculations, the county spent more than $130,000 in legal fees to create zoning laws that "would bring GTac to the table."[18] Community leaders wrote public letters of support to the Wisconsin state legislature suggesting that existing state and federal regulatory safeguards were sufficient and calling for reductions in water pollution limits for mining.[19]

Iron County leaders—all of whom were one and the same as the long-term residents who watched boom and bust transform their home community—offered two rationales for their support of the proposed mine. First, officials expected that the return of iron mining would repair the county's economic problems. The county's economic development organization framed the proposed mine as poised to "create badly needed jobs" and enable Iron County residents to once more earn a "decent living" in a county with one of the highest unemployment rates in the state.[20] In a statement on their website, the Iron County Resource Development Association (ICRDA) optimistically predicted that once the new mine was established, the region might "see the same economic benefits and revitalization of northern Wisconsin jobs and industry as it was in 1885, thanks to new and more advanced mining technologies." The organization expected that "the overall annual economic impact of operating a mine at a production level of 8 million tons would be $604 million"—nearly thirty times greater than the current operating budget of county.[21] The ICRDA promised that "direct jobs at the mine would be good paying, as similar jobs in Minnesota and Michigan average over $80,000 annually with wages and benefits."

Second, the mine made sense to local leadership because it echoed Iron County's symbolic origin story. Another generation of mining aligned with collective memories of the "good" industrial legacies of iron mining. Place names and memorials remind long-term residents that its raison d'être was iron ore. The county's formal motto is "live *liFe*"—emphasis on the chemical abbreviation for iron. Mountains of iron ore tailings punctuate forests. A drive east through the well-preserved company town of Montreal brings drivers to Hematite Street and between murals and mining equipment marked with permanent interpretive plaques. The ICRDA declared that because of "its history and deep roots in its mining culture Iron County stands ready to assist residents across the state to achieve the real economic benefits and job creation a revitalized mining industry would foster."[22] These discourses mirrored general, conservative political goal to return of industrial, blue-collar work to middle America. But Iron Countians pointed to the specific match between the new iron mine and their community's agreed-upon origin story rather than national rhetoric.

Emboldened by county-wide support and discourses of iron as identity, GTac sent lobbyists to the Wisconsin state legislature to offer "guidance" for a revision of decades-old mining laws. In the early 1980s, Wisconsin passed comprehensive mining legislation that increased permitting standards and remediation expectations for new ferrous metal mines. A decade later, the state added a moratorium on new nonferrous mines such as copper and nickel.[23] GTac urged the Wisconsin state legislature to revisit water pollution limits for ferrous mining, arguing that existing federal regulatory safeguards were sufficient. In 2013, the Republican-majority legislature modified the law to enable GTac's project to be permitted more quickly. While this decision was celebrated by the Republican majority in Iron County, environmental groups, nearby counties, and Indigenous tribes protested GTac's dubious commitment to protecting vulnerable wetlands and waterways in the northern reaches of the state.[24] Even as Iron County leadership attempted to lower bureaucratic barriers for GTac, neighboring (and majority Democratic) Ashland County passed jurisdictional limitations to hamper test drilling and, they hoped, disrupt the progress of the strip-mining company.[25] What followed was an explosive regional conflict reflecting the polarization around discourses of environmental regulation and blue-collar job creation.[26] This controversy spilled into Iron County itself, challenging taken-for-granted notions of reindustrialization as the best path out of economic depression

Controversy: Not Mined *This* Way

Initially most Iron County residents were supportive of a new iron mine. But as the proposal process expanded from months to years, even the most ardent supporters came to question if this was the right company—and industry—to bring the "good" home back. Doubts first emerged around the potential environmental impacts of the mine. Opponents of the mine raised concerns that the proposed mine would utilize techniques known to harm groundwater quality—it was to be a strip mine open to the elements and likely to leach heavy metals into northern Wisconsin's marshy water table.[27] When preliminary mapping predicted that the hydrological impacts of GTac's proposed mine would impact water sources far beyond the geological bounds of the iron deposit, a leader in the neighboring Red Cliff Band of Lake Superior Chippewa voiced concerns that their wild rice growing traditions would be directly threatened by the mine. He argued, "We would rather have clean water than jobs," even though his tribe had a 60 percent unemployment rate.[28] Motivated by these environmental anxieties, opponents organized protests at drilling sites and instigated shouting matches at public forums and town halls.

Initially, many Iron County residents found Ojibwe and environmentalists' concerns at odds with their own experiences with natural resource extraction. As part of Rupert's lobbying efforts, he explained, he would take visiting policymakers and protesters on a tour of the area. With a roguish grin, he asked me, "Have you seen the stockpiles at Montreal? Right at the foothills, there behind the old city hall, there's a little crick that runs beneath it. We had a cup there, and we scooped up the water to drink it. And they were looking at us, and we said, you want some?" The visitors always demurred, but Rupert would insist on taking a sip of the water to put point to how a lifetime of proximity to water tainted by iron mining caused him no ill effects. Look how "stunted" he was, he said with a laugh as he pushed back from his chair, opened his broad shoulders, and stretched to an intimidating six foot four. Rupert's illustration was humorous, but he admitted that this argument did not convince his audience. They'd counter that deep-shaft iron mining of high-quality hematite impacts water tables differently than do open-pit mines of low-quality ore. And, since testing of water sources adjacent to mines in the 1950s and 1960s was rudimentary at best, water pollution then cannot be compared with the potential of runoff today. With an exasperated sigh, Rupert enumerated these arguments before figuratively brushing them away with a swipe of his hand. It's not that he didn't care for the environment, he argued. He understood that "you have to have a great environment if we're going to have tourism." However, environmental regulation or activism is a form of environmental concern unfamiliar to many Iron Countians.

Dozens of other interviewees grappled with a disorienting contrast between their positive memories of iron mining and the threats of water toxicity. Leah argued that, as an avid trout fisher, she felt sensitive to pollution. "Like I said, I fish five miles downstream from that closed mine site. If I'm not catching trout down there [due to pollution], I don't want a mine. So, some people think I just want to go over and blow up the whole Gogebic Range over there. No! That's not true, that's not true. If we're going to do it, it needs to be done right." Leah, Rupert, and most other Iron Countians returned again and again to a collective environmental consciousness that anchored their view of economic development in a conception of nature as resource. Forests and water should be stewarded faithfully and enjoyed, certainly, but nonetheless leveraged for human benefit.[29] In the context of the proposed mine, such a collective, resource-centered environmentalism reflects the mechanics of Iron County's geography and demography: low population density combined with nearly one thousand square miles of forests would have rendered the new mine invisible between the folds of the Gogebic hills. In short, spacious geographies caused Iron Countians to argue that mining could coexist with environmental well-being.

Residents' perceptions of the motivations of environmentalists also fueled their initial resistance to anti-mine activism. Rural sociologists show that long-term residents in rural communities across the United States tend to be less concerned about environmental regulation and protection than do younger and newer residents.[30] Youth and outsider status showed up in interviewees' perceptions of anti-mine concern. Some Iron Countians argued that environmental anxieties were emerging not from neighbors and friends, but from college students and activists who lived outside of the county. Worries about water pollution were merely concerns of culturally and politically out-of-touch "professional troublemakers," various residents told me. Sure, a good environment mattered, but a blanket rejection of new mining, as some opponents desired, would hinder an economic revitalization for a county they did not call home.

But as the proposed mine incited more and more controversy over years of drawn-out permitting debates, even the most committed supporters of GTac wavered in their commitment to a new generation of iron mining. Laura hated how the environmental questions around the mine 'pitted families against families.' Leah was flustered that these internal conflicts contradicted her view that, "in Iron County, we truly like each other. We're a community that gets along. We get things done with our little limited resources." Even Rupert admitted that he was unhappy that the mine caused "a lot of controversy. It split up a lot of people. Most of Iron County was pretty good for it because we've been through the mining days—we knew. But then the outside areas, and the tribes—they were all against it." The proposed mine seemed to threaten locals' expectations of rural idyll (see chapter 4).

After nearly four years of wondering if the mine would begin operations, environmental conflicts transitioned into concrete anxieties about whether the company itself was truly a "good company" worthy of locals' support. On one hand, the company seemed to overreact to environmental protests. When a half dozen activists approached an active drilling location on county-owned public lands, GTac posted ex-military armed guards to protect their assets. A second direct action led to an aggressive altercation between armed guards, GTac representatives, and protesters. Several environmentalists were arrested and their cameras confiscated.[31] GTac's escalating response to those "outsider," environmental protesters at their mine-sampling sites shook local support, even for the people who were "pretty good for it," as Rupert put it. He shook his head with agitation when talking about the protest gone wrong. "You gotta respect people for their decisions. I have no problem with that. You still get along with them; you work with them."

On the other hand, the company frustrated local residents with half-truths and unfilled promises. Perhaps with the wisdom of hindsight, several interviewees voiced suspicions that the company's communications during its permitting process not only intended to mute environmentalists' activities but also meant to manipulate Iron Countians. For instance, the company promised to hire seven hundred employees to operate the mine but failed to explain that most of these jobs would require technical skills or training exceeding that of most working-age Iron Countians. Supporting industries might bring in more than one thousand new jobs, but they would be disappointingly "dispersed across a twelve-county region," according to one analyst.[32] Then, in early 2015, the mining company withdrew its application for the taconite mine. Company spokespeople cited the unfeasibility of remediating the wetlands located within the mine site, per federal environmental regulations, as the cause of their withdrawal. A close look at reports and media coverage suggest that the company's withdrawal was actually due to depressed metals prices, limitations in local and state legislative support, and issues with public opinion.[33] After the company abandoned its offices in Iron County in late 2015, locals grew angrier when the county newspaper revealed that the company left without paying several million dollars of lease payments to the county for use of its public lands.[34]

By the end of that saga, even the most ardent supporters of the proposed mine admitted that even if they wanted Iron County's pseudonymous natural resource to be mined again, it was not meant to happen *this* way. Locals were disappointed—not just at the company's withdrawal, but in the company itself.[35] GTac was not the "good company" of the nineteenth and early twentieth century, with managers who lived next door to workers and invested in their community's contentment. Rather, Iron County witnessed a modern and alienating version of corporate industrial operations. Paul frowned as he said, "Yeah, when GTac came in here, you know, they thought that they could come in here and walk all over everybody. That didn't happen; that's why they pulled out." Sheila continued, "When it started falling apart, I think everyone in the area got the impression—which probably was real from the beginning, but we were too happy about maybe having some industry in our area to really realize it—they were just here because they thought we were just a bunch of hicks . . . you know, that we weren't really able to see through the things that they were doing, and were going to just take us for everything that they could."

If a new mining operation was to actually follow in the footsteps of past iron mines that were "good to the people," as one interviewee told me, they would pursue a different approach. No missed payments to the county for access to land; no arrests of protestors; no half-truths about jobs; no "emotional rollercoasters" of bait and switch, as Pete, the head of the ICRDA, complained. Some interviewees remained hopeful that maybe a better company existed out there. Maybe, a second generation of mining could indeed solve the problems of joblessness, remoteness, and underutilization of the region's best natural resource. But although county leadership has continued to advertise its iron-rich lands to other speculators, there have been few bites. So, the county waits. Rupert said with a shrug, "What's there is going to be there. It's been there millions of years. It could be five hundred years from now, or twenty years from now . . . So yeah, it was a disappointment." He suddenly looked tired. "But we've had a lot of disappointments. You roll up your sleeves and you go on in life."

ABUNDANT NATURE: PUBLIC LAND AND OUTDOOR RECREATION

Second to iron ore, northern Iron County's "best . . . resource is abundant snowfall," Pete explained. Abundant is an understatement. This is Big Snow Country—between the first flurries in early October and the final melt in April, the northern half of the county accumulates between 160 and 200 inches of snow—an amount comparable to Colorado's Aspen or Vail.[36] Whereas ski destinations in the west gain their snow from the Rocky Mountains, Iron County's snow is a miracle of hyperlocal geography. Gary, fifty-six, explained it to me. "Twenty miles in either direction of Hurley, you have half as much snow! You know, we are right here in the bowl that catches it all." His hands mimicked scooping up air to demonstrate. The low ridges of northern Wisconsin form a unique microclimate that funnels the snow-building winds from Lake Superior into the core of Iron County and creates one of the most reliable snowpacks in the Midwest. Gary smiled enthusiastically. "That's a great thing when you get that kind of snow because, you know, the snowmobilers, the skaters, the cross-country skiers, the snowshoers, all the winter sports people come up and do stuff!"

Every year, thousands of downhill skiers and snowboarders flock to small but plentiful slopes at two ski resorts on either side of the Michigan-Wisconsin border. Nordic skiers glide across forty-six miles of groomed trails and parkland, staying the night in one of the two chain hotels or the local bed-and-breakfast in Montreal. Most lucrative for local businesses is the steady flow of snowmobile traffic that crisscrosses Iron County's four hundred and fifty well-groomed trails. On a typical winter weekend, thousands of snowmobilers pass through Hurley, stopping for food, drink, fuel, and rest.[37]

Even before iron mining collapsed, Iron County's white-powdered winters lured tourists. Since the 1930s, the wealthy from Milwaukee and Chicago would escape to second homes on lakes and huddle around roaring fireplaces in timbered ski resorts.[38] Following the "lost economy of mining," Pete explained, the Iron County Chamber of Commerce ratcheted up its advertisements for its "other natural resource." We sat in his office, cluttered with reports, spreadsheets, and brochures spilling across two desks and maps of Iron County overlapping on the walls. Pete steepled his fingers as he explained the draw of northern Wisconsin's outdoors: rolling hills of dense forest; the Milky Way spilling across the cloudless night sky in one of the least light polluted regions of the Midwest; and pristine winter weather, vibrant summers, and jewel-tone autumns. More than ninety percent of the county is covered in forests, and more than half of that land is designated as open to the public for hunting and driving ATVs.[39] When there isn't snow on the ground, sixteen waterfalls, three hundred miles of trout streams, and ample access to the clear waters of Lake Superior attract hikers, fishers, and boaters.[40] Echoing interviewees' stories of place attachment and identity discussed in chapter 4, the county's website hosts a series of pages for each category of nature-based amenities, such as "ATV & snowmobiling trails," "waterfalls," "campground and parks," "paddling," "fishing," and "Iron County 'Fall Color Tour.'" The website encourages visitors to "Live out your dream of pure outdoor recreation in Iron County, WI, where human-powered or motorized pursuits are numerous. There's much to enjoy here, so allow us to introduce you to the beauty and excitement of one of the prettiest places on the planet."[41]

Iron County locals and community leaders propose a form of environmentalism that uses, rather than isolates and regulates, natural resources. The county's website lauds the region's "numerous resource-based assets, including rivers and streams, forests, waterfalls, trails and parks."[42] Framing outdoor recreation in terms of natural resources allows Iron Countians to rationalize both their support for tourism and their continued interest in mining. Interviewees assured me that they were not concerned that water pollution from legacy mining or GTac's proposed project would dissuade tourists, nor were locals alarmed when hundreds of acres of county and privately owned land typically open for hunting and recreation were closed so that the company could do test drilling.[43] Remoteness of Iron County—while problematic for other economic pursuits—enables multiple land uses. Iron County has nearly forty acres of public forests per capita, and three times the land area of the whole city of Chicago with less than one percent of its population. There is simply so much open space in Iron County that the idea of industry compromising recreation or tourism seemed preposterous to long-term residents.

Furthermore, nature-based tourism overlaps with mining history. Infrastructurally, many of the same natural features that attract tourists—and which summoned passionate declarations of affection from long-term residents in chapter 4—are also vestiges of iron mining. For instance, on the eastern edge of the company town of Montreal, the old mining company administrative building now serves as a well-regarded, bed-and-breakfast for tourists.[44] Behind the town, snowmobile trails are evidence of the transformation of those deeply missed railroad tracks into flat woodland paths. "The reason we have such a great trail system here," Leah explained proudly, "is the tracks used to come up here, and we've used those as snowmobile trails.

We have a great, extensive snowmobile trail system up here. We have the best snowmobiling in the Midwest!" These trails are a big reason why, in 2009, Wisconsin's governor designated Iron County as the Snow Capital of Wisconsin.[45]

Tourism is so central to Iron County's economy that it is considered "recreation dependent" by the United States Department of Agriculture's Economic Research Service.[46] Tens of thousands of visitors spend $20 million dollars a year in Iron County, and tourism-related economic activities contribute nearly a third of the county's total economic output.[47] The Iron County Department of Forestry and Parks estimates that 650 jobs, or one out of every three in the county, are either partially or wholly dependent on tourism and recreation. The same low property values that make it hard to sell houses to permanent owners attract seasonal homeowners—people who live and work elsewhere in the state or region but spend a portion of each year in a secondary house. Secondary homeownership comprises a little more than half of Iron County's total livable housing.[48] This contrasts with the state's average vacancy rate of 12 percent and exceeds seasonal homeownership rates in Iron County's tourism-heavy neighboring counties by between 8 and 22 percent.[49] Pointing out the window of the historical society toward the town center, Cheryl explained to me that across the region, "a lot of people have bought houses—you can buy a really cheap house and that'll be your ski house."[50] Sure enough, the median house price in Hurley, the largest city at two thousand residents, is $60,000. Houses in the quaint company town of Montreal (see figure 5.1), which is listed on the National Register of Historic Places, are valued around $79,000.

There is, of course, an irony that the county has exchanged dependence on iron ore extraction for a different kind of environmental commodification. Iron County's economic dependency

FIGURE 5.1 Houses in Iron County's company town of Montreal.
Photograph by the author.

on outdoor recreation and nature-based tourism reflects a national trend. Since the 1980s, poor rural communities across the United States that lost some place-based, extractive industrial sector have increasingly turned to nature-based tourism and amenity development to manage economic declines. For instance, communities facing crises in ranching or mining in the American West have redesigned their landscapes—both infrastructurally and through media campaigns—to attract hikers, off-road ATVers, and seasonal homeowners.[51] Hardly ignorant of the gamble of economic dependency, many rural communities nonetheless accept this shift to the commodified "consumption" of place because it provides present residents one more chance at economic survival.[52]

In Iron County, tourists and their money do address many of the same problems that the proposed iron mine was expected to solve. Low housing values encourage in-migration of grocery-buying and tax-paying residents (however part-time or seasonal). Geographic remoteness is a lure rather than a curse, and visitors are satisfied to drive personal cars to their second homes rather than rely on rail or other missing transportation infrastructure. People who grew up in the area are also finding their way back home, drawn by the same nature-based recreation opportunities that attract tourists. Dennis explained that he bought his aunt's house when she died in the 1980s and returns multiple times a year to the town for snowmobiling or summertime reunions. "We still retain a house in Montreal. Our son's relatives are up here, so we come up." Similarly, Gary, who lives a few hours from his hometown but regularly visits, declared a hope that other people "would love to come to a place like this for a weekend and just forget the stress. I can see Hurley as a destination because it is a destination for *me*."

"Tourism Is Good but Not for Me": Limits to a Tourism-Based Economy

Even though natural amenities draw fierce devotion from locals, many of the same residents were ambivalent about the potential of nature-based tourism to fully solve the economic problems facing Iron County. Even with thousands of snowmobilers passing through or vanloads of visitors arriving to see the fall colors, tourism has never been "a boom, [although] it helped relieve a little bit of" economic depression, Pete explained. Sitting in the Iron County Historical Society, Dottie echoed Pete's admission. "Snowmobiling is huge," she agreed, "but they just go to the bars and have a burger." Her friend and fellow historical society volunteer, Cheryl, added. "The gas stations might benefit a bit." She continued, "Years ago, when the ski hills first came, everybody was opening," referring to restaurants, inns, and other businesses. Dottie interjected, "Because they'd come into town to eat." Cheryl said, nodding, "Now everything is at the hill." The all-inclusive ski resorts offer their own restaurants, housing, and souvenir shops. She shook her head with visible annoyance. "The ski hills figured out that the more they do, people don't leave there. They don't go into town to dinner; they have every-thing there for them. So, the towns, when it's ski season, don't get [the tourists]." Cheryl continued, "A lot of people who come for our beautiful scenery in the summer or fall, they don't spend a lot of money. You know, they don't." Data from the county's records underscore Cheryl's intuition. When compared to other Wisconsin counties, direct visitor spending in Iron County ranks sixty-fourth out of seventy-two counties. Due to a much smaller flow of tourists, tourist annual spending in Iron County is half of that in neighboring counties of Ashland and Bayfield.[53]

Tourism-based jobs are limited as well. While they provide wages for workers with little education or job experience, they tend to offer erratic schedules, low wages, few benefits, and limited opportunities for economic mobility.[54] In Iron County, annual incomes for tourism-related work range from $15,000–$30,000 a year.[55] Rupert grumbled that "tourism doesn't get you a 401k, it doesn't get you healthcare. It's a survival deal. That's why we need some good paying jobs." I heard echoes of this theme over tea in the Montreal Mining Company office-turned-bed-and-breakfast, where Deedee and her son Jimmy discussed the challenges of tourism as a livelihood strategy for locals. The ski hills in the area "do employ quite a few people in the season,"

Deedee said. But "people who do work there need to find other ways of making a living other than . . ." She waved her hand to encompass the woods and hills outside. "The season is only what—four or five months long? And then you have to find something else to do. There's only so many jobs. For me, I supplemented what I had when I first moved here by working at the ski hill. I worked in the office part, and I sold tickets. I worked there from the end of November until March." Deedee continued, "There's a lot of people who live here year-round that that's what they do—they hop from making wreaths to working at the ski hill to doing other things in resorts, finding jobs, housekeeping things like that whatever they can, just to stay in the area." Jimmy soberly agreed, "Some people got like three jobs."

Not only do tourism's part-time jobs fail to fully address the economic problems that people are most worried about in Iron County but seasonal homeownership also offers locals an unsatisfactory solution to the constrictions of contemporary community life. Dottie told me how she loves living among the matching white houses in Montreal, but when she flung back the curtain to point out her neighbors, she grimaced when she saw the house across the road—a small white bungalow that sold "for about the same price as a new car," she grumbled. After a fresh coat of white paint, the house was staged as a gift for some family member, complete with a huge red ribbon tied to the front door, she said with an eye roll. She's never met the new owners and only occasionally see lights flicking on and off on the odd winter weekend.

Home and hardly-lived-in houses are strange bedfellows. Partial residencies stand in contrast with the lives of those who "chose to stick it out," to return to Cheryl's claim from chapter 3. Being neighbors only a few weeks or months each year means no names are exchanged; no check-ins on the elderly occur; no in-kind mutual aid, like shoveling of others' sidewalks, happens.

Part-time residents have little need for grocery stores or gas stations, and no use for the local post office, community center, or church—all institutions that have reduced hours in the past decade. Home purchases by seasonal residents, who own a little more than half of Iron County's livable housing, haven't even driven up home values. While other studies of rural gentrification warn of the risks of pricing locals out of their own communities as wealthy outsiders buy up cheap properties, housing appreciation rates in Iron County have barely matched state averages.[56]

When considered in terms of both economic gains and community sentiment, Dottie summed up the generalized ambivalence many feel toward tourism: "Tourism is good, but not for me, or for the other neighbors, unless they work at the grocery store, or have a bar, or have another deal for tourists." But even for residents who do have a "deal" for tourists—like Deedee, the proprietor of The Inn Bed and Breakfast—the ebbs and flows of tourism dependency can be brutal. A rise in oil prices, a canceled marathon, a warmer-than-usual winter, or a pandemic can mean the difference between breaking even or shutting the doors for good. As COVID-19 halted travel plans in 2020 and 2021, the county experienced a 6.76 percent drop in visitor spending and lost 13 percent of tourism employment.[57] Residents are waiting to see if tourism will pull through again. Even in the best years, a dependency on recreation means that natural resources are still a matter of economic survival or collapse for many in Iron County.

Geographic remoteness—that problem called out by Rupert in the start of the chapter—is a double-edged sword—necessary to lure visitors seeking to escape to the woods and yet discouraging to those who are loath to travel far from home for their outdoor recreation. Darrell, the Iron County Resource Development Association board member, told me with irritation in his voice, "See, it's the attitude of what people think of the north. They think we're supposed to save everything for them to come up and enjoy when they want to make their one trip a year— if the gas price is low enough." For better or worse, tourism entangles economic success and community life in the whimsies not of a single company, as with large-scale industries, but on the perception of many potential consumers of a single, natural resource commodity.

For all the economic fragility that accompanies recreation dependency, at least it builds on residents' existing attachment to place. Some elements of the local tourism industry exist because civic associations and volunteer groups are invested in curating their favorite aspects of Iron County's wilderness. Two snowmobiling clubs team with county officials to maintain hundreds of miles of forest trails for their activities. One man has assumed responsibility to run a specialized attachment behind his snowmobile to groom paths in two local parks for cross-country and skate skiing. Private citizens maintain iron mining heritage sites as well, displaying machinery from the mines in their yards, trimming grass around informational signage put up by the county, and keeping their own company town houses well maintained.[58] While in practice, volunteers are fulfilling services typically funded by local governments, residents do not seem to resent performing upkeep that benefits visitors. Maintaining both wilderness and town is, for them, simply curating the best of their homes for themselves.

CONCLUSION

In a remote county that's a "great place to live, [and a] hard place to make a living," as Rupert put it, the exact form of future flourishing causes constant debate among residents. It's a debate born out of residential stability and attachment to place, emerging from people committed to diagnosing problems and questioning the efficacy of proposed solutions. But at its heart, it's a debate over what home could and should be. Home needs to exist within the intransigent infrastructural constraints of deindustrialization, like geographical remoteness and transportation limitations. Home should reverse demographic declines and an aging population while honoring the collective cultural values of a small but vibrant community. And, most fundamentally and most out of reach for everyday people, a thriving home in Iron County requires a thriving natural resource economy that raises standards of living for all.

The two economic development options dominant in Iron County—reindustrialization and tourism—reiterated both the durability and the flexibility of *who* and *what* home is for in Iron County. On one hand, the promise of a company interested in mining otherwise untapped geological riches resonated with political leaders and long-term residents eager for a familiar solution to problems of economic depression and geographic inaccessibility. On the other, the commodification of nature through tourism leveraged other natural resources—thousands of acres of public lands, dramatic seasonal variation, and locals' affection for place. Both strategies promise an economic boost that might return this forgotten corner of the Rust Belt to some sense of connection and centrality. But both reindustrialization and tourism create new versions of dependency—dependency on nature as resource and on capital. Large-scale mining is contingent on capital investments from a large company and, as locals ruthlessly identified, a new mine hardly guaranteed a return to the good jobs and mutually beneficial relationships of historic iron mining. Tourism might bring people, money, and jobs to the county, but the jobs are poorly paid and seasonal homeowners make lousy neighbors. As in the past, second-generation industry and nature-based tourism alike hang the economic fates of thousands of people on the fragility and whimsy of capital.

Today, those who still call Iron County home continue to work toward identifying what was good about the past and what is the best possible future given present constraints. For residents who experienced the midcentury closure of the mines, support for a new generation of mining was not purely a nostalgic expectation of a carbon copy of early twentieth century company town life. Rather, many were motivated by a much broader vision of an institutional intervention that, for the first time in more than sixty years, might be sufficient to generate a higher level of economic and social thriving. Through debating these possible futures for Iron County, residents actively weigh the trade-offs and promises of both paths toward renewed economic thriving and a revitalized home.

6

TANGLED LANDSCAPES

Southeast Chicago

The meaning or value of the same place is labile—flexible in the hands of different people or cultures, malleable over time, and inevitably contested.

—Thomas F. Gieryn, 2000.

People like General Iron and many other companies figure, this is a great place, that community's already dead, that soil's already dead, those people are already dying. They're a sacrificial zone. So let's come there. That's not acceptable to us anymore.

—Jade Mazon, cofounder of the Rebel Bells and member of the Southeast Environmental Task Force and the Southeast Side Coalition to Ban Petcoke, 2021.

Jamie stretched his legs out under the table and folded his hands behind his head. "I remember as a kid, when I was in high school traveling along 106th Street to get to St. Francis DeSales by bus, there was always the men getting off every morning and afternoon, on and off. The hard hats, everything, because the place was just pumping with jobs. And then"—Jamie snapped his fingers—"suddenly it was nothing.

I mean it was *vacant.*" Jamie rubbed his thick white beard and tipped his chair back onto two legs. "To see the mills collapse, to be demolished, and waiting for the next thing . . ." He shook his head as he let his chair thump to the ground. It echoed against the lofty ceilings of the Southeast Chicago Historical Museum, a single room located in the Calumet Park Field House. With a frown, he continued, "Will this neighborhood come back to what it was? It's not going to happen." Nodding out the open door, where a vast green lawn stretched into the blue horizon of Lake Michigan, he mused, "I mean, there's not going to be one place where 18,000 people are working, like there was with U.S. Steel South Works, and the industry and the ancillary industries that were created and stayed here for thirty and forty and fifty years. That's not coming back. The old Acme Steel has been demolished—or pieces are still standing, but a mighty wind will blow some of the stuff down. There are a few little companies in the property at Wisconsin Steel now. I don't know what they do." He grimaced, "But, I know they're industrial." Jamie concluded, "But something has to take its place. This can't just be a bedroom community, with all this land. . . . It has to be *something.* So, what takes its place?"

This is a landscape of lacunas—of people who used to be and things that once were there. Across the twenty-five square miles of the Southeast Side, the region feels more like the prairies of northern Indiana than the southern boundary of the Second City. Even though it holds ten times more people than Iron County, Wisconsin, postindustrial Southeast Chicago is still the most rural of the city's wards.[1] In between residential blocks, pocket parks, and small manufacturing and industrial sites, herds of white-tailed deer flit across regrown midwestern prairies. On six hundred acres of the former U.S. Steel site, parallel cement walls create two-thousand-foot-long valleys filled with grass and saplings. Fishermen sit with backs to these walls, perched on corrugated edges of the ore docks opening inland from Lake Michigan.

For the fifty thousand people who call this least-populated ward home, relative rurality is bittersweet. Sites of place attachment overlap with active environmental hazards and collective economic struggle. Locals know they cannot eat the fish they catch in the old industrial river. They cannot build houses or schools on most of the vacant land in the region due to physical or chemical residues from industrialization old and new.[2] Thousands of acres of underutilized urban land reflect the scarcity of employers. Since the 1990s, joblessness in these former steel neighborhoods has exceeded city averages by 25 to 50 percent.[3] Good work is rare—gone are local positions that pay well, offer benefits, and require minimal environmental risk. Vacant houses and unkempt lots in these former millgate communities keep property values frustratingly low, perpetuating a low tax base that strangles reinvestments in public services.[4]

Like in Iron County, deindustrialization undermined the local economy and created lasting problems for the Southeast Side. In both locations, residents are seeking economic fixes that honor their valued relationships to local geographies and community. On the Southeast Side, the focus of this chapter, long-term residents contest similar economic development proposals to those in Iron County, albeit in a very different context. On one hand, city policymakers have maintained the Southeast Side as a sacrifice zone for Chicago, enabling the establishment of new manufacturing and waste disposal industries through zoning, permitting, and tax policies. For decades, local and state political actors have framed new landfills, factories, recycling plants, storage depots, and fertilizer manufacturers as ideal solutions to the two most glaring problems in the Southeast Side—joblessness and property vacancy.[5] However, opponents to reindustrialization argue that the environmental costs are too high for too little economic gain. New industry, placed on old steel mill sites, abuts residential streets, public schools, and parks, creating significant health hazards. Today, the Southeast Side has the highest density of particulate air pollutants in the city while remaining one of Chicago's poorest neighborhoods.

Unhappy with the one-two punch of environmental and economic harms, or what I call *double disenfranchisement*, some activists and long-term residents propose outdoor recreation, heritage sites, and ecosystem restoration as an alternative to new industrial land use. In coordination with the city's Park District, private companies, and nonprofits, Southeast Chicago residents are transforming former steel mill and industrial waste sites into public parks. Though these parks do little to fix the economic problems on the Southeast Side, proponents argue that the growth of outdoor recreation infrastructures will challenge the taken-for-granted industrial purpose of this region.[6] Parkland offers residents and visitors a different relationship to the environment and provides experiences of place that build community connection and celebrate valued aspects of local geography.

While this bifurcation of land reuse echoes Iron County's redevelopment proposals, unlike the rural case, this urban end of the former commodity chain is characterized by more complex governance structures, top-down models of landscape management, and compounding environmental concerns. Whereas the hypothetical return of mining to Iron County sparked enthusiasm among many interviewees, residents of the Southeast Side are already too familiar with the disappointing wages and invasive environmental harms of new manufacturing to share their rural neighbors' optimism. Much more than in Iron County, the interests of Southeast Side political and economic institutions bump up against the diagnosed problems and hoped-for solutions proposed by on-the-ground residents. Residents, their political leaders, and their diverse social movement organizations often find themselves pitted against each other. Reindustrialization has been pushed by city leadership for decades, who frame another generation of manufacturing or waste disposal as a key strategy for returning good jobs to a struggling community. Opponents draw from their long residencies and experience in activism to resist the economic and environmental negatives of double disenfranchisement. While rural interviewees do not see reindustrialization and nature-based tourism as mutually exclusive, many Chicagoans do, and they propose green spaces for recreation, ecosystem health, or heritage preservation—spaces and uses that build community—would usurp new industries.

Even with so much contestation, advocates for the Southeast Side agree on the region's most basic needs: some combination of good jobs *and* livable landscapes to become a home that benefits all residents—an urban neighborhood that reflects the best of its thriving past, where residents benefit from local jobs, know their neighbors, and experience a shared sense of pride in their collective identity. In the city, recreating home means transforming its remnants into landscapes that provide residents economic solutions, social connections, and opportunities to access their valued places. This chapter articulates how Southeast Chicago's institutions and individuals diagnose problems and make sense of contradictory solutions to the long residues of deindustrialization.

TRACING THE TANGLE OF
PROBLEMS AT HOME

To diagnose their regions' economic challenges, interviewees drew my attention to the problem of postindustrial land—both its practical existence and its representation of disinvestment. As Jamie summarized, nearly two-thirds of the landscape of the Southeast Side is pockmarked by a complicated mix of green spaces, postindustrial properties, and new manufacturing sites. These land uses are dominant in large part because of the prevalence of poststeel brownfields—"abandoned, idled, or under-used" properties where "expansion or redevelopment is complicated by real or perceived environmental contamination," according to the U.S. Environmental Protection Agency (EPA).[7] Since the 1970s, federal guidelines mandate that any redevelopment of these properties follows strict remediation procedures since, if left unremediated, brownfields threaten to leach heavy metals like lead and chromium, toxins like arsenic, asbestos, and other industrial chemicals into water and soil.[8] Before being sold and repurposed, brownfields go through an expensive process of being tested, cleaned, sealed, retested, and, in some cases, left fallow for years.[9] Since so many steel companies in Chicago went bankrupt, their properties have lain vacant until a third party—typically the federal or state government—paid for cleanup.[10]

On the Southeast Side, pragmatic issues of maintenance, repair, and use of brownfield land have caused decades of conflict. For local government actors, the cheapest and most expedient solution to the area's problematic geography is to repeat the past: divert dirty properties into land uses that require the least remediation and provide the greatest number of jobs. One elected leader of the ward told me, "There's always a constant that I hear, you know, 'What's your biggest concern?' 'We need jobs, we need jobs, we need jobs!' And I mean, here's the thing, if you're not putting food on your table, how are you going to care about anything else? I mean, that's just a basic thing." They don't need just *any* jobs. In a neighborhood where 23 percent of families earn an income below the federal poverty level, the region needs diversified, entry-level jobs that can attract and hold young people, who are today the dominant category of unemployed on the Southeast Side.[11] And new jobs need to be local in a sprawling city where commute times keep stretching, wages are already low, and taxes and property values can directly benefit the neighborhoods where the jobs are located.[12] A new generation of manufacturing, waste management, or factory work demands very little brownfield cleanup and promises the most employment for desperate locals.

Yet even as the city repurposes some brownfield properties for job-creating industries, interviewees identified how both the vestiges and the renovation of local geographies perpetuate other economic and social issues. The mere presence of these properties—both those still abandoned and those redeveloped into unattractive industrial sites—depresses property values, dissuades repopulation, and, in Simonetta's opinion, inspires more systematic disinvestment in Southeast's residential neighborhoods. Speaking with me in her living room, Simonetta recalled how, without good employers, not only did most of her neighbors pack up and leave, but publicly funded services disappeared. "The community had been devastated already with [the steel mills] closing their doors. So, then they took our bus away . . . [and] if you take transportation away then people can't get to work. People can't get to school. So now you have an even *more* devastated community, and it's done intentionally. . . . Today, most of the Southeast Side is more than a mile from a bus stop." She grumbled, "We don't have anything. We're a food desert. We are a transportation desert. And we are a social service desert. There is nothing. And we still have children. We still have needs." She huffed a sigh and continued, "What's wrong with us? Why don't we deserve it? It's like, what makes us so less important than other people? You know what I mean?"

Conversations with both top-down city actors and long-term residents clarified how and why these two groups differently define the regions' problems and potential solutions. For the city's political actors and institutional representatives, the Southeast Side is a place for the city's waste and dirty industry. For people who still live in the neighborhoods, however, home contains multitudes. Yes, it's a proudly postindustrial neighborhood; but it's also a beautiful natural landscape, a collection of racially diverse working-class housing blocks, and a site for work, education, and leisure. Interviewees' discussion of land use stood in for more fundamental concerns about what a thriving Southeast Side community *should* look like.

The very act of living on the Southeast Side for a long time motivates people, like Simonetta, to invest in home—to engage, to fight, and to hold their political leaders accountable as they make choices about the region's postindustrial land. For decades, long-term residents have been confronting city leaders through grassroots, nonprofit, and activist organizations.[13] For example, in response to the accrual of deindustrialization's disinvestments, Simonetta formed a neighborhood Homeowners and Tenants Association to push the city government to address issues at the nearest public elementary school. "Every school should be a quality school," she declared. "Why shouldn't we have options for knowledge? Why shouldn't we have charter schools? Every public school should be a quality school. And I fought"—she said, her eyes narrowing—"and I sacrificed my daughter." In the 1990s, the elementary school's roof was sagging and classrooms were so understaffed that the principal had an open call for volunteers to manage the kindergarten classes. Simonetta's parents were shocked that she and Christopher didn't move out of their failing school catchment in order to send their kindergartener to a better public school. Shaking her head in vigorous objection to those past voices, she explained her commitment to stay in her neighborhood. She worked hard with the association to raise enough money and political attention to fix the school's roof and hire qualified teachers.[14] Her daughter thrived, Simonetta said with a smirk, pointing to a recent college graduation photo. "As they say, she's doing okay."

Again and again, I heard variations on these themes of disinvestment and engagement. Doubtful that the city would create either an economy or community that they wanted, many of my interviewees were deeply involved in grassroots organizing and civic engagement. They raised funds for fair housing or schooling, built community gardens, ran food banks, and self-funded arts programs for youth. Since the early 2000s, when brownfield reindustrialization became the city's formalized policy for postindustrial land use on the Southeast Side, citizen groups countered with nonmanufacturing commercial corridor plans, proposed protected green spaces, and protested dozens of polluting industries.[15]

Some residents directed their energy toward altering the political machinations of the city itself. Jamie declared that he tries to "put up the good fight" by backing political candidates committed to solving local economic and landscape problems. He said with a glint in his eye, "I have never missed an election since 1975, so I do what I can." A handful of my interviewees got directly involved in politics. Marcos, who I met at a monthly meeting of the Steelworkers Organization for Active Retirees, ran for alderman. He had stiff competition in the race, including Susan, a former public-school counselor and the daughter of a locally famous union organizer, who eventually won the position (with Marcos's vote, he admitted with a smile). Other longtimers work for city bureaucracies, like the Chicago Parks District, or citywide nonprofit organizations, such as Chicago's Friends of the Parks or Open Lands, to bring park development and environmental protection to the table. In a city characterized by career politicians and multigenerational power brokers, citizen involvement signals how committed Southeast Side residents are to rewriting the definition of home.

Interviewees were keenly aware that community disinvestment is a top-down process, solvable by institutional change rather than individual efforts. Ending gaps in school quality or deciding what to do with a hundred-acre brownfield requires massive funding initiatives, policy change, infrastructure renovation, and collaboration across governments, nonprofits, and companies. And yet, this region brims with everyday engagement, layered with rich legacies of multigenerational working-class families united by a fierce willingness to fight for collective good. The very process of contesting land uses—and the fundamental definition of home on the Southeast Side—illuminates long-term residents' dreams for a better future.

"ONE THOUSAND ACRES SUITABLE FOR MANUFACTURING": THE LOGIC AND LIMITS TO REINDUSTRIALIZATION

For four decades, government actors in Chicago have framed the reindustrialization of brownfields as an effective tool for transforming vacant or underused properties into sources of tax revenues and employment for the city. Writing in the preface to a Land Use Plan for the Southeast Side in 2005, the Chicago mayor Richard M. Daly suggested that economic success for the city as a whole required the perpetual use of formerly industrial land for new generations of industries.[16] Daly observed, "For over a century, the Calumet region has contributed to the prosperity of Chicago. . . . In a city where large tracts of vacant industrial land are needed but scarce, the Calumet area retains well over 1,000 acres suitable for manufacturing and other businesses. Almost 60 percent of land in Chicago that is available for industry can be found here." The Land Use Plan coordinated a suite of publicly funded tax breaks, loans, and grants aimed at attracting a new generation of "lighter" industries to the vast acreage on the Southeast Side.[17] Daly institutionalized a strategy of urban redevelopment that, by the end of the twentieth century, was already popular among mayors and state political leaders.

Daly not only rationalized new tax abatement and incentive strategies but enshrined existing zoning rules. Reindustrialization relies on top-down zoning policies to preserve certain spatial relations in dense cities. In the 1990s and early 2000s, Chicago set aside nearly one-third of land and water on the Southeast Side as a planned manufacturing district (PMD)— a special zoning designation intended to preserve manufacturing jobs by protecting industrial firms from encroachment by land uses incompatible with manufacturing.[18] PMDs are "sticky" properties that are nearly impossible to rezone for nonindustrial uses. Another third of properties in this region are zoned for factories, junkyards, and other manufacturing uses. This secondary form of property zoning is, in theory, easier for aldermen to change than a PMD designation. However, given the persistent political interest in preserving the Southeast Side as an industrial corridor for the city, ward leadership is often loath to spend limited political capital on rezoning petitions. The few successful rezoning appeals have transitioned manufacturing properties into city-managed parks. In the past twenty years, the number of acres zoned for parks and open spaces has grown to nearly a quarter of the Southeast Side.[19]

Top-down incentives and zoning policies aimed at preserving existing property uses are not unique to Chicago. The geographer David Harvey observed that in the 1970s, city managers across the United States came to prioritize market mechanisms, rather than publicly funded systems, to solve social, economic, and environmental problems.[20] Policymakers keen to lure private companies to their economically strapped, postindustrial cities proposed incentive structures now recognizable as neoliberal—tax deferrals and abatements, reduced regulatory expectations, city-funded grants, or subsidized property prices. Specifically in deindustrialized cities, the reindustrialization of brownfields was attractive to city bureaucrats because it offered a roadmap for transforming vacant land into job-producing businesses capable of rescuing flailing local economies.[21] Not only did reindustrialization cost less, as federal law requires only minimal remediation for polluted properties returning to manufacturing uses, but keeping dirty properties dirty also allowed cities to prevent more financially valuable greenfields from entering a city's brownfield cycle.

State and regional governments have also adopted reindustrialization as a strategy for larger-scale economic development. For instance, in the 1990s, the governor of Illinois and mayor of Chicago collectively marshaled $100 million to lure the Ford Motor Company to the city.[22] In exchange for a guarantee that Ford would create jobs and invest in underutilized property, the city offered the company a ten-year tax break through its Economic Development for a Growing Economy (EDGE) program.[23] Since the largest lots of vacant property were located on the Southeast Side, as Daly observed, neighborhood leaders added to the incentives being offered to Ford by tapping into a ward-specific pool of money to repair infrastructures and remediate a 113-acre site for the new Ford Supplier Park.[24] This publicly funded incentive structure succeeded and today, Ford's factory pays nearly five thousand workers to assemble Explorers and police cars.[25] More recently, in 2015, the state of Illinois categorized the majority of the 10th ward as an Enterprise Zone. One of only six such zones in Chicago, this program rewards businesses that create or retain a certain number of jobs through tax exemptions on utilities, building materials, and, perhaps most significantly for large manufacturers, purchases of property. Here's the catch: on the Southeast Side, this tax exemption only applies to manufacturing companies that are operating a "pollution control facility."[26] The accumulated consequence of city, regional, and state policies means that today, neighborhoods on the Southeast Side share space, by design, with dirty industries. A drive down a major throughfare passes a cement manufacturer, a company that renders plant and animal waste into fertilizer, three oil-refining byproduct depositories, five electricity generation stations, and two large-scale recycling sites.

In Southeast Chicago, I heard the most support for reindustrialization as policy and practice from interviewees in positions of political or economic power. Consistently, these interviewees framed new industrial job sites as the most effective way to solve economic problems. For instance, Bill, a white, middle-aged coordinator at a job training center located just outside of the 10th ward, voiced support for new manufacturing work as the most appropriate solution to local economic issues. He directed my attention from his office window to a rooftop wind turbine rhythmically reflecting the afternoon sun. Beneath the turbine, a soap factory churns out products and a greenhouse produces high-priced salad greens for downtown markets. This factory, Bill declared, was his model and motivation—not just to shuttle young people into *any* job but to "get more, clean, sustainable industry into the area . . . to get more jobs so that we can get more young people into those positions—especially in the manufacturing jobs."[27]

Organizations, like Bill's, tasked with training young people for employment echo this vision. The top majors at the local community college are logistics and warehouse management; trade unions call for apprentices in manual labor; job training centers affiliated with city government prioritize channeling local youth into manufacturing work.[28] An elected ward leader admitted to me that, given the desperation many of her constituents feel when looking for work, she'd be happy to have any new businesses take up residence in her ward. She winced a little as she admitted, "Even industrial!" She clarified, "Not at the expense of people's health or anything like that, it's just . . . people have to be able to provide for their family. I mean, I really truly believe that."

"Perpetual Struggles": Resisting Economic and Environmental Costs of Reindustrialization

Reindustrialization reproduces taken-for-granted ideas of what the Southeast Side should *mean* to the city of Chicago. Policies and practice have entrenched this solution to problems of land reuse and economic depression in local landscapes. If executed well, perhaps another generation of this familiar category of blue-collar work could return the region to the best version of its past. But even in the face of double-digit unemployment numbers, reindustrialization hasn't captured the imaginations of many long-term residents in Southeast Chicago. Residents are seeking economic fixes that don't merely follow the path of least resistance; they want jobs that build back community. Zoning and financial incentives that favor reindustrialization reproduce the logic of industrial dependency without providing the benefit-rich, family-supporting jobs that locals remember. Even at Ford, the region's reindustrialization success story, only one hundred of its five thousand jobs are full-time and salaried. The remaining 4,900 jobs are hourly positions with few avenues for advancement.[29] While these jobs are located in Southeast Chicago, they don't exclusively employ local residents. Steel mill jobs pulled from labor pools located within walking distance, but contemporary industrial workforces are much more dispersed. In a phone interview, the local alderperson explained that while she has no legal leverage to force businesses to hire from the local pool of job seekers, each year, she sits down with any willing managers and encourages them to hire through local trade unions or ward-specific vocational programs. But, she admitted, last year, only two companies acted on her suggestions—and Ford wasn't one of them.

Beyond the limits of employment, interviewees voiced concerns that many of these newer industrial land uses have a heavy environmental footprint. The U.S. EPA hosts a website just for Southeast Chicago, listing its seventy-five investigations into companies possibly violating the Clean Air Act and three significant "enforcement actions."[30] Even with this close attention by the EPA, smaller manufacturing companies can often fall through regulatory loopholes.[31] Geographies remember and toxins accrete. Ninety percent of all landfills in the city of Chicago exist on the Southeast Side, making it one of the largest waste disposal clusters in the United States.[32] In 2019, soil samples revealed high levels of manganese and lead contamination in a youth league baseball field on the Southeast Side.[33]

Unlike in Iron County, on the Southeast Side, the past haunts rather than inspires. Environmental justice researchers have shown again and again that garbage and toxic wastes tend to be dumped in poor neighborhoods with open spaces and few regulations.[34] These practices are reproduced, in turn, through representations of what a place is *for* inscribed both on paper and in the local imagination. On the Southeast Side, maps, policies, and historical narratives have normalized the exploitation of local landscapes. Roy made this point to me as we sat in a McDonald's with cooling cups of coffee clutched in our hands. "You're never going to get a steel mill here again. And what we have been getting are bulk material facilities along the river because they're buying up the properties very cheap because it's contaminated. And because it's contaminated, they almost perpetuate it by saying, 'Hey, now we can bring in dirty industry because we're already contaminated!' We have to get rid of that thinking." Striking the table with the flat of his hand, he continued, "For the longest time, the City Department of Planning and Development ignored us. Just because it's on a map downtown somewhere that it's industrial, they thought that's all we are. It's just the attitude, you know? We've had a succession of mayors who really didn't consider this as . . . prime territory over here. . . . So, we've always been the poor stepchild down here, you might say, and the dumping ground."

Zoning and incentive policies codify a vision of the Southeast Side as industrial because this vision is useful to policymakers. From a planning perspective, city governments want to keep land in reserve as a "sacrifice zone"—a location deemed disposable by people in power because it was historically impaired by environmental damage and economic disinvestment and, in this case, because it serves as an easy repository for the dirty industries necessary for the city to function.[35] Logics of disposability are not unique to the twenty-first century. As discussed in chapter 1, since the nineteenth century discourse about the growth of Chicago has been linked to the designation of the Southeast

Side as an industrial region. But in light of the environmental harms and economic limitations to reindustrialization, new industries and the policies that attract them have faced increased scrutiny by critical observers across the United States.

In a 2018 essay, the Editorial Board of the *Chicago Tribune* critiqued reindustrialization on the Southeast Side as an "imbalance in City Hall's vision for how Chicago should grow." The authors quipped, "For years, South Siders have watched developers gobble up North Side tracts with feeding-frenzy appetites while their neighborhoods languish. The North Side gets glitzy glass and steel—and the South Side gets the scraps."[36] A growing chorus of skeptics argue that incentive-based public policies reward companies seeking to win the race to the bottom for wages and pollution disposal while starving local communities of desperately needed funding.[37] Incentives "carry a steep public cost," according to a *Chicago Tribune* critique of the EDGE program that funded Ford's establishment. "Every dollar awarded to a company is a dollar not collected to fund basic public services like education, transportation and health care."[38]

For as long as policymakers have preserved the 10th ward as a naturalized repository for the distasteful byproducts of Chicago's economy, long-term residents have been resisting. In the 1980s, a group of African American and Latino women living within the "toxic donut" of waste repositories a few miles west of the steel region organized protests that directly influenced the city's policy on landfills. In the 1990s, the city proposed building a regional airport near Lake Calumet. A new generation of activists galvanized to successfully block the large-scale erasure of neighborhoods for the planned project.[39] In the same time frame, the long-term resident Marian Byrnes coordinated the efforts of thirty grassroots organizations in opposition of a garbage incinerator proposed for the former Wisconsin Steel site.

Her organization, the Southeast Environmental Task Force (SETF), still runs point for complaints to the U.S. and Illinois EPA, organizes protests against persistent polluters, and offers "Toxic to Treasures" tours, which bus visitors and locals through industrial sites and into new park developments.

SETF, in coordination with the Natural Resources Defense Council, the Active Transportation Alliance, and other grassroots organizations, plays a vital role in protesting proposed industries today. For instance, late 2019, General Iron, a metals recycling plant located in north Chicago, gained city approval to transfer its shredding processes to the Southeast Side.[40] This permitting request faced no resistance from city policymakers, at least initially, because it merely expanded the footprint of a metals recycling company that had already been functioning on the Southeast Side for thirty years. General Iron did not require changes to zoning laws, nor did the move challenge any presuppositions of appropriate land use. SETF first challenged the proposed company move when grassroots organizers learned that the company was already marred by persistent complaints of airborne pollution—"shredder fluff," lightweight particulate residual materials from the metals recycling process. City officials assured protesters that the new recycling plant would include an enclosed shredder equipped with suction hoods, high-efficiency filters, solar panels, and air-monitoring technologies.[41] But, based on decades of personal experience, the activists (who are also long-term residents) were skeptical that the recycling company would build or retrofit their processes without firmer state or federal regulatory pressure. Frustrated by silence from the city and the Illinois EPA, the protests escalated. In 2020, a group of twenty nonprofit workers, students, and teachers from the high school located across the street from the proposed expansion site began a hunger strike.[42] By risking their bodies' health voluntarily, these hunger strikers drew attention to the involuntary exposures of reindustrialization. After nearly three years of contentious public meetings, weekly protests, and national press coverage, intervention by the federal EPA motivated the city to deny the proposed plant relocation in 2022.[43]

Fierce resistance to reindustrialization in a former steel mill neighborhood might be surprising to observers. After all, living with a polluting industry is nothing new to most long-term residents. Due to the tight geographic overlap of work and home, families of steelworkers swept soot from their porches, shut windows against smoke from smelters, and fertilized their gardens with dredgings from industrial waste-filled catchment ponds. Even decades after closure, workers experienced respiratory issues from clouds of dust and gusts of hot, toxic fumes from metals and fuel. On a walk through the old U.S. Steel site with Jesús and Marcos, descendants of Mexican steelworkers, Jesús told me that through their kitchen window, they could hear "the ore boats . . . coming in or when the mill was blasting. So, we grew up, literally, right in front of the mill." As he stopped to touch old taconite pellets littering the ground, he said, "One of the things that we all remember here—I know Marcos will remember—is when they would throw the graphite in the air." Marcos laughed and nodded. Jesús continued, "We were actually exposed to the graphite, thinking that it was sparkly, silver rain, and we would play in it!" They two men groaned and shook their heads at their childish naivety. In small amounts, the U.S. Center for Disease Control does not consider graphite dust harmful.[44] But not only can decades of inhalation of any particulate matter cause severe respiratory issues, graphite is often a visible signal of more insidious and otherwise invisible airborne toxins.[45]

Simonetta, who lived a few houses away from Jesús, recalled the daily coating of her porch and windowsills with the sparkling particles. Her face twisted in anger. "We used to sweep like that much dust"—she measured an inch with her pointer finger and thumb—"off the porch every morning." She continued with a frown, "One day I walked home and my mother was sitting next door on the stairs, and she was all silver because of all the graphite that had been in the air, and she looked like the tin man. I cried. I actually cried! And I said, 'Oh my, this is the shit that we're breathing in, that we're living in!'" In the early 1970s, when the steel mills were still running and the newly formed U.S. EPA first established a Chicago office, Simonetta "used to call [them] every day" to complain about the particulate matter. The local representative ignored to her objections. He would snidely remark that it was either dust or unemployment for her husband and every other working-age man on the block. She retorted that the mills "have the money to put in for pollution control, and they won't. They will *not* spend the money." When the mills closed, her anxieties about her family's economic crisis were colored with disappointment that the company "would rather *close* than . . . invest" in protecting locals' health.

The EPA representative was echoing a narrative popular across the U.S. industrial corridor—that environmental and health risks were acceptable trade-offs for middle-class wages for blue-collar work.[46] At least there were jobs accompanying steel's emissions. But the risk-benefit calculus of the 1970s is not recognizable today. Twenty-first century industrial jobs are dirty and low wage. Industrial properties still abut millgate communities—a useful community layout when those industrial jobs meant middle-class wages and a walkable commute but a bitter entanglement today as residual brownfields combine with reindustrialization to create localized, environmental risks without good jobs.[47]

This pattern of double disenfranchisement—poor environment and poor jobs—has changed the narrative of on-the-ground residents on the Southeast Side. Roy crushed his now-empty coffee cup with his fist. "I think the average person in this area today is more concerned about earning a living, their kids being able to go to a decent school, get an education, and being able to pay the mortgage, and being able to breathe clean air is important to them, we've found," he said, referring to conversations he and his fellow volunteers in a local environmental group had been having with neighbors. "And where people, in the past, were very willing to make that exchange of having to have dirty air and more dust and more grime on their clotheslines and their cars and everything, because 'Hey, that's where I get my paycheck, just shut up, that's what puts the bread on the table.' But today, it's not there. People are saying, 'No, our health is more important than these jobs that you want to bring in here and you want to pay just a little bit over minimum wage to bring them in. No.' "

Every year, dozens of new manufacturers express interest in opening new plants here. While new jobs are tempting, social and environmental organizations find themselves sucked into a cycle of protest and resistance because, as the environmental group SETF summarizes on their website, conflict is "necessary to strike a balance between economic life, human welfare, and the environment—struggles that define the Calumet Region."[48] The work of protest is driven by the commitment of long-term residents to their home, and more precisely, to intentionally contradicting the definitional work of political leaders intent on calcifying the geography of the Southeast Side as set aside *for* new industry. Even observers near to the halls of power are calling out the one-two punch of the city's passive disinvestment from the Southeast Side and its active targeting of the neighborhood as a sacrifice zone. Pointing to the unequal spatial distribution of industrial pollution, the ward alderperson told a Chicago-based reporter, "We're tired of being the city's dumping ground. . . . We want and deserve good things too."[49] Not all redefinition work is successful. But through active conflict over the use of the region's ample geographies, residents make space for new definitions of home—ones that resist further economic disenfranchisement, challenge the mindless repetition of the past, and honor long legacies of community connection and affection for place.

"PRESERVING THESE ECOLOGICAL GEMS": BUILDING TWO THOUSAND ACRES OF PARKS IN CHICAGO

On a windy Earth Day, I joined a group of Southeast Chicago birdwatchers on a walk through a marshland. My companions pointed out a green heron there, a gull here—and could that be a rare least bittern in the distance? Tucked between smokestacks and warehouses is a patchwork of three thousand acres of marshlands that the National Audubon Society considers an Important Bird Area vital for songbird and waterfowl migrations across the highly urbanized southern region of Lake Michigan.[50] Some of this land is still owned by nearly defunct steel mills; other acreages are capped landfills; and still other properties belong to the Chicago Park District (CPD). For two decades, the CPD has been coordinating a coalition of nonprofits, volunteer organizations, private companies, and city agencies to build a quiver of public parks, nature conservation sites, and industrial heritage monuments on the Southeast Side. In 2010, the CPD announced a goal to administer more than two thousand acres of nature space on the Southeast Side.[51] By 2021, the CPD had exceeded that goal, with one-quarter of its citywide 8,800 acres of its properties found in six parks on southern marshlands or brownfield prairies. These parks provide recreational infrastructures ranging from "heart-pumping adventures like rock climbing and mountain biking, to more passive activities like fishing, birding, or trail walks," according to the CPD website for Southeast Side parks (see figure 6.1).[52]

Many long-term residents and their organizations view park development as the best opportunity to redefine the Southeast Side.[53] In a 2011 Chicago newspaper article, a local environmental leader said, "Here on the Southeast Side of Chicago, all we get is more industry. So, what we're hoping is that by preserving these ecological gems that eventually they become our assets.

FIGURE 6.1 Rock climbing wall in Steelworker's Park, Southeast Chicago.
Photograph by the author.

Perhaps we could do eco-tourism here, bring people from outside of the community to our community."[54] Toward that end, each year, hundreds of members of the regions' environmental organizations—ranging from Open Lands to the SETF—collaborate with the CPD to build and maintain access to green spaces. Roy joins the Chicago Audubon Society's annual Calumet Marsh Bird Survey to count breeding birds in protected wetland habitats. He recalled how the powerful citywide nonprofit Friends of the Parks "say they want to see . . . the lakefront all unspoiled and unbuilt. So that may occur here on the south end of the lake, too, which would give us a nice strip of lakefront property. And then Lake Calumet and the bike paths and things that are going on out here—the marshes, the parklands, the bike park, and all these things." He then proposed reframing of land reuse in his neighborhood. "We no longer have to just look at ourselves as a polluted end of the line for everything that the city wants to get rid of. [We want] to rebrand ourselves, to be the playground of the city instead, and a place where people can come out and camp, fish, and hike and bike ride, and things like that. Why not?"

Proponents of new parks may dislike reindustrialization, but people who argue for reindustrialization are generally supportive of park development. In fact, many economic development organizations see efforts to make parks as part of a multipronged strategy for revitalizing the region.[55] For instance, Bill, from the job training center, paired his hope for new, greener manufacturing with a parallel vision of a future of cleaned-up "brownfield areas [to] get them back into productive use, or if it's going to be an open space, get it open so that it's clean enough to use by community people for recreation purposes or birdwatching or whatever." Bill was inadvertently echoing the formal position of the Millennium Reserve (later renamed the Calumet

Collaborative), an organization started in 2015 by the state of Illinois and the city of Chicago that focused on redevelopment of the southern edge of the city. In a cached version of their website, this organization formally declared, "The abandoned industrial landscape and closed landfills of the Calumet area are being re-imagined for new commercial and 'green' industrial developments, as well as habitat restoration, historic heritage parks and active recreation."[56]

Groups both for and against reindustrialization do agree that park development benefits local residents by quite literally making new and accessible geographies. Since the mid-1800s, the Southeast Side of Chicago has been reorganized, dissected, and cordoned off to prioritize the flows of industry over the easy movement of everyday people. At the turn of the century, marshy rivers were corralled into canals and cemented into docks, and open fields were crisscrossed with industrial-sized railroads and streets. When companies were open, steelworkers belonged on this landscape; they walked to work via footbridges and pedestrian paths that crisscrossed river and field. But with deindustrialization came locked gates and a mess of restrictive land tenure arrangements, toxic properties, off-limits waterways, and convoluted public transportation routes. The creation of public parkland not only redraws mental maps and rewrites narratives about the purpose of brownfields on the Southeast Side, but it also practically enables access to properties once off-limits to the public. Many recreational or habitat landscapes use brownfield properties that are nearly impossible to repurpose for new buildings because they are pockmarked with "hard residues," like steel building foundations or capped landfills.

Indeed, parks promise environmental good in a community too familiar with environmental harm. A case in point is Big

Marsh Bike Park—one of the newest parks located on a city-owned, three-hundred-acre plot of land that was once a waste and slag dumping site for the now-bankrupt Acme Steel. On land that for decades barred foot traffic, this park now offers several miles of walking paths and a pump track, a circular paved path with artificial hills that mountain bikers and skateboarders use to gain speed and practice jumps. Reuben, the director of this park's volunteer group, hoped that increased access to this landscape would benefit community members worn thin from years of fighting the worst of reindustrialization. "My hope is that the people who have been part of the environmental justice movement can benefit from access to green space in their backyards. I think it can be about equity."

Most interviewees were pleased that parks were transforming landscapes abandoned in the wake of the steel collapse of the twentieth century into assets in their too-often overlooked home. Roy is a stocky white man more at ease with binoculars than on a bike. "It wasn't my idea, having a bike park there," he gruffly stated. He explained that he was "in that category" of naturalists who would rather let such wildland lie untouched by humans in an urban region where "there's such little habitat left anymore. But"—he held up his hand as a caveat—"we have been—for 20 years!—endeavoring to get it cleaned up and more inviting to members of the community. You see other areas of the city getting all the benefits, like up on North Side." He pointed with his chin northward toward the skyline barely visible in the distance. "The 606 and the Lakefront and downtown and everything," he said, referring to a multimillion-dollar investment in several new park projects in the city center. "And, we're saying, 'Hey, look at this remote area out here. Look at how degraded it has been,' and 'Don't we deserve something out here? At least clean things up.' So, I think it's a good thing in that regard, that we're finally getting some attention down here."[57] Park development requires an intentional reimagining of place and provides a new way for people to experience an industrial area. As people move through and to the marshlands of the Southeast Side, their presence, experiences, and stories are slowly changing the narrative about the purpose of these thousands of acres.

For long-term residents of the Southeast Side, certain parks provide sites to ground collective stories of belonging to community and geography. On a sixteen-acre section of the U.S. Steel property at the mouth of the Calumet River sits Steelworker's Park—one of the first to be managed by the CPD. In 2002, U.S. Steel—one of the few mills that didn't go bankrupt in the twentieth century—donated this land to the city. Because thirty years had passed since the mill was active, this lakefront property was no longer considered dangerous to visitors by federal or state standards. But any redevelopment that required digging deep was limited by foundations of the once-massive steel mill complex, cement pads reinforced with steel and embedded with a network of small rail tracks, and walls that paralleled the narrow ore dock abutting Lake Michigan.[58] Within these residues, a park was born. After years of debate over what to do with century-old ore walls, the CPD installed rock climbing holds and harness clips. On Saturdays in the summer, people from the community can rent shoes, strap into belaying harnesses, and scramble up the wall.[59] Summer is also when Shakespeare in the Park sets up a stage, the alderman's office sets off Fourth of July fireworks, and early morning fishermen shuffle through the remnant half-inch rounds of taconite iron pellets to cast a line into Lake Michigan.

Vestiges of the region's largest steel mill are more than merely the backdrop for this community park. They offer a canvas for telling stories about industry and home. Back with Jesús and Marcos at Steelworker's Park, Jesús drew my attention to a nearly life-size sculpture of a man in a hard hat, arms wrapped around a woman, and a small child tucked between their knees. Jesús, now a well-established artist, beamed with pleasure at his name on the plaque. "Believe it or not, we've been talking about leaving a monument for the steelworkers for over 20 years. When the mills first closed, we started talking about leaving a monument there." When he was finally asked by the CPD to design and cast a sculpture, he jumped at the chance. "I wanted to make something that . . . nobody would look at it and identify it. So that's why there's no faces, because if you could look at it, and then you could see whatever you want in the faces. That was very important to me. And the other important thing is that we were a family. It wasn't a man by himself; it was a family. A steelworker was not just *one* [person]." Jesús and Marcos know this personally. They were in their early twenties when they lost their jobs at U.S. Steel—last hired, first to go. Although they were able to find new jobs—Marcos worked his way up the ranks at the local fire station, and Jesús runs an art studio—their fathers and uncles struggled to redefine their identities without industrial economic structures.

For these two men, this park offers a physical site to hold the grief of past crisis in tension with their ongoing connection to the artistic, athletic, and social versions of the modern Southeast Side. Public art, birdwatching outings, and bike parks not only challenge the dominant policy and practice of returning postindustrial land to new industrial uses, but these uses transform the nothingness of deindustrialized lands into spaces for new stories about home and beacons for reinvestment. Parklands make the Southeast Side more than the sum of its industrial pasts.

Better than the Alternative: Ambivalent Embrace of Parklands Economics and Accessibility

While reindustrialization inspired fierce resistance due to its contradictions with valued components of home, park building summoned more measured hesitation from interviewees. Park development is often framed by stakeholders as a welcome reduction of land available for industrial sacrifice. And yet, disappointment in the capacity of parks to repair economic problems emerged often in interviews. Bicycling, birdwatching, and educational activities are essentially free, and the Southeast Side offers no notable hospitality industry to house overnight visitors.[60] On the smallest scale, parks proponents had hoped that increased traffic to Big Marsh would produce noticeable economic gains for nearby businesses. Since 2019, the number of cars crossing a traffic counter in the park increased by 400 percent—from an average of 30 to 122 cars per day. In August 2021, the park had a peak day of 349 cars. The hope is that this influx of drivers will spend money at gas stations and buy lunch from the Chicago-famous smoked seafood shack on the bridge over the Calumet River. Perhaps large events, like cycling competitions or the annual Christmas bird count, will bring customers to corner diners.

Certainly, for those gas station owners, food shack cooks, and waitresses serving coffee, an increased customer base is welcome. However, any aggregate economic boon from those small economic injections has been negligible.[61] Unlike in Iron County, Southeast Chicago is hardly dependent on recreation. On one hand, parks offer little by way of employment. Friends of Big Marsh pays their director and one assistant to coordinate programing and apply for grants. The CPD hires people to perform maintenance and build parks, but those employees live in neighborhoods across the city. Even work performed by hyperlocal land trusts or organizations requires teams of merely three to five employees. The head of the citywide Friends of the Parks group explained that, on the Southeast Side, her board wrestled with the contradictions between enthusiasm from "our base that just wants a pretty park" and local residents who "care more about, 'Right, yes, I'd like more parkland—but I want a job!'"

On the other hand, other economic benefits of park development, such as increased property values that typically characterize urban blocks with attractive green spaces, have also failed to materialize. Based on past research on urban park development in deindustrialized cities, a decade of aggressive green space development on the Southeast Side *should* have attracted higher-wage residents and aspirational companies. This economic shift, known as green gentrification, is both bad and good. At its worst, gentrification displaces vulnerable residents by driving up rental costs and property taxes. In some cities, the displacing effects of park investments have become so concerning to many urban residents that some collectively resist green gentrification through protests, as the sociologists Ken Gould and Tammy Lewis observed.[62] At its best, however, gentrification brings an influx of much-needed capital investment to marginalized communities.

For better or for worse, no such economic development—or collective resistance—has emerged in this neighborhood. When I asked Reuben if he and his team at Big Marsh were concerned that their park would exacerbate gentrification, he responded carefully. "I don't want to be naive, right," but gentrification is "not at a point where it's come up consistently" in community meetings or in conversation with his local Big Marsh volunteer board. Reuben reflected, "I'm sure somebody would disagree

with me, but the far Southeast Side is still sort of outside of most
of the gentrification network in Chicago." Similarly, Louisa, the
neighborhood's elected representative to city council, told me
with a laugh, "I don't at all think that we're gentrifying South
Chicago." She expected that the most the region could hope
from park development was an economic "shot in the arm."

Housing price data backs up both Reuben and Louisa's intu-
itions. For decades, the neighborhoods surrounding Big Marsh
and other natural areas have maintained some of the lowest
housing prices in the city—even with the pandemic-driven,
national price hike for houses in less densely populated regions
in 2020 and 2021.[63] At first glance, this might be surprising—
the verdant marshlands, sparkling lakefront views, and inex-
pensive housing seem a siren's call to wealthy newcomers seeking good residential and commercial investments. But even
with low population density and access to nature, the Southeast Side is not attracting wealthy residents. The shadows of
industries past and present might be limiting economic investments. The Southeast Side is fifteen miles from downtown
with few public transportation options. The city's only industrial river still moves with freight traffic. Houses, schools, and
churches sit tucked between power plants. And public parks
gleam green beneath a cloak of some of the city's highest concentrations of particulate matter, leading to jokes overhead in
public meetings that bikers and hikers would need to "hold
their breath" while visiting the Southeast Side for outdoor
recreation.

This lack of direct economic stimulation compounds
issues of public disinvestment. While property taxes provide
most funds for city parks, currently, private funding contrib-
utes significantly to CPD activities. Its website for Southeast
Side's parks lists thirty private donor organizations as key

"collaborators."[64] Private capital is key to park development, but ultimately increases parks' vulnerability. For instance, Big Marsh bike park exists only because the city government has been significantly aided by private companies.[65] In the early 2000s, REI, the outdoor recreation gear cooperative, and SRAM, a bike part manufacturer, were interested in funding a recreational cycling park and approached the CPD. In exchange for access to city-owned brownfields, the companies' philanthropic branches funded 95-percent of the Friends of Big Marsh operating budget. The remaining 5 percent of the budget covers maintenance work completed on an as-needed basis by the CPD. Even the onsite environmental center is privately funded. Ford Motors—the same company responsible for employing thousands of people—opened the Ford Calumet Environmental Center in 2021. In fulfillment of a decades-old community benefits agreement that accompanied its entry into the community in the 1990s, Ford funded the construction of the state-of-the-art building for educational programming.[66]

Private funding is core to park development. However, because the entirety of park function is not publicly funded (meaning it appears as a line item in the city budget), the city will not be prepared to take over bills historically footed by companies if and when those companies decide to end their philanthropy. If REI, SRAM, and Ford stop funding Friends of Big Marsh Park, the management organization for this open space will face the chopping block. In short, privatized park funding creates a new generation of dependency on company benevolence. While not as extreme as when steel companies built neighborhoods, maintained infrastructures, and provided social safety nets, this funding structure means that companies still play a foundational role in the construction and perpetuity of a significant form of land use on the Southeast Side.

Finally, park development incited ambivalent opinions from some interviewees because of the overlapping geographies of industrial landscapes and green space. Even as parkland opens formerly fenced-off brownfields to the public, past and present industrialization restricts access to these spaces. Reuben admitted the tangled mess of industrial infrastructures, transportation networks, and city zoning policy makes his park particularly hard to get to. "The only reason there's a 300-acre park for the City of Chicago . . . is because it's sort of not in the most accessible place." His lips formed a thin line in concentration as he explained the logistical problems of the park's location. The street leading to Big Marsh Park from the East Side neighborhood "dead-ends at the tracks. It's officially railroad property." The railroad companies are nervous about liability issues if kids cross the tracks, he said, but biking on the main road has its own problems. "It's really hard for local kids to access the Big Marsh bike park from the East Side (one of the neighborhoods on the Southeast Side). They have to bike six miles to get to the entrance of a park that is, geographically, three-quarters of a mile from their neighborhood." Since bicycling to the park from residential neighborhoods in the 10th ward is so difficult, it creates an awkward class and age stratification for users of the park. At a public meeting, Carlie, a young white woman who volunteers with a local teen group to coordinate group rides to the park, voiced concern that they either have to "risk heavy traffic" and flat tires or cycle "miles out of their way" to safely get to the bike park. Parks like Big Marsh might be most exciting and accessible to residents who do *not* live amid active industries—who can drive around infrastructural problems and leave when the pollution feels oppressive. The park's embeddedness in an active, industrial sacrifice zone still structurally excludes and symbolically alienate some young people and those without access to cars.[67]

Furthermore, in this majority Latino and African American neighborhood, these issues of accessibility offer local residents racially inequitable imaginaries of nature. As the geographer Carolyn Finney articulates, *who* feels like they belong in landscapes set aside for "recreation, scenic viewing, scientific understanding, [and] education" mirrors American legacies of racial exclusion.[68] For decades, communities of color on the Southeast Side have comprised the core of environmental activist movements rather than the visionaries for park development. A few interviewees bluntly stated that Big Marsh was too hard to get to and, as a bike park, probably wasn't "for them." Two others mentioned concerns about performing outdoor activities in one of the parts of the city with the highest concentrations of particulate air pollution.[69] And then there's the views. Everywhere you turn, vistas of industry obscure the horizon. Large and busy roads funnel trucks past neighborhoods; electricity plants groan and crackle; ammonia from a fertilizer manufacturer wafts over houses on humid days; and, even looking out at Lake Michigan, plumes of emissions from the last steel plant in Gary, Indiana fog the horizon. At a public meeting about a proposed pocket park along the banks of the Calumet River—accessible only via a small towpath between two industrial buildings—one resident, Maria, a Latina in her mid-fifties, said, "Our Calumet River has a hard landscape. It's discouraging that we can't have a pretty view." Another participant in this meeting complained, "We do have all the wildlife, we just don't have a chance to stop and see it."

So, if park development isn't successfully creating jobs or directly addressing the source of reindustrialization's pollution, then what is it for? Parks are for attention—a way to bring new people to the most geographically remote, "forgotten part of the city," as the alderwoman said.[70] When those flows of people run aground on the complicated infrastructures of their still-industrial community, some locals hope that the city will be forced to send funds to repair crumbling infrastructures.

CONCLUSION

In Southeast Chicago, ideas about the past have constrained options for the future. Decades of policy and practice have pushed former steel mill neighborhoods down the commodity chain from a site for large-scale manufacturing to dumping grounds for waste disposal. Zoning rules, tax abatements, and policy categorizations have reified these former millgate neighborhoods as the city's sacrifice zone—a convenient location for hiding Chicago's wastes and smelly industrial processes out of sight and out of mind (to some). For proponents of reindustrialization, bringing back good jobs is core to rebuilding community life because economic thriving was central to neighborhood function before deindustrialization. However, many more interviewees were concerned that more recycling plants, small factories, oil byproduct storage locations, and large warehouses are not producing the kind of home that local residents need or want. Activists and everyday observers complain that top-down policies, combined with the dense, patchwork geography of the Southeast Side, create new environmental harms without generating much-needed employment. Many residents call for reprioritization of community health over such poor economic gains.

Park development offers an alternative land use and, for some proponents, a better vision for home and well-being in the local community. New parks remove brownfields from circulation and challenge the dominant framing of the Southeast Side as the city's dump. Even though parks hardly address economic problems, proponents of park development emphasize that their approach presents a different vision of home than does reindustrialization. They imagine a future where deindustrialized landscapes are transformed into sites for greater access, connection, and collective affection for place.

Stepping back into both communities central to this book, it is striking that in both Iron County and Southeast Chicago, reindustrialization and green space development emerged as parallel economic development solutions to economic, geographic, and community problems. Comparison highlights how each case's position on the iron and steel commodity chain and relationship to local landscapes differently shapes contemporary options. Industrial history offered a model of a "good company" for Iron Countians supportive of reindustrialization, and rurality enabled locals to overlook potential impacts of a new mine on nature-based tourism. In contrast, interviewees in Southeast Chicago make clear how the ways in which people in power define the purposes of "home" impact what policies are crafted, where is protected, and where people stash their unwanted wastes. But across mining and manufacturing communities, long-term residents share in common a goal to reimagine their home in a way that fixes economic problems while still honoring components of geography and community that they collectively value.

CONCLUSION

T his book is not just a deindustrialization story. It is a story about home. We all want a functional and stable home—landscapes, nature, and buildings that anchor us in place; people to whom we belong; clearcut ways to make ends meet. For many of us, however, home is characterized more by change than stability. For some the familiarity of home might be upended by a new job, an exciting educational opportunity, or a compelling social duty pulls them away. For others, homes transform beneath our feet and against our wills. In some places, climate change is fundamentally reshaping home. Increasingly frequent hurricanes are eroding land beneath houses; rising sea levels are scraping away the sandy beaches of childhoods; warming waters are killing the fish eaten to survive; and costs of repairing and preventing these disasters are pricing people out of their homes. In other communities, macroeconomics is colliding with politics to make places harder to live in. Rural farmland is becoming more costly to keep in agriculture. Urban gentrification is pushing to the periphery people living in neighborhoods deemed high value by planners or politicians. States and municipalities are battling increasingly polarized panics of pandemics, economic recessions, and housing shortages that are expelling residents. The pace and intensity of these crises have become only more prevalent in the past several decades, making a changing home an increasingly everyday experience.

Through a close study of two formerly integrated nodes of the midwestern iron and steel commodity chain, this book provides a new way of thinking about how home is made, threatened, and renegotiated in a world constantly in flux. Instead of viewing home as unchanging, I have embraced crisis as core to the social construction of home. Questions about the implications of these crises are fundamentally questions about home—sociological puzzles about what gives place meaning and, thus, what is lost, retained, or renegotiated in the wake of transformation.

Across boom and bust, I found that three consistent building blocks comprised home—*geography, community,* and *economy*. First, home is fundamentally geographical—home is *here*, not there, because it is embedded in place-based, material resources and spatially connected to other places. Second, when people talk about home, they're talking about *who* is home—who belongs to one another as family, workmates, employers, or friends. These relationships shift as structural contexts transform, but remain important. Finally, home is always tangled up with economic relations of everyday life. Not only do paying a mortgage and working a job root people in places and in social networks, but accomplishing these material needs is its own way to be human, express creativity, and establish a sense of belonging.

In this book, narratives offered by working-class folks who have lived in Iron County or Southeast Chicago since before company closures illuminate how the three aspects of home ebbed, flowed, and overlapped over time. The book begins where interviewees began: home existed *because* of industry. In the nineteenth and early twentieth centuries, iron and steel firms in

Southeast Chicago and Iron County laid physical and cultural foundations for community life, physical landscapes, and economic well-being that would long outlast the companies themselves. Companies constructed residents of these communities as worker-citizens—laborers whose experiences of both home and employment were entangled in a landscape organized around the interests of capital. Home, for worker-citizens and their descendants, reflected industrial companies' power to integrate economic interests and worker control into geographic landscapes.

Understanding *how* home was made in Iron County and Southeast Chicago enables the naming of *what* was lost when companies began to close in the mid-twentieth century. As the economic floor disappeared, entire communities of workers and their families tumbled from blue-collar, middle-class wealth to poverty. The disaster of deindustrialization erased the economic foundation for an entire region's blue-collar middle class, threatening the recognizability of worker-citizens' social relationships and physical surroundings. Without the centrifugal force of one industry providing both well-paid work and infrastructural maintenance for these villages, the material basis for residents' presence as both workers and citizens faded away. In short: when work disappeared, worker-citizens lost their country.

And yet, while the characteristics that made these two communities feel like home for workers and their families disorganized, they did not disappear. Unlike many analyses of deindustrialization which stop at the moment of company closure, my book tracks the stories and strategies of residents navigating decades of localized economic upheaval. In the detritus of significant structural change, a small but persistent remnant population remained. The people who became long-term residents recreated home—not as some abstract thing but as a real, material set of resources and social relationships, geographically located in a place that has been in Great Depression–level economic crisis for five decades. Interviewees explained how, in their pursuit of new employment, they moved within rather than away from familiar landscapes and community relations. As years became decades, income became less central to interviewees' reasons for staying and, thus, less vital to their definitions of home. When asked why they still lived in their deindustrialized communities, interviewees spoke of worthwhile trade-offs and attachment to what remained. Homeownership offered both sunk costs and emotional stability; disconnected geographies limited economic productivity while also engendering affection for nature; and communities smaller, older, and poorer than generations before still offered communality and familiarity today. The place-based nature of financial, social, and symbolic investments both tied them down and enabled them to thrive. Like a prism held up to changing light, the idea and practice of home remains a clear, if shifting, beacon of hope for many long-term residents.

In bringing the story up to date, we see how and why the concept of home motivates action and inspires decisions. Through their ongoing presence—their engagement with the origin stories of their places, their attunement to the trajectory of boom, bust, and loss, and even their contestation of economic redevelopment options—long-term residents shape the trajectory of their home community. Today, the people who still call these deindustrialized places home are seeking economic fixes that honor remnant components of geography and community that they personally and collectively value.

In the coming pages, I reflect on my definition of home and speak to how this framework can inform other research. I link core contributions of this book to debates about choice, mobility, and place, and conclude with new questions to moti-vate further explorations of issues of home in understudied settings.

PERMUTATIONS OF HOME: GEOGRAPHY, COMMUNITY, AND ECONOMICS

As they told stories about their own residential persistence, offered strategies for improving their lot at home, and expanded expectations of what—and who—their home should be for in the years to come, three themes kept emerging. Again and again, long-term residents used vocabularies of geography (place attachment, infrastructural limitations, and spatial remote-ness), community (social networks, community attachment, and demographic change), and economy (incomes, class status, and trade-offs). Breaking down the overlapping components of home into three observable elements draws attention to how and with what consequences structures persist, but meanings change.

Across the arc of this book, we see how home is a physical location that records priorities and purposes in its institutions and landscapes. The first two chapters of the book demonstrated how iron and steel companies not only organized geographies but set the terms of conflict, belonging, or exclusion within worker communities and rendered entire regions contingent on their continued economic success. Today, industrial homes are rife with palimpsest landscapes—properties and policies that, like historical parchments erased for reuse but still bearing visible traces of their earlier forms, continue to catch and alter contem-porary plans.[1] Century-old creations of industrial capital reiter-ate long-defunct priorities of the American Midwest: massive walls, unused brownfields, four miles of unused lakefront, houses, place names, and empty fields reproduce origin stories in both Southeast Chicago and Iron County. These physical presences—combined with the many losses of deindustrialization—have propagated a new generation of parallel policies aimed at transforming relative rurality, physical acreages, and eroded infrastructures into productive land uses. Through zoning policies, land tenure rules, and tax codes, government and legal actors in both rural and urban communities are prioritizing outdoor recreation and reindustrialization as the dominant economic development options. These land uses make sense to policymakers and many interviewees because of the persistence of industrial structures (the physical stuff of these places) and cultures (ideas about what a place is for).

Thinking about how institutions and landscapes reproduce priorities inspires questions about how these patterns might change. Within the (often literal) space formed by the ongoing processes of deindustrialization, residents strategically and often optimistically interacted with the durable remnants of their industrial places. As industrial scaffolding for economic thriving dismantled in the mid- to late-twentieth century, people leveraged what remained of geography, community, and economy to reimagine their priorities, actions, and identities. Without one thriving and central economic engine for their communities, many interviewees increased their valuation of community and geography. They leaned into attachment to place and community as rationale for remaining at home and selected practices that supported that meaning. As time passed, the people who became long-term residents created new stories about what their home should be *for*. Today, longtimers want jobs, beautiful spaces, and top-down investments in infrastructure; they want to inspire mobility in other people, drawing tourists or new residents to a viable and interesting community. Residents run for office, join nonprofits, and continue to negotiate both the material residues of and competing ideas about the meaning and purposes of their place within their region. Their choices, made within the material limitations of deindustrialization and woven into individual and collective stories of identity, affection, and purpose, scaffold their hopes and dreams for the future. Even as historical structures and stories constrained options, residents challenged, revised, and leveraged the vestiges of home.

A study of deindustrialization through the theorization of home shows how home is both fluid and constrained, impacted by everyday decisions accumulating over decades, and structured around immutable structures and powerful histories. Undergirding these tensions are fundamental building blocks of home that persist across space and time. Even as crisis weakens geographies, communities, or economies, people can and do redistribute the weight of these components of home relative to each other in order to practically problem solve and maintain a sense of belonging. Residues of the past don't foreclose the impact of individual or collective action. Rather, they set only part of the vocabulary for community change, cultural meaning, and individual identities. Considering how people shift the weight of each component of this generative triad enables researchers to ask better questions about a wider range of social life in this era of endless crisis.

CHOICE, MOVEMENT, AND THE SACREDNESS OF STABILITY

Rethinking the familiar tale of deindustrialization in terms of the social construction and renovation of home reframes how we— as sociologists, policymakers, and everyday people—approach two sociological puzzles. First, this book draws out dynamics of choice and constraint in the face of crisis. There is a long-standing debate in sociology about how much our personal choices and actions are shaped by dominant social structures, such as family dynamics, economic opportunities, or structural breakdowns, like war or disaster. In particular, some analyses of residential stability or mobility often pits agency against structure.[2] What begins as an innocent question—"Why don't you move?"—too quickly devolves into assumptions that failure to move is caused by a structurally enforced diminishment of agency.[3] Within the contexts of ruin or rubble, it often appears that the residentially stable are stuck: either they cannot make the "rational" choice to move due to structural reasons, or they have agency but are choosing poorly.

Deindustrialization certainly upended social structures and limited economic options in Iron County and Southeast Chicago. But the data in this book suggests that hard contexts also created a fluid dialogue between practical constraints and residents' choices. Without the company setting the rules, home was a site of nearly constant decision-making. As depressed house prices, upended landscapes, and local disinvestments collapsed the material and symbolic hold of industrial companies on home, residents intentionally exercised their agency in countless small decisions made. They leveraged residual natural resources and fraying social relations to find work, remain housed, create a sense of stability for family in the face of tremendous upheaval, and rationalize their resistance to outmigration. These many decisions further eroded industrial definitions of geography, community, and economy.

Certainly, the residues of deindustrialization limited possibilities in Southeast Chicago and Iron County. Chapters 5 and 6 delineate how historic policies and practices capped the menu of options available in both city and country. To overlook these structural residues would be to fall prey to the inverse temptation of overlooking structural challenges in favor of celebrating individualized "resilience." Some politicians, nonprofit organizers, and public voices too enthusiastically assume that people always have enough agency to upend the structural losses of crisis. A deeply American revision of the 'bootstrap' narrative, the resilience framework relies on inspiring cases of individuals and communities who, imbued with some inherent quality, bounce back in the face of trauma to overcome tremendous odds.[4] Resiliency discourses tend to individualize choices and valorize ideal types of successful routes through and out of crisis.[5] Individual stories are always partial stories when abstracted from macrostructural contexts. After all, no individualized capacity could keep the bottom from falling out of the American iron and steel market. The volunteerism, activism, and community work of many of my long-term residents can only chip away at issues of infrastructural disconnection, misguided tax or zoning policies, or top-down disinvestment. Real solutions to structural breakdowns of economy, policy, or environmental health require financial investment and top-down coordination. Beyond deindustrialization, the breed of trouble characterizing climate change, global pandemics, or other disasters that our places and people are facing overwhelms individual grit.[6]

Second, embracing the give and take of structure and agency attunes observers to a greater range of emotions experienced by decision-makers who have had their resources most depleted by structural collapse.[7] Residential stability was not one choice made among many equal options. Thus, as they reflected on why they stayed at home, interviewees often expressed sentiments of hesitation, awkwardness, or ambivalence. While some interviewees were committed to stay from the moment industry closed, others remained in place out of habit or coincidence, and still others felt trapped by homeownership. Tangled feelings about choice reflects a collision between challenging contexts and social roles, interests, and values. Rather, ambivalence is a sentiment of hesitation that is "built into the structure of social statuses and roles," according to the sociologist Robert Merton, and, as the environmental sociologist Michael Carolan proposed, merely a "product of our sociological and ecological embeddedness."[8]

Indeed, complex choices, and ambivalent feelings about those choices, do not foreclose agency. After all, how often do any of us have the privilege of making decisions about our lives completely free from external limitations or contradictory sentiments? We *all* live in contexts where our social roles and our sense of self-worth collide with the buildings and budgets of everyday life. Like long-term residents in postindustrial communities, we are often performing the tiring work of creating something new within the structural residues of the past. Making choices through these pros and cons—embedded in specific places and reacting to circumstances beyond our control—doesn't extinguish agency. It merely makes us human. Our geographies, communities, and economies might set the rhythm and beat for the music of everyday life, but, like jazz musicians, we improvise.

In sum, what do long-term residents in Iron County and Southeast Chicago teach us about choice and constraint? In landscapes that are polluted, geographically marginalized, and socially transformed, long-term residents have had to survive, strategize, and dream within existing limitations and opportunities. Whether interviewees became long-term residents intentionally or accidentally, their decades of small and everyday decisions— and the stories they told about who and where they were—transformed their postindustrial homes. Long-term residents are not only tradition-keepers; as every decision, large and small, further embedded them in place, they also became their homes' advocates, seeking solutions to community-wide problems beyond individual-level resilience. Residential persistence maintained certain social networks, which in turn reduced the likelihood of neighborhood or village erasure through gentrification or abandonment. In telling their story of staying, they reworked stories of the past to motivate a collective vision for the future.

A second contribution of this book is its attention to understudied variations of movement, migration, and mobility. Centering people who prioritized staying at home challenges common conceptions of mobility. From rural outmigration to urban transience,[9] from neocolonial global flows of agricultural commodities to the infiltration of markets by transnational corporations,[10] commodities, capital, and people seem to be constantly on the road. In pursuit of conceptualizing the modern "space of flows," scholars often gloss over the action of stability as immobility or inaction.[11]

Focusing on residential stability alters our perceptions of what *counts* as movement. While thousands of workers and their families did permanently move out of Iron County and Southeast Chicago in search of employment in other cities and states, I argue that there also existed a qualitatively different kind of movement. From the moment when unemployment dropped the floor out from beneath them, job seekers wishing to stay in the deindustrialized Midwest were on the move—driving across their swiftly changing landscapes between part-time gigs, beyond state lines during the week but back home over the weekends, and to and from retraining programs or night classes. In the face of capital flight and mass outmigration of neighbors and friends, these nonmigrants traveled, hustled, and rationalized their persistence within the geographic bounds of economic crisis. In turn, staying in place strengthened ties and reconstructed frayed social structures for the newly unemployed. Moving within rather than away from an inhospitable economic landscape revealed the interplay between pragmatic strategies of making ends meet and symbolic rationales of attachment motivating certain residents' commitment to "sticking it out," as chapters 3 and 4 showed.[12]

Shifting attention toward those who stay not only recenters alternative forms of mobility but illuminates how spatial relations of place shape the contexts of everyday problem-solving. The geographic location of home, as I've conceptualized in this book, matters to movement. People are staying or leaving *somewhere*. Place is a seat of meaning and a structure for daily life; it reflects institutions, absorbs constraints, and shapes people's personal and collective identities. Most of daily life occurs in locations that people can touch and describe, adore or ignore, and historicize or prognosticate. The *where* of everyday life circumscribes people's menus of options and their perceptions of agency. For instance, rural and urban places differently shape the economics and sociality of residential stability. As chapter 3 discussed, commuting looked very different in the southernmost neighborhood of metropolitan Chicago than in the remote northeastern corner of Wisconsin. Multiweek, rural megacommutes threatened Iron Countians' family and community relationships much more than did urban commutes. Inversely, however, population density and urban development policy in Chicago created contexts for environmental health issues that were unimaginable in rural iron mining villages. Thus, centering residential stability demands a closer read of how the resources of place condition the choices available to those who live there.

Finally, a focus on residential stability foregrounds the people who, in staying, challenge the stories other people tell about how places *should* be used. Residential longevity troubles developers' stories of empty places in need rehab and renovation. It blurs the line between desirable and forgotten neighborhoods, or between a countryside turned worthless and one worth staying for. By centering the people who still live in—and make choices in—hard places, this book demands the reconsideration of definitions of certain places as left behind, peripheral, or, as Wendell Berry put it, *desecrated*.[13] Those sticks-in-the-mud who refuse to leave demand that we pause, listen, and recognize their claim to home.

GEOGRAPHY, COMMUNITY, AND ECONOMY: ASKING NEW QUESTIONS OF HOMES IN CRISIS

Fundamentally, this book demonstrates that home is constantly changing. What home is and should be continually requires negotiation of geography, community, and economy. By considering themes of place, choice, and movement within my fluid typology of home, this book equips us to ask new questions about places in crisis. Who is actually in that place? Why are they there? How do different social groups understand and negotiate geography, community, and economy?

The research I conducted for this book hinted at three areas for further study of how the components of home show up in other contexts and with other populations. First, we need more information about the agency and actions of youth who still live in hard places. In my research for this book, I focused on the generation of residents who had experienced the arc from boom to bust. However, I noted that new generations of young people—youth who are very aware of the persistent, economic limitations of their home region—are nonetheless choosing to stay and live in their postindustrial, childhood homes. How do young people who have grown up in the residues of a prolonged economic or environmental crisis perceive and interpret their environments, and how do these perceptions relate to migration decisions? How do young people conceptualize a "good home"? Does their different connection to the past mean different things for the strategies they pursue? How do their explanations of their residential persistence contrast with narratives of older generations?

In Wisconsin, I talked to young people bucking the trend of youth outmigration. I found them working the front desk at the hotel, playing gigs at bars on weekends, or going four-wheeling with childhood buddies. They were aware of better economic options elsewhere—most had gone to college or trade school far from home before returning home. But they liked the cheap houses, being able to check in on grandma, and plugging into a rural culture that they had grown up with. Likewise in Chicago, some of the children and grandchildren of the steel mill generation stayed in place, commuting to jobs offering higher wages or more opportunities for advancement located far beyond the boundaries of their neighborhood. This generation pointed to their deep ties to local social networks and valued their neighborhood's collective steel mill heritage. In both cases, these younger residents seemed to prioritize the social components of home over the convenience of living closer to stronger economic options elsewhere. More systematic research into these younger, residentially stable—but potentially economic mobile—social groups is needed.

Second, I suggest further research into returnees and return visitors—former residents who have lived away from their childhood homes for decades and yet who, due to job changes or upon retirement, choose to return to their home regions. What rationales do returning residents offer to explain their decisions to come back to a community still struggling with the economic residues of deindustrialization? How do they interpret their place in a social world that has changed while they were away? Particularly in the Wisconsin case, there was a stickiness about Iron County for a subgroup of interviewees. Half of my rural Wisconsin interviewees specifically discussed the seasonal or permanent return of older people who had out-migrated in the 1960s, 1970s, and 1980s. At the county fair and several summer parades, I talked with a dozen people who had established careers far from Iron County but who make an annual summer pilgrimage back home for multiple weeks or months. These returnees spoke freely of their perceptions of the costs and benefits of moving for better jobs or exciting educational opportunities; of their ties to other families in other locations; and of the people and landscapes that drew them back, year after year, to Iron County.

One interaction particularly captures the hold of home on departees. Waving his copy of the latest issue of the local paper, the *Daily Globe*, with his Houston home address stamped on it, Bill described the pull he felt to permanently move home to Iron County once he retired from his job in the Texas oil fields. "If you know anything about mallard ducks, where the young ones are fledged, where they learn to fly, they come back to the same place." He rubbed his gray-streaked bearded chin, carefully forming the metaphor. "This is where we learned to fly, so to speak. And we wanted to come back to visit. Anyway, that's the analogy I would use. Just home, this is home." It remains to be seen how an influx of retirees will change or challenge local culture. Some research suggests that these returned residents bring higher levels of purchasing power, education, and class expectations.[14] Will their intentional return reinvigorate community life or introduce new demand for a diversified economy? Or will there be little economic or cultural difference because of retirement status and shared origin stories?

Finally, the geography, community, and economy framework for theorizing home calls for new questions about the in-migration of residents previously unfamiliar with their new locations. How do new arrivals differently interpret and value established home cultures and structures? How permeable are definitions of home that are situated in the palimpsests of the past? Who belongs, and what is place for? How do long-term residents negotiate meanings of community and place in light of the clashing expectations of in-migrants? Are there anxieties about the "other"?

These questions particularly emerged during my research with long-term residents in Chicago. Since 2000, a new generation of Latin American migrants have increased Southeast Chicago's population and decreased the average age to thirty-five.[15] While I did not get to talk to this newer generation of migrants, a few long-term residents referred to clashes between the social and economic priorities of these "new Mexicans," as Jesús and Marcos dubbed them, and those of the extant steel mill culture. Scholarly research and popular media alike signal that the arrival of newcomers often instigates economic anxieties and cultural clashes.[16] Particularly in writing about the American Rust Belt, the relationship between home and newcomers often seems to be defined in terms of exclusion and a xenophobic fear of "the other."[17] This book calls for more fine-grained questions. For instance, because home is geographically located, so are conflicts between new arrivals and longtime residents. Living in Southeast Chicago means dealing with the vestiges of the steel industry on a daily basis—from fenced-off brownfields that abut neighborhoods to railroad tracks that crisscross residential streets to policies that encourage the region to remain the city's industrial sacrifice zone. Even as new migrants bring their own conceptions and expectations of work, community, and landscape to the Southeast Side, how do they reckon with the physicality of their new home?

In rural communities, COVID-19 spurred an explosion of migration that raised similar questions about how migrants might experience home differently than long-timers. In Wisconsin, a handful of residents eagerly hoped that Iron County would become a "zoom town," as remote work enabled people to move to affordable, rural communities with high densities of natural resource amenities.[18] Gary, who grew up in the area, mused, "We can't be miners anymore. . . . The tourist industry is only going to take it so far. . . . What could happen here? What kind of industry can flourish here? Well, you know, in the dot com age, why wouldn't you want to live in a place like this and work from home? You know?" Pete, the county's economic development coordinator, has been trying to make this dream come true. He had been working for years to grow the rural county's broadband internet access. He painted a picture for me of white-collar workers, with laptops and headphones, filling the local cafés or tucking into cozy corners of their Northwoods cabins for year-round, remote work that would buoy local economies and enliven an aging social world. Iron County is not becoming a "zoom town" quite yet. But as federal policies enable the further expansion of broadband internet, residents may yet need to weigh the pros and cons of this new form of economic and demographic revitalization. After all, in-migrants without place-based jobs and with more economic resources can bring their own challenges to an established rural community. New arrivals can drive up housing prices and displace locals. Cultural conflicts can emerge between long-term residents and newcomers who are more interested in outdoor recreation and less interested in investing in the fullness of local community life.[19] More research is needed to understand the contours of these place-based economic and cultural clashes.

These questions are just a start; the typology of home developed in this book can and should travel to new cases. By taking seriously the puzzle of why and with what consequences people stay in regions on the edge of extinction we can understand the interplay of the material requirements for people to survive and the implications of the ideas they, and others, assign to these places.

CONCLUSION

Deindustrialization is an entry point into a broader conversation about crisis, home, and finding our way in a changing world. Probing the stories and silences of home among blue-collar laborers in two formerly connected industrial communities illuminates the relationships between the individual and social structure, stability and mobility, and work and home. Deindustrialization offers stark context for residential persistence in the face of crisis. Many of us have not experienced such an extreme case of the construction and reconstruction of home as did those in Iron County and Southeast Chicago—the intentional, top-down construction of home by extractive and manufacturing companies, its subsequent, large-scale dismantling, and its effortful renegotiation by residents. Nonetheless, this is also our story. Climate change, pandemics, and other forms of displacement are already forcing more and more of us to reconfigure home, to deal with the residues of the past, to reframe our own agency within constraints of the present, and to make vital decisions about moving or staying in geographies wracked by crisis. In the decades to come, many of us will need to grapple with fundamental transformations of the places we call home—places that we rely on for economic well-being as well as for social and personal sense of meaning.

APPENDIX A

NOTES ON METHODS

PLACING MYSELF IN IN THIS RESEARCH

This research emerges from my own experience in the American Rust Belt. I grew up in a low-income village in the foothills of the Appalachians, crisscrossed with creeks that are tinged orange from iron oxide seeping from long abandoned mines. In Herminie, Pennsylvania, population 856, my neighbors are the stuff of Steinbeck: elderly, poor, and full of stubborn wildness. Mrs. Cooper and Mr. Miller would often remind me that their people *made* this western Pennsylvania town; their grandfathers came here in the late nineteenth century, when a wide seam of bituminous coal was discovered ribboning through the foothills of the Appalachians. In 1893, the Berwind-White Coal Mining Company opened Ocean No. 1 Mine and built fifty company houses on the steep slopes to house 271 miners.[1] The life of this little town lasted exactly forty-five years. In 1938, the mine closed due to "excessive water" and many workers followed the company to nearby coal seams.[2] But some people remained. They found jobs in the steel mills of Pittsburgh thirty miles away or created their own mom-and-pop grocery stores, diners, laundromats, or notaries. But Herminie didn't have much economic strength.

When Pittsburgh's steel industry collapsed in the 1980s and 1990s, the ensuing regional economic depression crushed wages, propelled out-migration, and shuttered stores. This was my childhood. I lived the disinvestment in public schools and libraries, lack of employment opportunities, weed-covered railroad rights-of-way, bare grocery shelves, and consistent invisibility in postindustrial America. In the grocery store and across kitchen tables, I had long conversations with friends and family about whether to stay or leave for opportunities elsewhere. But there were also whispers that there we were part of something bigger in the most sinister sense—that the tangled fates of city and country extended far beyond this small corner of western Pennsylvania. Across America, the working class was paying the price for the cataclysmic shift in macroeconomic policies and practices.

While Southeast Chicago and Iron County might not be *my* place, both communities do feel a little like home. When, in the context of inviting interviewees to participate in my research, I explained my roots to people living in both rural and urban locations, their faces softened. "You get it," one man said in Chicago. Across states bordering the Great Lakes and its rivers, the systemic contraction of manufacturing and mining industries collapsed the economic core of working-class villages and cities. Throughout this project, I found myself walking the fine line between adopting a scholar's detached gaze and sharing my familiarity with the emotions, losses, and fundamental questions that deindustrialization raised about the value of place to people and to the economy. On one hand, this book certainly benefited from what bell hooks called dual membership. I was positioned in the study as an "indigenous ethnographer . . . one who enters culture where they resemble the people they are studying and writing about."[3] My lived experience with both rural and urban deindustrialization sharpened my intuition about what mattered to interviewees. Good research emerges not in spite of the intimacy of my position but rather, as the sociologist Bryant Keith Alexander reflects, "because I am so embedded in the storied histories of these sacred places." Like Alexander, my position allows me to "represent without reducing culture, to simultaneously capture and release, to celebrate but not exoticize, to signal and signify without "reading" culture."[4]

And yet, any story of people who stay in place is inherently *not* my story. While this book derives from my personal experience of childhood in a postindustrial region, I left my hometown for college, benefiting from the wealth of my white, middle-class parents. After nearly two decades away for travel, school, and work, I am a stranger to my village and a tourist in Pittsburgh. My childhood experiences were sometimes incongruous to the challenges faced by long-term residents, and my lack of true "insider" status limited my access to some people who were skeptical of my intentions.

As a whole, however, I found the tension between familiarity and detachment honed my research skills and sharpened my analytical intuition. To compare and analyze Southeast Chicago and Iron County, Wisconsin, I bring to bear the academic training I received while I lived far from home in Madison, Wisconsin, in Chicago, and even now, in Philadelphia. As a discipline, sociology and its allied social sciences offer a powerful set of tools that enable researchers to not only identify and diagnose persistent problems but also explore the viability of possible solutions. With this training and life history, I entered interviewees' homes, perused tenderly maintained local archives, handled relics of long-defunct steel mills and iron mines, and listened to many stories. It is at this blurred line between observer and participant that I begin and end this book.

METHODS FOR DATA COLLECTION AND ANALYSIS

In researching and writing this book, I have attempted to produce new insights into the lives of working-class people and the postindustrial places they call home. This book draws from three categories of data gathered in both Iron County and Southeast Chicago: close reads of thousands of archival documents tracing the histories of both locations, two years of episodic ethnographic observation of everyday life, and 120 in-depth conversations with long-term residents and community leaders. I also relied on descriptive demographic, economic, and historical data extracted from governmental records and previously published books and reports to map my original data onto the bigger story of economic change. In this methods appendix, I explain my methodological sources and process and discuss the choices I made through data collection and analysis.

Historical documents were my first stop in learning how home was originally constructed in these two communities. Since very few local records were digitized, I spent portions of my visits capturing (via photograph) and organizing several thousand historical documents from five local and regional archives, as well as personal collections of artifacts kept in houses, closets, or small museums run by volunteers. For my rural case, I gathered archival materials from the Iron County Historical Society, Ashland Historical Society, Wisconsin Historical Society, and the Ironwood, Michigan Historical Society. For the Chicago case, I researched in the archives of the Chicago History Museum and the Southeast Chicago Historical Museum. From these archives, I analyzed company employment records, maps of railroad routes, blueprints of mine shafts and housing plans, and articles from local and state newspapers, as well as amateur photography from the early twentieth century, autobiographical essays, and handwritten letters commemorating the anniversaries of the closure of mines or mills. Additionally, I drew from a dozen publicly available oral histories of southeast Chicago millworkers and northern Wisconsin miners conducted between 1990 and 2001 by each location's respective historical societies.

I supplemented this historical data with descriptive statistics. I tracked net out-migration through historical data from the U.S. Census and the American Community Survey. These sources, combined with more localized data from Wisconsin's Applied Population Lab and Chicago's CityData, informed my analysis of neighborhood-scale economic outcomes, homeownership patterns, poverty and unemployment rates, and demographic changes.

My broader ethnographic approach built from this historical data. I conducted multiple short-term field visits over four years—a "patchwork" of one to fourteen days of intensive field visits.[5] When contrasted with traditional, multiyear, sited ethnographies common in sociology and anthropology, a patchwork approach may appear quite fragmentary. However, it provides ample opportunity for rigorous, contextual knowledge-building. Short visits allowed me to conduct a comparative project within a reasonable amount of time. In three multiweek field visits, occurring between August 2015 and July 2016, I conducted interview, historical, and ethnographic research on-site in northern Wisconsin, and from December 2015 until April 2017, I lived in Chicago and conducted weekly trips to the Southeast Side. I walked and drove across landscapes with community members, spent hours in historical societies, and drank coffees and nibbled cookies with residents. In Southeast Chicago, I joined months of meetings for retired steelworkers in Southeast Chicago and, in Iron County, I attended class reunions, parades, and county fairs.

While historical data and ethnography were vital to this project, its lifeblood was open-ended interviews. In this section, I discuss my interview protocol, sampling approach, and how I attempted to mitigate some limitations to interview data. I employed a life-history interview model, offering a minimally structured set of questions that invited speakers to offer rich and detailed stories about their experiences with deindustrialization, rationales for continued residence in economically depressed regions, current problems, and possibilities for the future. The interviews followed four categories of questions: 1) personal history, 2) community history, 3) industry history, and 4) today and the future. (I include the full interview question list at the end of this appendix.) I printed out these questions on one page and placed it visibly in front of both me and my interviewees. Counterintuitively, this visible prop enabled me to encourage my interlocutors to diverge from the prepared interview questions. Interviewees often seemed relieved to understand the scope of my curiosity about their lives and felt greater authority to direct our interview in their preferred direction. Some chose to adhere to the questions provided, treating them like a checklist to guide what stories they wished to tell. Others immediately diverged from the specific questions and offered me narratives that reorganized the themes I presented to better transform the episode of deindustrialization disruption into organized contrasts between "before" and "after."[6]

While my interviews often felt more like open-ended conversations than systematic information-gleaning sessions, I was intentional about the format of follow-up or probing questions. I asked *how* questions more often than I asked *why* questions. I found that *why* questions tended to incite guarded reactions, as evidenced by Simonetta and Christopher's defensive—if revealing—answer to my question of why they stayed (see chapter 4). *How* questions called forth smaller and stepwise explanations of strategies and practices. In recalling an unfolding series of decisions within situational constraints, interviewees did not feel pressured to commit to a single motivation or prior intention. As trust developed across the course of the interview, I posed more *why* questions in ways that cued that a variety of answers would be appropriate. For instance, in many of my interviews, I explained that in talking with many people who have continued to live in or departed from Rust Belt communities, I heard a lot of different reasons for people coming back or never leaving. Highlighting the community's heterogeneity seemed to reduce "ego threats," or fear of judgment by the interviewer, and encouraged respondents to explore a wider variety of rationales and motivations.[7]

These interviews lasted between forty-five minutes and two hours. I digitally recorded interviews with the permission of interviewees, placing my recorder within eyeshot but not as a central focus. If I noticed that a speaker was visibly anxious about being recorded, glancing repeatedly at the red light of the tape recorder, I checked if they were still okay being recorded. If so, I would slide the recorder under a napkin or beneath a stack of papers and continue our conversation. In Wisconsin, I took the visibility of audio recording to another extreme: I rented large microphones and a high-quality recorder to conduct a grant-funded oral history radio project, which was broadcast on the local AM station in Hurley. The project provided interviews that were notably shorter than my typical interviews, averaging ten minutes, instead of sixty to ninety minutes. The final product is available on my website, www.amandamcmillanlequieu.com.

Sampling

When selecting interviewees, I purposively sought firsthand accounts of long-term residents—people who had experienced some portion of industrial boom and bust and lived in or near their home community for at least two decades (see table A.1).[8] Approximately 70 percent of people with whom I spoke fell into this category. Half of my interviewees had been living in the region for more than forty years. The remainder were either younger people who had departed and returned to their hometowns or leaders of nonprofits or government agencies who were invested in the local region but didn't necessarily have multigenerational roots in Southeast Chicago or Iron County. I focused my interviews on long-term residents because, when we look at the long view of deindustrialization—the fifty-some years of everyday life that continued on following company closures—long-term residents disproportionally shape the culture and narrative of the region. How they understand their own pasts directly informs their engagement with the future of their place. These are the locals who have outlasted the life spans of the industrial companies that founded their home regions in the first place. In describing their experience of residential persistence, long-term residents volunteered tales not of *one* great out-migration but a multitude of departures, returns, long commutes, and reunions. Today, they sit on boards and run for local government; they protest, vote, volunteer, and persevere.

How did I find my interviewees? In both cases, several local people quickly bought into this project and became key to seeding my access to wider networks of interviewees. In Iron County, three enthusiastic volunteers affiliated with the Iron County Historical Museum arranged my first dozen interviews with their friends and family. I continued to benefit from the museum's rooms and resources as I conducted several dozen more interviews through snowball sampling—relational connections where previous interviewees encouraged their friends or families to speak with me. In Southeast Chicago, gaining access to interviewees was a more circuitous and time-intensive process. The Southeast Chicago Historical Museum offered a warm site for many of my initial interviews. Monthly Steelworkers Organization of Active Retirees meetings at Local 1093 connected me with a very different group of long-term residents. Attending community events also brought me into meaningful conversations.

I directly requested interviews with community leaders whose organizations or formal positions emerged as central to community function. Often, other interviewees recommended I speak with specific people who they felt might offer representative or contradictory perspectives. Close readings of local newspapers, Facebook pages, or historical documents also pointed me to members of a particular group or political position which needed to be represented in my project.

While 90 percent of my interviews were conducted from 2015 to 2017, during the COVID-19 pandemic in 2020 and 2021, I conducted follow-up research. I benefited from new methods of digital ethnography, conducting follow-up interviews with community leaders in both cases to fact-check contemporary issues, attending six public meetings in Chicago via Zoom, and analyzing dozens of emails and social media posts concerning contemporary conflicts over land use and development in both cases. In 2022, I also returned in person to Southeast Chicago to see a new suite of park development projects that had been built since my last visit.

There are two limitations of my sampling approach. First, a focus on long-term residents meant I did not explore the experiences of in-migrants or visitors. As I discuss in the book's conclusion, this gap offers exciting avenues for future research. For the purposes of this project, however, I found that to answer my questions about homes in crisis, I needed to focus on residents with the longest tenancies (see Table A.1). Long-term residents who had watched boom and bust were the best suited to shed light on the shifting meanings and material contexts of home in transition. Second, prioritizing long-term residents meant that approximately half of my interviewees were between the ages of sixty and eighty, and one-quarter were between the ages of forty-six and sixty. The remaining one-quarter were split between interviewees younger than forty-five and older than eighty (see Tables A.2 and A.3). This skewed age grouping

TABLE A.1

Combined cases: Interviewee demographics	N = 120
Women	45%
Long-term residents	65%
Returnees/former residents	30%
Race: White	85%
Race: Hispanic	10%
Race: African American	5%

TABLE A.2

Chicago: Interviewee demographics	N = 58	Population = 50,000
Women	45%	52%
Long-term residents	65%	Likely 30–50% of the ward
Returnees/former residents	30%	—
Mean age	43	31
Race: Hispanic	40%	58%
Race: African American	10%	15%
Race: White	50%	27%

TABLE A.3

Wisconsin: Interviewee demographics	N = 62	Population = 6,000
Women	52%	54%
Long-term residents	85%	Likely 30–50% of county
Returnees/former residents	35%	—
Mean age	60	55
Race: Hispanic	—	—
Race: African American	—	—
Race: White	100%	99.8%

reflects both the higher average age of people who experienced industry and the cohort bias inevitable within snowball sampling. To better reflect the voices of other generations, I sought out younger cohorts through theoretical sampling and intentionally incorporated ethnographic observation across the generational divides.

Data Collection and Management Decisions

With the help of several undergraduate research assistants, I transcribed interviews, processed archival documents (captured by a photograph and converted to optical character recognition PDFs), and compiled quantitative data for analysis. With the exception of three interviews where recording was not possible and I took handwritten notes, quotations are verbatim based on recorded and transcribed audio. Very rarely, quotes are edited for clarity. I removed filler words as long as it did not change the meaning of the sentence or phrase.

In notes and final write-ups, I use real names of places, businesses, and organizations. To protect the identities of participants, I initially designed this research to change all interviewees' names to pseudonyms. Pseudonyms grant speakers a valence of privacy, useful for life narratives like these, where people are sharing about family, friends, and significant (and sometimes very personal) life events. I retained descriptors of race, age, gender, and residential longevity. In many conversations, my interlocutors looked visibly relieved when I explained that I would use a different name linked with their direct quotes and life stories. At times, people wanted merely to keep personal stories of loss and misadventure private; others, particularly those who were in political leadership or connected to community organizations, wanted to avoid escalating local conflicts by saying the wrong thing at the wrong time. Changing names consistently alleviated these concerns for this subgroup of participants.

Other interviewees vocally objected to the practice of obscuring their identities. More than one interviewee quipped, "I've got nothing to hide!" In a few cases, I did decide to use real names. For instance, when local leaders were quoted by name in newspapers, I did not change names, as to do so would threaten the accuracy of the documents themselves. If this project was solely historical, I could have treated these instances with the ethical framework of a historian considering archival documents. But my research blurred the lines of past and present; in several instances, I conducted multiple interviews with those same quoted political leaders. This raised a conundrum with pseudonym usage. How could I consistently honor my commitment to change interviewees' names—particularly those, like political leaders, who were sensitive about speaking to an outside researcher? If I changed names but kept identifying, personal details consistent (i.e., the political leader of XX location/group), a savvy reader could easily parse who was who. I solved this challenging problem in two ways. In a few cases, in coordination with my university's Institutional Review Board policies, I went back to these local leaders and had them sign a waiver to use their real name; otherwise, I used the pseudonymous names but extracted their personal stories from their political presence by referring to their positions without names (for example, "as the leader of the Historical Society said . . .").

It is standard practice to link verifiable identities with oral histories, and I used two compilations of oral histories as part of the data for this book. First, I quote from a set of a dozen original stories that I recorded in Iron County in 2016 as part of a side project for a podcast that I edited and played on the local radio station. Working with my university's Institutional Review Board and benefiting from the wisdom of the oral history librarian at the University of Wisconsin, I offered participants in this side project written releases to sign that would allow me to use their real names for both my book project and the podcast. Second, in Chicago, I relied on a rich set of oral histories conducted in the early 2000s by a group of high school students, transcribed and paired with signed releases for name use, and stored at the Southeast Chicago Historical Museum. Thank you to all participants and project organizers for recording stories for future generations.

Data Analysis

Using MAXQDA (qualitative data analysis software), I iteratively read the data I collected—memos from ethnographic fieldwork, interview transcripts, historical documents, and quantitative data—using an inductive open-coding approach. This means that I looked for and recorded similarities and differences across the data and labeled shared themes as they emerged over multiple reviews. My primary focus was on how interviewees explain, justify, and rationalize their past behaviors and present expectations in light of the challenges of living in a hard place. When considering the past, people do not simply recite facts or chronicle the order of events. They discuss events "in a setting or scene and in the unfolding of a plot with characters who act and react in particular ways," as the social scientists Scott Peters and Nancy Franz articulated.[9] Storytellers choose a particular beginning and ending to their story, emphasize certain themes, and leap over space and time to make legible complex processes, actors, and causal linkages. A narrative approach to interpretation is powerful because this meaning-making process is as externalized, collective, and entangled as the landscapes central to this study.

A common critique of narrative analysis is concerned with speakers' interpretations of the past: Are people retroactively expressing motives to explain a past action? This retrospective interpretation points to "the fact that a person's views and interpretations change over time; past behavior is reinterpreted in light of new information and experiences."[10] The stories told in this book, anchored as they are in a prolonged disaster, are certainly laced with reinterpretation—with judgments of causality, condemnation, or justification. What I analyze is *how* they tell the story of crisis, change, and coping. In moments of crisis, narratives become all the more vital to social life. In my study, the breakdown of cultural structures required reinterpretation of common meanings of place, middle class, or natural resources.[11] "Stories," Charles Tilly sums up, "provide simplified cause-effect accounts of puzzling, unexpected, dramatic, problematic, or exemplary events"[12] It is through story that people make sense of their experiences of crisis and the very real consequences of deindustrialization that they continue to live with every day.

A focus on story does not foreclose the importance of the historical record. I triangulated interviewee statements about historical events with secondary sources (other published books, newspapers, and articles) as well as community history found in museums and newspaper archives, demographic histories pulled from census and community survey data, and other interviewee recollections of dates, places, and people. I included historical statements from interviewees only when their story or event was similarly reported in at least two other historical documents. I also hired two local people to fact-check the historical information in this book against archival resources and their personal knowledge. Rod Sellers in Chicago and Julie Morello in Iron County have each dedicated themselves to a lifelong study of their community's histories and archives.

INTERVIEW PROTOCOL DOCUMENT

Below is the document that I printed for interviewees to review before and during the interview. This document was also provided to my university's Institutional Review Board.

This interview is very open ended. I am interested in exploring the history and future of your community, particularly in light of the closure of the mine/factory some years ago. I would like to understand if and how the mine/factory was important to community life here, and to you personally, and how you think the closure of the mine/factory changed life here. You can choose at any time to stop the interview or to skip any questions.

Before we continue, let me get a better sense of your personal history in Wisconsin/Chicago:

PERSONAL HISTORY
- When did your family move here?
- Why are you still living here?
- Do you have other family or close friends in the area?
- Where do/did you work?

Now let's shift to the broader community:

COMMUNITY HISTORY
- Where are the boundaries of this community? Where does ____ end and (a neighboring community) begin?
- Before the mine/factory closed, were there events that were important to community life? How about now?
- When the mine/factory closed, who left, who stayed, and why?
- Are the people who live/visit here now different than people who were your neighbors/visitors when the mine/factory was open?

INDUSTRY HISTORY
- Did you know that the mine/factory would close?
- How did you feel when you found out that it was closing?
- Do you think anything could've been done to keep the industry open?
- Was there resistance to the mine/factory closing and/or attempts to open it back up?
- What did people who worked in the mine/factory do after the industry closed?
- How did the closing impact the community?
- How did the closing impact you and your family?

TODAY AND THE FUTURE
- What do you think the future holds for this place?
  - If you could dream up the best future for this community, what do you think it'd look like?
- Did the industry affect the environment?

Do you have any other stories you'd like to share? Anything that seems important for me to know that I haven't asked?

Thank you so much for your time!

APPENDIX B

TEACH THIS BOOK

n addition to this book contributing to the literature on economic change, place, environment, and identity, this book can be used as a teaching tool for upper-level undergraduates and graduate students in the social sciences. Instructors could use this book to challenge students to think historically about contemporary social issues such as economic decline, capital and residential mobility, environmental transformation, and community development. In this section, I propose five teaching frameworks with suggested readings and provide a list of discussion questions.

FIVE APPROACHES FOR INSTRUCTIONAL ENGAGEMENT

Economic History: Build this book into courses committed to covering the long timelines and broad spatial relations of economic history. This book engages substantively with existing research on the boom, bust, and rusting of America's industrial corridors. While much of this scholarship is limited to temporally immediate impacts of industrial closures in either rural or urban settings, this book considers a multigenerational, temporal range and an urban-rural spatial scope when considering canonical questions of out-migration, unemployment, and environmental crises following plant or mine closures. Such comparisons enable a more precise analysis of how the passage of time and relative geographical remoteness affects place attachment, socioeconomic challenges, and possible futures in postindustrial landscapes. I recommend that students read the introduction and chapters 1 and 2 with a comparative sensibility. Have students pay particular attention to how rural and urban contexts offer differing sets of resources for processes of economic development and dismantling. Ask students to debate questions of path dependence and identify how macroeconomic structures might limit options for on-the-ground residents. Complementary readings include High's *Industrial Sunset* (2003), Cowie and Heathcott's *Beyond the Ruins* (2003), and Mah's *Industrial Ruination, Community, and Place* (2012), as well as case-specific studies from Bensman and Lynch (1989), Dudley (1994), or Hackworth (2019).

Place and space: Integrate this book—particularly the introduction and chapters 1 and 4—into lectures on theories and experiences of place. I converse with conceptions of space and place offered by classical geographers such as Tuan (1971 and 1990) and Relph (1976), as well as more contemporary work that contemplates the changing nature of place in the face of globalization, such as Massey (1994). My discussions of the meanings of place for long-term residents draw on both rural sociological research on community affection for rural landscapes and livelihoods (e.g., Harrison 2012; Wuthnow 2015) and place attachment scholarship concerned with the social-psychological forms of attachment between individuals and their landscapes (e.g. Low and Altman 1992, Stedman 2003). My analysis of the landscape-scale change of the late nineteenth and early twentieth century, as well as the return to nature on postindustrial landscapes today, builds on work on the changing social construction of nature done by environmental historians such as Cronon (1991) and environmental sociologists such as Pellow and Park (2011).

Rust Belt experiences and the working-class: Pair this book with other writing on emotions and the American Rust Belt, particularly from and about the role of the working class in contemporary politics. Have students compare and contrast books that address perception and affect of working-class voters with chapters 2, 5, and 6. See work by Wuthnow (*The Left Behind*, 2018), Hochschild (*Strangers in Their Own Land*, 2016), or Cramer (*The Politics of Resentment*, 2016). Notably, even though my research took place before and after Trump's election, when populist sentiment seemed to be driving a return to far-right political opinions particularly in rural and white regions, these themes did not emerge in my research process. In Chapters 5 and 6, my interviewees voiced discontent with the government. But it was local governmental failings rather than national level policy-making to which my interviewees vociferously objected. Likely they were simply too familiar with the realities of both macroeconomic trade policies and the logistical challenges of their long-deindustrialized communities to put much stock into presidential campaign rhetoric about bringing factories back home.

Trauma, disasters, and risks: Drawing from scholarship on disasters and hazards, offer students alternative cases of crisis and ask them to trace how and why historical processes of the social construction of home—and specifically geography, community, and economy—shape outcomes. Students can use my typology of home to consider theories of risk, material entanglement, and cultures of loss offered by environmental sociologists researching their own case studies of residential stability in the face of acute environmental crisis. Students should read Chapters 1 and 2 in tandem with Erikson's classic *Everything in Its Path* (1976), Jerolmack's *Up to Heaven and Down to Hell* (2021), Elliot's research on climate change and loss in *Underwater* (2021), Kimbro's book *In Too Deep* (2021), or Gray's *In the Shadow of the Seawall* (2023).

Globalization and mobility of people and capital: Students can bring this book into conversation with scholarship on globalization and its attendant flows of capital and people. Chapters 2, 3, and 4, respond to scholars of migration, both classical (e.g., Blau and Duncan 1967) and contemporary (Rapport and Dawson 1998), by highlighting how and why people may *not* out-migrate after a localized, economic collapse. Students could read chapters 1 and 2 to engage with commodity chain literatures, particularly those concerned with the flows of natural resources across time and space (e.g., Bunker and Ciccantell 2005), those interested in what happens when a commodity chain disarticulates (e.g., Werner and Bair 2011), and those committed to tracing the transnational consequences of the mobility of capital (e.g., Broughton 2015). Finally, chapters 5 and 6 might be placed alongside environmental historians' and sociologists' insights into the environmental health consequences of such immobility, like Brown's *Toxic Exposures: Contested Illnesses and the Environmental Health Movement* (2007), Taylor's *Toxic Communities: Environmental Racism, Industrial Pollution, and Residential Mobility* (2014), or Pellow's *Garbage Wars: The Struggle for Environmental Justice in Chicago* (2004).

CHAPTER-BY-CHAPTER DISCUSSION QUESTIONS

INTRODUCTION

1. How do the people introduced in the two vignettes discuss the problems and potential of their deindustrialized homes?

2. What assumptions do you have about how people could and should respond to large-scale disasters or crises like deindustrialization?

3. What three concepts will be used to build the definition of home in this book? How do you see those three concepts in your personal experience of home, place, and crisis?

4. What are the core methods used to gather data for this book?

5. What is gained from looking at two cases rather than just one?

CHAPTER 1

1. What was the role of metals companies in establishing housing in Iron County and Southeast Chicago? How did these nineteenth-century firms exert control over geography, community, and economy?

2. What are some possible impacts of paternalistic company oversight in formerly industrial towns/neighborhoods after the closure of these companies?

3. What is a "worker-citizen"? How did companies create this category? And why is it important to understand interviewees' interpretations of capital, place, and home?

4. Describe how companies used paternalism to manage employees in both Iron County and Southeast Chicago. Although company paternalism was most explicitly popular at the turn of the twentieth century, paternalism still exists today as a managerial strategy. Think of some examples of companies

providing "nonincome benefits" today. Discuss the wins and losses of this approach for employees.

5. How did companies organize community relations in both cases? What stories did the iron and steel industry tell about the purposes of social life? What was the role of unionization? How did race and gender show up in neighborhood-building?

6. How did interviewees' experience of "boom" mirror popular conceptions of the midcentury American middle class? Did company dominance over the social construction of home intensify or alter worker-citizens' expectations for the economic boom?

CHAPTER 2

1. What macroeconomic forces drove the steel industry's collapse? How did these abstract economic changes materialize for residents?

2. How did interviewees interpret these changes? Who did they blame for their changed circumstances? What emotions did they express in interviews?

3. Describe how company closures shifted locals' definitions of home. Specifically, discuss how economic changes altered worker-citizens' experiences of their local geography, community function, and economic well-being.

4. How were the shutdowns of the mines in Iron County and the steel mills in Southeast Chicago communicated and executed differently? Why did these differences impact residents' ability to react to these closures?

5. How did unions in the two cases react differently to company closures?

6. What options did the newly unemployed have to solve their most basic economic problems?

CHAPTER 3

1. What types of jobs did residents take on after industry closures removed many jobs in their areas? What external structures constrained residents' options for finding work?

2. Discuss how job seekers leveraged what geographic and community resources were left behind following company closure in pursuit of economic problem-solving.

3. Define informal labor. This form of work is not only a strategy for the newly deindustrialized. Today, people manage economic risk through variations of informal labor. Provide some examples of informal labor today, and discuss the wins and losses of this strategy for making ends meet.

4. What is megacommuting? Why would unemployed miners choose this strategy to earn an income?

5. What remaining materials and structures did residents rely on for work following mine or mill closures? How do these jobs reflect the continuation of values that were established prior to deindustrialization?

6. What trade-offs did residents have to make when searching for jobs back home?

7. After mines and mills closed, women entered the workforce en masse. Discuss why, and identify some of their employment and educational paths introduced in this chapter.

CHAPTER 4

1. What reasons did residents give for staying in their deindustrialized towns? Describe where each of these reasons would fall on a gradation between material and symbolic rationales.

2. Discuss how homeownership offers benefits and costs? If you were in the same position as the homeowning interviewees in this chapter, what decision would you have made about selling and moving or staying at home?

3. How do rationales interviewees offer for residential stability connect to the histories of their formerly industrial towns and neighborhoods?

4. Through the stories interviewees tell, how do you see residents' definition of home—specifically, geography, community, or economy—shifting? What are some examples of how the long-term residents revised the weight or rewrote the meaning of their home region?

5. How do landscapes and nature matter for interviewees in Southeast Chicago vs. Iron County? How do community relationships keep people at home?

CHAPTER 5

1. When asked about the potential future for their home, what are the core concerns for Iron County residents? How do issues of geography, community, and economy emerge in residents' diagnoses of shared problems?

2. How did the history of mining shape residents' reactions to the GTac mine proposal?

3. What is the concept of a "good company" to Iron County residents? And how did this concept frame discussions about a new generation of mining?

4. Where was there conflict between interviewees concerning various proposed futures for their community?

5. Rurality is a gradient. Using information from this chapter, describe how rural Iron County is. How would you identify the level of rurality in other places?

6. What are the advantages and disadvantages of tourism in Iron County? Why do mining and tourism not conflict in residents' interpretations of future economic prospects?

7. What would be an ideal future for Iron County according to most interviewees? And why? What do you think would be a good future for the region? Why?

CHAPTER 6

1. When asked about the potential futures for their home, what are the core concerns for Southeast Chicagoans? How do issues of geography, community, and economy emerge in residents' diagnoses of shared problems?
2. How does Southeast Chicago's industrial history impact zoning in the area? How do top-down definitions of what the Southeast Side is *for* structure potential futures for this region?
3. What factors must Southeast Side residents weigh when considering industrial growth in their area? How have attitudes toward industry changed since the steel mills closed?
4. What are some examples of how residents are contesting the status quo of second-generation industry?
5. Why is park development a common alternative land use in the region? Why do some residents express ambivalence to park development? In your opinion, are parks a success? Why or why not?
6. Compare and contrast chapters 5 and 6. What similarities do you see between problem diagnosis, economic development options, and the reconstruction of home in each location? How do characteristics of place—extreme remoteness in rural Wisconsin or a peripheral location within a very large city— shape these two cases in different ways?

CONCLUSION

1. How does place-making change for residents of a deindustrializing space?
2. How do the economic hopes for residents reflect expectations established during industry booms?
3. How does this book recontextualize the options and choices of the residents from formerly industrial towns?

4. After reading this book, do you consider residents' ties to place material, emotional, or both? Why, and in what ways?

5. How do these concepts inform your own understanding of "home" and how we create that feeling in geographic locations?

NOTES

INTRODUCTION

1. As is typical in much social science writing, interviewees were given pseudonyms. Pseudonyms grant speakers a valence of privacy, useful for life narratives such as these, where people are sharing about family, friends, and significant (and sometimes very personal) life events. Through the book, I retain descriptors of race, age, gender, and residential longevity. Their quotations have not been altered: when I use double quotation marks, I am directly quoting from interviews that I recorded, with the speaker's oral or written permission. When I use single quotation marks, I am quoting my closest approximation from ethnographic observation—often taking place in an on-the-move interview (such as in a car or on a walk) or through an on-the-ground conversation with a larger group of people. In a few instances where an interviewee's role is very public and core to how the reader might interpret what the speaker is saying, I asked interviewees for permission to use their real names.

2. Matthew Wilson, Anish Tailor, and Alex Linares, "2017 Chicago Community Area Economic Hardship Index," Great Cities Institute, December 13, 2019, https://greatcities.uic.edu/2019/12/13/fact-sheet-chicago-community-area-economic-hardship-index-2017/.

3. I base this claim on several data sources. First, I contrast rates of out-migration with in-migration over the decades since company closures. In both cases, populations declined by 20–30 percent from date of first company closure. This simple calculation does not account

for population churning, however—rapid in-migration of new residents to replace people who fled closures. To account for this gap, I use a second measure—homeownership—to track some degree of residential permanence. Higher rates of completed mortgage payments communicate that homeowners have lived in a particular house for between fifteen and thirty years, the lengths of typical mortgages. As of 2019, the national average of free-and-clear homeownership is 37.9 percent. Ninety percent of Southeast Chicago's housing units are occupied, with homeowners living in more than 60 percent of those houses. This contrasts with the city as a whole, where only 45.7 percent of houses are owner-occupied. William Erbe, *Local Community Fact Book: Chicago Metropolitan Area—Based on the 1970 and 1980 Censuses* (Chicago: Chicago Review Press, 1985). Thirty-five percent of Chicago houses are owned free and clear. In Iron County, 80 percent of housing is occupied full-time (distinct from part-time occupation by seasonal homeowners or tourists). More than half of Iron County homeowners own their houses free and clear. United States Census Bureau, "DP04: Selected Housing Characteristics 2017–2021," American Community Survey 5-Year Estimates, 2021, https://data.census.gov/table?q=DP04; United States Census Bureau, "Quickfacts: Chicago City, Illinois. Quickfacts: Owner-Occupied Housing Unit Rate, 2017–2021," 2021, https://www.census.gov/quickfacts/fact/table/chicago cityillinois/HSG445221#HSG445221; United States Census Bureau, "DP04: Selected Housing Characteristics: Iron County, Wisconsin, 2015–2019, American Community Survey 5-Year Estimates," 2019, https://data.census .gov/cedsci/table?g=0500000US55051&tid=ACSDP5Y2019. DP04&hidePreview=true; United States Census Bureau, "DP04: Selected Housing Characteristics: Chicago City, Illinois, 2017–2021, American Community Survey 5-Year Estimates," 2021, https://data.census.gov/table ?q=DP04&g=1600000US1714000&tid=ACSDP5Y2021.DP04.

4. Since 1965, at least 14 percent of Iron County has lived below the federal poverty line. In 2023, the poverty line as set by the Department of Health and Human Services is an annual income of $14,580 for an individual, $30,000 for a family or household of four, and $50,560 for a family or household of eight. "How the Census Bureau Measures Poverty," 2023, https://www.census.gov/topics/income-poverty/poverty /guidance/poverty-measures.html; Department of Health & Human

Services, Office of the Assistant Secretary for Planning and Evaluation, Poverty Guidelines, 2023, https://aspe.hhs.gov/poverty-guidelines.

5. Iron County Forestry and Parks Department, "Iron County Outdoor Recreation Plan 2016–2020," 2016, https://www.nwrpc.com/965/Iron -County-Outdoor-Recreation-Plan-2016; "Wisconsin Settlement Data," 2016, https://population.us/settlement/wi; More generally, see analyses of general trends of recreation dependency and poverty in Thomas L. Daniels and Mark B. Lapping, "Small Town Triage: A Rural Settlement Policy for the American Midwest," *Journal of Rural Studies* 3, no. 3 (1987): 273–80.

6. Jan W. Duyvendak, *The Politics of Home: Belonging and Nostalgia in Europe and the United States* (Basingstoke, UK: Palgrave Macmillan, 2011); Douglas J. Porteous and Sandra E. Smith, *Domicide: The Global Destruction Of Home* (Montreal and Kingston, CA: McGill-Queen's University Press, 2001).

7. Many studies of deindustrialization center on its economic effects, such as labor market dislocation (job/income loss), increased employment precarity as jobs shift toward the service sector, and disinvestment in community services by capital and austerity-seeking local governments. Justin R. Pierce and Peter K. Schott, "The Surprisingly Swift Decline of US Manufacturing Employment," *American Economic Review* 106, no. 7 (2016): 1632–62; Justin R. Pierce and Peter K. Schott, "Trade Liberalization and Mortality: Evidence from U.S. Counties," *American Economic Review: Insights* 2, no. 1 (2020): 47–64. A secondary literature focuses on the social repercussions—physical suffering, health effects, community disintegration, alienation, and their ramifications for democracy and population health. See Gábor Scheiring and Lawrence King, "Deindustrialization, Social Disintegration, and Health: A Neoclassical Sociological Approach," *Theory and Society* 52 (2022): 145–78. For example, the term "Rust Belt," coined by the politician Walter Mondale in the 1980s, refers to decay and loss of functional, industrial machinery. See Christopher Byron, "Booms, Busts and Birth of a Rust Bowl," *Time*, December 27, 1982; Anne Trubek, "Why the Term 'Rust Belt' Matters," *Belt*, April 15, 2016, https://beltmag .com/why-rust-belt-matters/. Even environmental benefits of industrial demise like the clearing of air once polluted by unregulated industries become telling markers of loss, as the journalist Edward McClelland

reflects in his monograph *Nothin' But Blue Skies: The Heyday, Hard Times, and Hopes of America's Industrial Heartland* (New York: Bloomsbury, 2013). As time passed and industrial infrastructures became ruins, people experienced the anomic ambivalence of "devastation but also home," in Alice Mah, "Devastation but Also Home: Place Attachment in Areas of Industrial Decline," *Home Cultures* 6, no. 3 (2009): 287–310.

8. Art Gallaher and Harland Padfield, *The Dying Community* (Albuquerque: University of New Mexico Press, 1980).

9. John Kenneth Galbraith, *The Nature of Mass Poverty* (Cambridge, MA: Harvard University Press, 1979).

10. Reflecting on the cycle of boom, bust, and residential mobility in his 1985 essay on deindustrialization, the journalist James Fallows surmised, "If there is one widely accepted symbol of today's changing economy, the 1980s version of the allegorical Joad family hitting the road during the Depression is the proud steelworker who gets laid off in Youngstown." Fallows, "America's Changing Economic Landscape," *The Atlantic Monthly*, March 1985, 57.

11. The linear push-pull model of migration posits that humans will move away from places that are economically constrained or environmentally degraded and toward places that are less degraded or more predictable. Opportunities pull migrants, while constraints push them. See Hannah Gosnell and Jesse Abrams, "Amenity Migration: Diverse Conceptualizations of Drivers, Socioeconomic Dimensions, and Emerging Challenges," *Geography Journal* 76 (2011): 303–22; Shawn Malia Kanaiaupuni, "Sustaining Families and Communities: Nonmigrant Women and Mexico-U. S. Migration Processes," Center for Demography and Ecology, July 2000, 41; Lori M. Hunter et al., "Rural Outmigration, Natural Capital, and Livelihoods in South Africa: Migration and Environment in Rural South Africa," *Population Space and Place* 20, no. 5 (2014): 402–20.

Out-migration can have a positive effect on communities of origin, such as the reduction of population pressures on scarce resources and increased economic infusion through remittances. Migration reallocates household labor supply to diversify risk and manage economic losses at home. See Julie C. Keller, *Milking in the Shadows: Migrants and Mobility in America's Dairyland* (New Brunswick, NJ: Rutgers University Press,

2019); Paul A. Lewin, Monica Fisher, and Bruce Weber, "Do Rainfall Conditions Push or Pull Rural Migrants: Evidence from Malawi," *Agricultural Economics* 43, no. 2 (2012): 191–204; Jürgen Scheffran, Elina Marmer, and Papa Sow, "Migration as a Contribution to Resilience and Innovation in Climate Adaptation: Social Networks and Co-Development in Northwest Africa," *Applied Geography* 33 (2012): 119–27; K. van der Geest, "North-South Migration in Ghana: What Role for the Environment?" *International Migration* 49, no. S1 (2011): e69–e94. Larry Long, *Migration and Residential Mobility in the United States* (Thousand Oaks, CA: Russell Sage Foundation, 1988).

A more nuanced perspective that emphasizes the uneven distribution of historical, political, economic, and social contexts has shifted push-pull rhetoric. For instance, scholars of economic change and class realized how the same macroeconomic transformations in the late twentieth century that killed industrial work meant that the most job growth across the country occurred in the "precarious" service sector. Moving away from economic crisis didn't inherently guarantee better employment options. See Michael Mayerfeld Bell and Giorgio Osti, "Mobilities and Ruralities: An Introduction," *Sociologia Ruralis* 50, no. 3 (2010): 199–204; Arne L. Kalleberg, "Precarious Work, Insecure Workers: Employment Relations in Transition," *American Sociological Review* 74, no. 1 (2009): 1–22; Marcel Paret, "Towards a Precarity Agenda," *Global Labour Journal* 7, no. 2 (2016): 111–22.

12. Some scholars argue that environmentally-related migration is a household strategy to diversify risk (new economics of labor migration theory). See J. Edward Taylor and Alejandro Lopez-Feldman, "Does Migration Make Rural Households More Productive? Evidence from Mexico," *Journal of Development Studies* 46, no. 1 (2010): 68–90. A prevalent critique of this literature is its tendency to assume some level of environmental determinism—that certain environmental factors consistently cause certain kinds of movement. This alternative perspective shows that social, environmental, and economic factors do matter to mobility decisions, but households also rationalize their decisions through narratives of permanence. See Zygmunt Bauman, "Migration and Identities in the Globalized World," *Philosophy and Social Criticism* 37, no. 4 (2011): 425–35; Lori M. Hunter, Jessie K. Luna, and Rachel M. Norton,

"Environmental Dimensions of Migration," *Annual Review of Sociology* 41, no. 1 (2015): 377–97; and Eva Rosen, "Horizontal Immobility: How Narratives of Neighborhood Violence Shape Housing Decisions," *American Sociological Review* 82, no. 2 (2017): 270–96.

13. Chad Broughton, *Boom, Bust, Exodus: The Rust Belt, the Maquilas, and a Tale of Two Cities* (New York: Oxford University Press, 2015); Yolande Pottie-Sherman, "Rust and Reinvention: Im/migration and Urban Change in the American Rust Belt," *Geography Compass* 14, no. 3 (2020): 1–13.

14. Harry Caudill, *Night Comes to the Cumberlands: A Biography of a Depressed Area* (Boston: Little, Brown, 1963); Alice Mah, *Industrial Ruination, Community, and Place* (Toronto: University of Toronto Press, 2012); Adam A. Millsap, "The Rust Belt Didn't Adapt and It Paid the Price," *Forbes*, January 9, 2017, https://www.forbes.com/sites/adammillsap/2017/01/09/the-rust-belt-didnt-adapt-and-it-paid-the-price/; Stewart Lockie et al., "Coal Mining and the Resource Community Cycle: A Longitudinal Assessment of the Social Impacts of the Coppabella Coal Mine," *Environmental Impact Assessment Review* 29, no. 5 (2009): 330–39; Jack Metzgar, "Blue-Collar Blues: The Deunionization of Manufacturing," *New Labor Forum* (Spring-Summer 2002): 20–23; Robert Wuthnow, *The Left Behind: Decline and Rage in Rural America* (Princeton, NJ: Princeton University Press, 2018).

15. Thomas F. Gieryn, "A Space for Place in Sociology," *Annual Review of Sociology* 26, no. 1 (2000): 469, 475.

16. Barry Bluestone and Bennett Harrison, *The Deindustrialization of America: Plant Closings, Community Abandonment, and the Dismantling of Basic Industry* (New York: Basic Books, 1982).

17. Hunter, Luna, and Norton, "Environmental Dimensions of Migration," 392, notes that while "migration is a long-standing form of adaptation to environmental change, although migration may not be an option for particularly marginalized households and may further marginalize those most impoverished."

18. I join a small but rich tradition of attempting to name and theorize complex narratives of loss after economic (or environmental) crisis. For instance, Mindy Thompson Fullilove, in *Root Shock: How Tearing Up City Neighborhoods Hurts America, and What We Can Do About It* (New

York: New Village, 2016), identified grief following urban development and gentrification as "root shock", and Glenn A. Albrecht, in *Earth Emotions: New Words for a New World* (Ithaca, NY: Cornell University Press, 2019), dubbed the disorientation of climate-change-fueled-loss '*solastalgia*', or a "homesickness you have when you are still at home." Karen E. Till, in "Wounded Cities: Memory-Work and a Place-Based Ethics of Care," *Political Geography* 31, no. 1 (2012): 3–14, linked memory, place, and community recuperation after economic-based trauma. Focusing on the trauma of "natural" disasters, Kai Erikson, in *Everything in Its Path: Destruction of Community in the Buffalo Creek Flood* (New York: Simon & Schuster, 1976), 200, described cultural crises emerging from topographic erasure. Centering on the Rust Belt specifically, Tim Strangleman, in "'Smokestack Nostalgia,' 'Ruin Porn' or Working-Class Obituary: The Role and Meaning of Deindustrial Representation," *International Labor and Working-Class History*, no. 84 (2013): 23–37, questions the voyeuristic lure of rubble, ruins, and other physical markers of loss, and more recently, Sherry Lee Linkon, *The Half-Life of Deindustrialization: Working-Class Writing About Economic Restructuring* (Ann Arbor: University of Michigan Press, 2018), highlights alternative literary voices emerging from middle America that tell stories of resistance and creativity in place.

19. Richard Florida, *The Rise of the Creative Class (New York: Basic Books, 2019)*; Richard Florida, "Returning to the Rust Belt," *Bloomberg*, August 31, 2017, https://www.citylab.com/life/2017/08/returning-to-the-rust-belt/538572/.

20. Arlie Russell Hochschild, *Strangers in Their Own Land: Anger and Mourning on the American Right* (New York: New Press, 2016); Michèle Lamont, "Addressing Recognition Gaps: Destigmatization and the Reduction of Inequality," *American Sociological Review* 83, no. 3 (2018): 419–44; Anna Rhodes and Max Besbris, *Soaking the Middle Class: Suburban Inequality and Recovery from Disaster* (New York: Russell Sage Foundation, 2022); and Jennifer M. Silva, *We're Still Here: Pain and Politics in the Heart of America* (Oxford: Oxford University Press, 2019).

21. David L. Harvey, "Globalization and Deindustrialization: A City Abandoned," *International Journal of Politics, Culture and Society* 10, no. 1 (1996): 175–91. I build on geographers' conceptions of place—that a particular constellation "of material things that occupy a particular segment

of space and have sets of meanings attached to them." Tim Cresswell, "Place: Encountering Geography as Philosophy," *Geography* 93, no. 3 (2008): 135. To be at home is to be in a physical place in which one dwells, according to Heidegger—that in situ action that renders meaningful a place and interpretable, broader human experience. Martin Heidegger, "Building, Dwelling, Thinking," in *Basic Writings: From Being and Time* (San Francisco, CA: Harper, 1977). Similarly, the geographer Doreen Massey summarized that because of the resource dynamics of regional chains, "different social groups, and different individuals are placed in very distinct ways in relation to these flows and interconnections. . . . [They] have distinct relationships to this anyway differentiated mobility." Doreen Massey, "A Global Sense of Place," in *Space, Place, Gender* (Minneapolis: University of Minnesota Press, 1994): 26.

22. Shannon Elizabeth Bell, *Fighting King Coal: The Challenges to Micromobilization in Central Appalachia* (Cambridge, MA: MIT Press, 2016); Karida L. Brown, *Gone Home: Race and Roots Through Appalachia* (Chapel Hill: University of North Carolina Press, 2018); Ellie Byrne, Eva Elliott, and Gareth Williams, "Poor Places, Powerful People? Co-Producing Cultural Counter-Representations of Place," *Visual Methodologies* 3, no. 2 (2015): 77–85; Jefferson Cowie and Joseph Heathcott, eds., *Beyond the Ruins: The Meanings of Deindustrialization* (Ithaca, NY: ILR, 2003); Steven High, *Industrial Sunset: The Making of North America's Rust Belt, 1969–1984* (Toronto: University of Toronto Press, 2003); Colin Jerolmack and Edward T. Walker, "Please in My Backyard: Quiet Mobilization in Support of Fracking in an Appalachian Community," *American Journal of Sociology* 124, no. 2 (2018); Cheryl Morse and Jill Mudgett, "Longing for Landscape: Homesickness and Place Attachment Among Rural Out-Migrants in the 19th and 21st Centuries," *Journal of Rural Studies* 50 (2017): 95–103; Sonya Salamon, "From Hometown to Nontown: Rural Community Effects of Suburbanization," *Rural Sociology* 68, no. 1 (2003): 1–24; Ronald Tobey, Charles Wetherell, and Jay Brigham, "Moving Out and Settling In: Residential Mobility, Home Owning, and the Public Enframing of Citizenship, 1921–1950," *American Historical Review* 95, no. 5 (1990): 1395–422; and Wendy Wolford, *This Land Is Ours Now: Social Mobilization and the Meanings of Land in Brazil* (Durham, NC: Duke University Press, 2010).

23. Interviewees claimed varying levels of intensity of attachment to certain places or social networks. These variations may be linked to the number of years they've lived there, as the social psychologist Maria Lewicka (2011) suggests. Additionally, highly emotional experiences of making ends meet in the decades after mine and mill closure might have heightened residents' sentiments of affection for place, according to environmental psychologists. Alison Hope Alkon and Michael Traugot, "Place Matters, but How? Rural Identity, Environmental Decision Making, and the Social Construction of Place," *City and Community* 7, no. 2 (2008): 97–112; Patrick Devine-Wright, "Beyond NIMBYism: Towards an Integrated Framework for Understanding Public Perceptions of Wind Energy," *Wind Energy* 8, no. 2 (2005): 125–39; Per Gustafson, "Meanings of Place: Everyday Experience and Theoretical Conceptualizations," *Journal of Environmental Psychology* 21, no. 1 (2001): 5–16; Maria Lewicka, "Place Attachment, Place Identity, and Place Memory: Restoring the Forgotten City Past," *Journal of Environmental Psychology* 28, no. 3 (2008): 209–31; Maria Lewicka, "Place Attachment: How Far Have We Come in the Last 40 Years?" *Journal of Environmental Psychology* 31, no. 3 (2011): 207–230; Setha M. Low and Irwin Altman, eds., *Place Attachment* (New York: Springer, 1992); Lynne C. Manzo, "For Better or Worse: Exploring Multiple Dimensions of Place Meaning," *Journal of Environmental Psychology* 25, no. 1 (2005): 67–86; Christopher M. Raymond et al., eds., *Changing Senses of Place: Navigating Global Challenges* (Cambridge: Cambridge University Press, 2021); Richard C. Stedman, "Is It Really Just a Social Construction? The Contribution of the Physical Environment to Sense of Place," *Society and Natural Resources* 16, no. 8 (2003): 671–85.

24. Daniel R. Sundblad and Stephen Sapp, "The Persistence of Neighboring as a Determinant of Community Attachment: A Community Field Perspective," *Rural Sociology* 76, no. 4 (2011): 515, called for the scholarly attentiveness to both structural and socioemotional bonds to community *over time*, ones that "measure . . .[the] feeling of being at home in or bound to a geographic community and *then* evaluate the extent to which structural and social conditions influence this sense of attachment."

25. Certainly, not all actions need to have motives—"it is erroneous to assume that consciousness of [. . .] alternatives and therefore choice is

necessarily given before every human action, and that in consequence all acting involves deliberation and preference." Alfred Schutz, "Tiresias, or Our Knowledge of Future Events," *Social Research* 26, no. 1 (1959): 71–89. Yet in this study, interviewees repeatedly voiced rationales for staying *as* motives—drivers that encouraged or at least explained their particular action. I am more interested in how and why speakers justify their actions than in testing the 'true-ness' of their motivation at the time of decision-making.

26. Kerri Arsenault, *Mill Town: Reckoning with What Remains* (New York: St. Martin's, 2020); Japonica Brown-Saracino, "Social Preservationists and the Quest for Authentic Community," *City and Community* 3, no. 2 (2004): 135–56; Rebecca Elliot, *Underwater: Loss, Flood Insurance, and the Moral Economy of Climate Change in the United States* (New York: Columbia University Press, 2021); William Firey, "Sentiment and Symbolism as Ecological Variables," *American Sociological Review* 10, no. 2 (1945): 140–48; Ken Gould and Tammy Lewis, *Green Gentrification: Urban Sustainability and the Struggle for Environmental Justice* (New York: Routledge, 2016); Rachel Tolbert Kimbro, *In Too Deep: Class and Mothering in a Flooded Community* (Berkeley: University of California Press, 2022); Karen E. Till, "Wounded Cities: Memory-Work and a Place-Based Ethics of Care," *Political Geography* 31, no. 1 (2012): 3–14.

27. Katherine Roberts, "The Art of Staying Put: Managing Land and Minerals in Rural America," *Journal of American Folklore* 126, no. 502 (2013): 407–33, suggests that even social responses to crisis that look like acquiescence to the status quo are often intentional strategies to resist or redirect hegemonic influences. She observed how rural folk in Appalachia relinquished rights to gas and mineral leasing on their land in order to further the more important value of keeping land under family control. These self-positioning strategies may, to outsiders, appear inactive and ambivalent, but they are in fact active and critical choices constrained within a hegemonic context.

28. Wendell Berry, "It All Turns on Affection," National Endowment for the Humanities Jefferson Lecture, Washington, DC, April 23, 2012, https://www.neh.gov/about/awards/jefferson-lecture/wendell-e-berry-lecture. Also see Wallace Stegner, *Crossing to Safety* (New York: Modern Library, 2002); bell hooks, *Belonging: A Culture of Place* (New York:

Routledge, 2008); and Robert Macfarlane, *The Old Ways: A Journey on Foot* (New York: Penguin, 2013).

29. Terry Tempest Williams, *Refuge: An Unnatural History of Family and Place* (New York: Vintage, 1992).

30. bell hooks, "Homeplace: A Site of Resistance," in *Yearning: Race, Gender, and Cultural Politics* (Boston: South End, 1999).

31. Gastón R. Gordillo, *Rubble: The Afterlife of Destruction* (Durham, NC: Duke University Press, 2014).

32. Home is a place "to which one withdraws and from which one ventures forth," (Yi-Fu Tuan, "Geography, Phenomenology, and the Study of Human Nature," *Canadian Geographies* 15, no. 3 (1971): 189). One must be rooted in a local place to claim a sense of home, according to David M. Hummon, "Community Attachment: Local Sentiment and Sense of Place," in *Place Attachment*, ed. Irwin Altman and Setha M. Low (Boston, MA: Plenum Press, 1992): 253–78. "Like breathing in and out, most life forms need a home and horizons of reach outward from that home. The lived reciprocity of rest and movement, territory and range, security and adventure" characterize what it means to be human, according to Anne Buttimer, "Home, Reach and the Sense of Place," in *The Human Experience of Space and Place*, ed. Anne Buttimer and David Seamon (London: Croom Helm, 1980): 166–87, 170.

33. Jennifer E. Cross, "Conceptualizing Community Attachment," Rural Sociological Society Annual Meeting (2003); John D. Kasarda and Morris Janowitz, "Community Attachment in Mass Society," *American Sociological Review* 39, no. 3 (1974): 328; Harvey Molotch, William R. Freudenburg, and Krista E. Paulsen, "History Repeats Itself, But How? City Character, Urban Tradition, and the Accomplishment of Place," *American Sociological Review* 65, no. 6 (2000), 791–823; Lee Shaker, "Community Attachment," in *Oxford Bibliographies in Communication*, 1–2, last modified September 30, 2013, http://www.oxfordbibliographies .com/view/document/obo-9780199756841/obo-9780199756841-0136.xml.

34. Mario Luis Small, *Villa Victoria: Origins of Network Inequality in Everyday Life* (Chicago: University of Chicago Press, 2004); P. Sharkey and J. Faber, "Where, When, Why, and for Whom Do Residential Contexts Matter? Moving Away from the Dichotomous Understanding of Neighborhood Effects," *Annual Review of Sociology* 40 (2014): 559–79.

35. Gillian Rose, *Feminism & Geography: The Limits of Geographical Knowledge* (Minneapolis: University of Minnesota Press, 1993); Iris Marion Young, "House and Home: Feminist Variations on a Theme," in *Intersecting Voices: Dilemmas of Gender, Political Philosophy, and Policy* (Princeton, NJ: Princeton University Press, 1997), 134–64.

36. Karl Marx, *Capital*, vol. 1: *A Critique of Political Economy*, trans. Ben Fowkes. (Toronto: Penguin, 1990); William Julius Wilson, *The Truly Disadvantaged: The Inner City, the Underclass, and Public Policy* (Chicago: Chicago University Press, 1987); Viviana Zelizer, *Economic Lives: How Culture Shapes the Economy* (Princeton, NJ: Princeton University Press, 2010).

37. David Bensman and Roberta Lynch, *Rusted Dreams: Hard Times in a Steel Community* (Berkeley: University of California Press, 1989); Katherine M. Dudley, *End of the Line: Lost Jobs, New Lives in Postindustrial America* (Chicago: University of Chicago Press, 1994); Steven High, *Industrial Sunset: The Making of North America's Rust Belt, 1969–1984* (Toronto: University of Toronto Press, 2003), 16.; Matthew E. Kahn, "The Silver Lining of Rust Belt Manufacturing Decline," *Journal of Urban Economics* 46, no. 3 (1999): 360–76; William Kornblum, *Blue Collar Community* (Chicago: University of Chicago Press, 1974); Cecily Neil, Tykkyläinen, Markku, and Bradbury, John, eds., *Coping with Closure—an International Comparison of Mine Town Experiences* (London: Routledge, 1992); John C. Raines, Lenora E. Berson, and David M. Gracie, eds., *Community and Capital in Conflict: Plant Closings and Job Loss* (Philadelphia: Temple University Press, 1982); New York Times, ed., *The Downsizing of America: Millions of Americans Are Losing Good Jobs. This Is Their Story* (New York: Random House, 1996); Christine J. Walley, "Deindustrializing Chicago: A Daughter's Story," in *The Insecure American: How We Got Here and What We Should Do About It*, ed. Hugh Gusterson and Besteman, Catherine Lowe,(Oakland, CA: University of California Press, 2010), 113–39.

38. Charles Tilly, *Big Structures, Large Processes, Huge Comparisons* (New York: Russell Sage, 1984).

39. Phillip McMichael, "Incorporating Comparison within a World-Historical Perspective: An Alternative Comparative Method," *American Sociological Review* 55, no. 3 (1990): 386.

40. On community studies: Mario L. Small, *Villa Victoria: Origins of Network Inequality in Everyday Life* (Chicago: University of Chicago Press, 2004); Gene F. Summers and Kristi Branch, "Economic Development and Community Activism," *Annual Review of Sociology* 10 (1984): 141–66; William R. Freudenburg, "The Density of Acquaintanceship: An Overlooked Variable in Community Research?" *American Journal of Sociology* 92, no. 1 (1986): 27–63.

On commodity chains, see Marion Werner and Jennifer Bair, "Commodity Chains and the Uneven Geographies of Global Capitalism: A Disarticulations Perspective," *Environment and Planning* 43, no. 5 (2011): 998–1015; Stephen Bunker and Paul S. Ciccantell, *Globalization and the Race for Resources* (Baltimore, MD: Johns Hopkins University Press, 2005); Paul S. Ciccantell, David A. Smith, and Gay Seidman, *Nature, Raw Materials, and Political Economy* (Amsterdam: Elsevier, 2005); Jane L. Collins, "New Directions in Commodity Chain Analysis of Global Development Processes," *Research in Rural Sociology and Development* 11 (2005): 1–15; Terence K. Hopkins and Immanuel Wallerstein, "Capitalism and the Incorporation of New Zones into the World Economy," *Review* 10 (1987): 763–79.

41. Writing in 1996, the rural sociologist Linda Lobao reflected on the "continual spatial loosening of elements once considered indicative of differences between rural and urban areas." Linda Lobao, "A Sociology of the Periphery Versus a Peripheral Sociology: Rural Sociology and the Dimension of Space," *Rural Sociology* 61, no. 1 (1996): 89.

42. William Cronon, *Nature's Metropolis: Chicago and the Great West* (New York: Norton, 1991).

43. Michael Mayerfeld Bell, *Childerly: Nature and Morality in a Country Village* (Chicago: University of Chicago Press, 1995); Michael Mayerfeld Bell and Loka Ashwood, *An Invitation to Environmental Sociology*, 5th ed. (Thousand Oaks, CA: Sage, 2015).

44. Natalie Moore, "On the Grounds of an Old Steel Mill, Could Chicago Create a Piece of Utopia?" *Chicago Sun Times*, January 19, 2019; Christine J. Walley, *Exit Zero: Family and Class in Postindustrial Chicago* (Chicago: University of Chicago Press, 2013).

45. This contrasts with 1.2 acres of public land per person in the state of Wisconsin as a whole. Iron County Forestry and Parks Department,

"Iron County Outdoor Recreation Plan 2016–2020," 2016, https://www
.nwrpc.com/965/Iron-County-Outdoor-Recreation-Plan-2016.

46. Colleen Connolly, "Get to Know Your Ward: 10th Ward," *NBC Chicago
and Ward Room*, January 27, 2015, https://www.nbcchicago.com/news
/local/chicago-politics/get-to-know-your-ward-10th-ward/97973/.

47. Data tracing the residential movement of individuals or subgroups of
residents can be methodologically challenging, particularly when the
geographical measurement area changes over time (like in the Chicago
case). Census data focuses on net in- or out-migration and cannot consistently speak to return migration (people who leave and then return
"home") or (until recently) age-cohort outmigration. As of 2022, new
data is available on young people moving out in the 1990s and 2000s at
county-by-county level—useful for my Wisconsin case but not for the
smaller community-areas of my Southeast Chicago case. United States
Census Bureau, Migration Patterns, "Young Adult Migration," https://
migrationpatterns.org/.

48. Gökçe Günel, Saiba Varma, and Chika Watanabe, "A Manifesto for
Patchwork Ethnography," Society for Cultural Anthropology, Member
Voices, June 9, 2020, https://culanth.org/fieldsights/a-manifesto-for
-patchwork-ethnography.

49. The sociologist Sarah Damaske reflects how "accounts can be under-
stood as the product of the negotiation between actions taken in the
cultural meanings attached to those actions." Sarah Damaske, "Work,
Family, and Accounts of Mothers' Lives Using Discourse to Navigate
Intensive Mothering Ideals: Work, Family, and Accounts of Mothers'
Lives," *Sociology Compass* 7, no. 6 (2013): 436–44.

1. CAPITALISM MAKES PLACE: CONSTRUCTING AN INDUSTRIAL HOME

The chapter epigraph is by John Urry, riffing off of John Berger, *Selected
Essays and Articles: The Look of Things* (Penguin, 1971), 35–41, found in
Derek Gregory and John Urry, eds., *Social Relations and Spatial Struc-
tures* (MacMillan Publishers Ltd., 1985), 30.

1. As mentioned in the preface and introduction and discussed further in
the methods appendix, all interviewees were given pseudonyms. Their

quotes have not been altered—when in double quotation marks, I am directly quoting from interviews that I recorded, with the speaker's oral or written permission. When in single quotation marks, I am quoting my closest approximation from an on-the-move interview or on-the-ground conversation with a larger group of people. I retained descriptors of race, age, gender, and residential longevity.

2. William F. Cannon, Gene L. LaBerge, John S. Klasner, and Klaus J. Schulz, "The Gogebic Iron Range—a Sample of the Northern Margin of the Penokean Fold and Thrust Belt," U.S. Geological Survey Professional Paper 1730, 2007.

3. While logging and trapping had lured handfuls of white immigrant settlers northward in the seventeenth and eighteenth centuries, most permanent settlements only sprang up because of the discovery of iron in the late 1800s and the integration of what came to be known as the Gogebic Iron Range into Midwestern steel commodity chains. Gwen Schultz, *Wisconsin's Foundations: A Review of the State's Geology and Its Influence* (Madison: University of Wisconsin Press, 1986), 52.

4. Hector Fernando Burga, "Traditions of Placemaking and Fundamentalisms of Practice: The New Urbanism in the Context of Globalization," *Traditional Dwellings and Settlements Review* 20, no. 1 (December 2008): 15; Kelly Main and Gerardo Francisco Sandoval, "Placemaking in a Translocal Receiving Community: The Relevance of Place to Identity and Agency," *Urban Studies* 52, no. 1 (2015): 71–86; Yolande Pottie-Sherman, "Rust and Reinvention: Im/Migration and Urban Change in the American Rust Belt," *Geography Compass* 14, no. 3 (2020): 1–13.

5. "South Chicago: The County Commissioners at Calumet Harbor," *Chicago Daily Tribune*, May 29, 1872.

6. William Cronon, *Nature's Metropolis: Chicago and the Great West* (New York: Norton, 1991), 35, citing the newspaper editor William Bross, from his paper "Chicago and the Sources of Her Past and Future Growth," published in 1880.

7. The environmental historian Bill Cronon discussed the role of industrial boosters in fanning the flames of speculation and investment in Chicago. Boosters argued that the exact locations of these new industrial projects were natural: steel mills could only be built adjacent to water and rail transportation, while iron mine shafts only worked if

the right geology aligned with beneficial land rights. "They saw the engine of western development in the symbiotic relationship between cities and their surrounding countrysides." William Cronon, *Nature's Metropolis: Chicago and the Great West* (New York: Norton, 1991), 34.

8. "Gogebic: Its Unbounded Wealth," *The Herald*, April 23, 1886, www .wisconsinhistory.org/turningpoints/search.asp?id=694; Oglebay Norton, *Oglebay Norton Company: Montreal Mine, 1886–1962* (Cleveland, OH: Iron County Historical Society, 1962); Oglebay Norton, *Oglebay Norton Company: 125 Years* (Cleveland, OH: Iron County Historical Society, 1979).

9. Hector Fernando Burga, "Traditions of Placemaking and Fundamentalisms of Practice," 15; Main and Sandoval, "Placemaking in a Translocal Receiving Community," 71–86.

10. In the "wild-garlic place" of Chicagou, the Potawatomi tribe of the much larger Anishinaabe people group traded, battled, settled, and foraged across the thousands of acres of glacier-flattened prairie. Near the southernmost tip of Lake Michigan, these prairies were segmented by sluggish rivers that, during wet seasons, bled into the surrounding lowlands to form a sprawling marshland. In the rainiest summers, the waters rose enough to allow a canoe to travel west from that lake across those small rivers and south to the Gulf of Mexico through the Mississippi. Those skillful enough to brave the open waters could point their prows toward the northern horizon of Lake Michigan and find its meeting place with the other Great Lakes and their peoples, including the Ojibwe, who were located in the iron-rich forests near Lake Superior. Nineteenth-century settler-colonists followed these waterways and trade routes to lay claim on comfortable village settlements and established trade networks across lakes and rivers. The movements of the Anishinaabe peoples were soon choked off by a U.S. government eager to expedite the westward expansion of its settlers. The Potawatomi were marched to western reservations in 1833, and in the 1850s, the Ojibwe of Lake Superior were condensed and resettled on much smaller reservations in the Upper Midwest. The easternmost Odawa were the first to meet white settlers and were thus the first to be forced to cede their land in the early nineteenth century. Helen Dwyer and Sierra Adare, "Ojibwe History and Culture," Wisconsin First Nations, n.d.,

https://wisconsinfirstnations.org/ojibwe-history-and-culture/; "Potawatomi History," Milwaukee Public Museum, n.d., https://www .mpm.edu/plan-visit/educators/wirp/nations/potawatomi/history; Richard White, *The Middle Ground: Indians, Empires, and Republics in the Great Lakes Region, 1650–1815* (Cambridge: Cambridge University Press, 1991).

11. The French started exploring Lake Superior in the 1620s. The first fur traders to come to Wisconsin arrived in 1659, building a crude fort on Chequamegon Bay (present-day Ashland) and wintering at Lac Courte Oreilles (today, Sawyer County). Arnold Alanen, "The Planning of Company Communities in the Lake Superior Mining Region," *Journal of the American Planning Association* 45, no. 3 (1979): 256–78; Henry E. Legler, "The Great Boom on the Gogebic," in *Leading Events of Wisconsin History* (Milwaukee: Sentinel, 1898), 310–15; Matthew Liesch, *Ironwood, Hurley, and the Gogebic Range* (Chicago: Arcadia, 2006); and Edward Marek, "Ashland's Iron Ore Docks, a Fascinating History," *Wisconsin Central: The People, the Land, the Culture,* accessed October 3, 2015, https://web.archive.org/web/20150306173109/http://www.wisconsin central.net/Culture/Culture/AshlandOreDocks.html.

12. Herbert Casson, "The Romance of Steel and Iron in America," *Munsey's Magazine,* April 1907, Chicago History Museum, HD 9510 C27 1906.

13. Iron ore initially brought to Chicago's steel mills from Pennsylvania, New Jersey, and New York was quickly usurped by hematite iron ore. Cheap water-based transportation from the newly exploited Marquette Range on the Upper Peninsula of Michigan, Minnesota's Mesabi Range, and the Gogebic Range in Wisconsin and Michigan via the Great Lakes meant that the Lake Superior mining district dominated the country's iron ore trade for nearly a century; Marek, "Ashland's Iron Ore Docks, a Fascinating History"; United States Work Projects Administration, "History of Iron County," 1938, http://content.wisconsinhistory .org/cdm/ref/collection/wch/id/58348.

14. Communities that grew around a mine were called locations— i.e., Cary Location for the Cary Mine, or Montreal surrounding the Montreal Mine. Today, some small villages in the region retain their mine location monikers. "Mountains of Iron," *Chicago Times,* July 25, 1886, accessed from Wisconsin Historical Society, Wisconsin Local History

& Biography Articles, https://www.wisconsinhistory.org/Records/Newspaper
/BA15164.

15. Will Harrington, "Lake Superior Iron Mining Today," *The Age of Steel*
(August 13, 1898): 19.

16. Terry S. Reynolds and Virginia P. Dawson, *Iron Will: Cleveland-Cliffs
and the Mining of Iron Ore, 1847–2006* (Detroit: Wayne State University
Press, 2011), 95.

17. Terry S. Reynolds, "Muting Labor Discontent: Paternalism on the
Michigan Iron Ranges," Center for U.P. Studies, n.d., accessed January
25, 2018, https://www.nmu.edu/upperpeninsulastudies/muting-labor
-discontent-paternalism-michigan-iron (quoting a miner in Michigan,
1881). See also Alanen, "The Planning of Company Communities in the
Lake Superior Mining Region," 256–78.

18. For a contemporaneous, if fictional, account of the region, see Edna
Ferber, *Come and Get It* (London: William Heinemann, 1935). This
novel was partly based on Ferber's visit to Iron County's Burton House
(hotel) in Hurley, Wisconsin.

19. Oglebay Norton, *Oglebay Norton Company: 125 Years*; Oglebay Norton,
Oglebay Norton Company: Montreal Mine 1886–1962. When the discovery of ore in Iron County was announced in national newspapers, John
D. Rockefeller immediately bought a plot of land on the Gogebic from
the newly incorporated state of Wisconsin and asked a friend of his,
the Cleveland mining magnate David Norton, "to dig the ore out and
send it to market." Norton, with his partner E. W. Oglebay, would come
to dominate parts of the Iron County market. The next year, Oglebay
arrived in the county to explore "the efforts to produce ore from the
new discovery by means of a small open pit." He returned to Ohio
with a proposal for his partner: their company, Oglebay Norton, should
serve as an ore-selling agent that would manage the most productive
mines in the Gogebic on behalf of steel companies like Rockefeller's
and transport ore on their fleet of Great Lakes freighters east and south
to manufacturing plants in industrial cities across the Midwest. When
the volatile market crashes of the late 1890s ruined small iron and steel
companies, nearly two hundred independent companies consolidated
into a handful of iron and steel company holdings. By 1900, only four
steel companies controlled nearly three-quarters of the Lake Superior

region's iron ore output. As one of the few companies that remained in the Gogebic range, Oglebay Norton thus became a potent player in the nascent mining community of northern Wisconsin and one that shaped the place in lasting ways. In 1901, Rockefeller sold most of his mines to Carnegie's U.S. Steel Corporation, further consolidating Carnegie's influence on steel pricing and availability. Oglebay was already managing and selling ore from mines in the Upper Peninsula. By the turn of the twentieth century, "the Bessemer fleet of ore carriers numbered 38 vessels, carrying 3.5 million tons in one season. Cleveland's iron ore industry had risen from a few companies and 800 people to several hundred companies employing some 8,000 workers." Oglebay Norton, *Oglebay Norton Company: 125 Years*, 6. (Note, this is not to be confused with Bessemer, Michigan—the town in Michigan is named after this iron-ore refining process known as Bessemer refining). By 1901, the founders, Oglebay and Norton, were both wealthy enough to retire but stayed on in leadership until 1924. Crispin Oglebay, a nephew, was elected president. In 1960, Oglebay Norton bought the taconite mines in Minnesota that would eventually put the company's deep-shaft mines out of business. Although the firm would remain a notable presence on the Wisconsin Gogebic Range, Oglebay Norton's Montreal Mining Company remained one of the smaller operations in the Lake Superior mining district of Minnesota, Wisconsin, and Michigan. The business structure of Oglebay's company embedded what would become Iron County into regional steel commodity chains, enabling steel companies across the Midwest to produce a seemingly endless and always growing flow of consumer-facing products.

20. Oglebay Norton Company was the company contracted by Rockefeller to "dig up the ore" two decades earlier.

21. Montreal Mining Company, "A Report on 'Home Owning Plans' for the Montreal Mining Company," Iron County Historical Society Records, 1922; National Register of Historic Places, "Montreal Company Location Historic District, Montreal, Iron County, Wisconsin," Reference Number 80000141, 2016, http://www.wisconsinhistory.org/Content.aspx?dsNav=N:4294963828-4294963813&dsRecordDetails=R:NR1905.

22. A newspaper article in 1939 described how, "of the 400 homes in the city, 140 neat frame buildings are owned by the company and rented to

miners at a cost of $1.50 a room per month. The other homes have been built on property leased to the owners by the company." Ralph Werner, "Down 3,000 Feet; See Wisconsin's Noted Montreal Mine," *Milwaukee Journal*, June 25, 1939.

23. Even miners wishing to build their own homes also relied on the mining company for land to rent. The mobility of iron ore instigated the active establishment and maintenance of a stable company community even before Roosevelt's Federal Housing Administration altered conditions for homeownership. See Sally A. Shumaker and Gerald J. Conti, "Understanding Mobility in America: Conflicts Between Stability and Change," in *Home Environments*, ed. I. Altman and C. M. Werner (New York: Springer, 1985), 237–53.

24. Peter Benzoni, *Beyond the Mine: A Steelworkers Story* (Superior, WI: Savage, 1997).

25. Holly Fellman, "'Everything's a Rustin,'" *Iron County Miner*, June 5, 1964, 6. Physical copy photographed by author as a clipping in Hilda M. Lake's White Binder, Iron County Historical Society. Also accessible at https:// www.newspapers.com/image/358689505/?terms=Fellman&match=1.

26. "South Chicago: The County Commissioners at Calumet Harbor," *Chicago Daily Tribune*, May 29, 1872, 6.

27. Bowen argued that Chicago's proximity to newly discovered iron ore, combined with a new steel refining technology capable of mass-producing steel, promised to make the Second City competitive in a booming East Coast steel market. The best source for Bowen's involvement with the opening of the Joseph H. Brown Mill in 1875 is the *History of Cook County* by Alfred T. Andreas (1884). Irondale is the former name of South Deering. See https://archive.org/details/bub_gb_V_A1AQAAMAAJ/page/n579/mode/2up. Also see the Bowen biography here: https:// archive.org/details/bub_gb_V_A1AQAAMAAJ/page/n557/mode/2up.

28. Ann Durkin Keating, "Chicago's Harbors: From the Chicago to the Calumet Rivers," *The Electronic Encyclopedia of Chicago* (2005), https:// encyclopedia.chicagohistory.org/pages/300013.html.

29. "Finished: Closing Ceremonies of the Jubilee. Excursion by Lake and Rail to Calumet," *Chicago Daily Tribune*, June 8, 1873, 1.

30. According to Frank Stanley, a former volunteer at the Southeast Chicago Historical Museum, the former president of the Southeast

Chicago Historical Society, and an executive at U.S. Steel South Works, during World War II, employment approached twenty thousand but never surpassed that number. In 1925, the iron- and steel-producing plants in Southeast Chicago were Illinois Steel Company, U.S. Steel South Works, Youngstown Sheet and Tube Company, Federal Furnace Company, Wisconsin Steel Company, and Interstate Steel Company; John B. Appleton, "The Iron and Steel Industry of the Calumet Region—a Study in Economic Geography" (PhD dissertation, University of Chicago, 1925); Dominic A. Pacyga, *Chicago: A Biography* (Chicago: University of Chicago Press, 2009), 48–65; Rod Sellers, "Chicago's Southeast Side: Industrial History," 2006, http://www.csu.edu/cerc /researchreports/documents/ChicagoSESideIndustrialHistory.pdf.

31. William Dillingham, William Jett, and Alexander E. Cance 1911. *Immigrants in Industries (In Twenty-Five Parts).* United States. Immigration Commission (1907-1910). 402.

32. The steel and iron industries contributed significantly to midwestern population growth. The influx of immigrant labor for steel helped Chicago's population grow from 300,000 in 1870 to 2.7 million in 1920. While the federal government restricted the influx of Asian immigrants at the turn of the twentieth century, the nation preserved de facto open borders for all European immigrants until a quota system was first established after World War I through the Emergency Quota Law of 1921. See "1921 Emergency Quota Law," n.d., University of Washington–Bothell Library U.S. Immigration Legislation Online; Russell M. Magnaghi, *Miners, Merchants, and Midwives: Michigan's Upper Peninsula Italians* (Marquette, MI: Belle Fontaine, 1987).

33. Eugene J. Bluffington, "Steel," *The Chicago Visitor,* vol. 1 (Chicago: Chicago History Museum, 1930).

34. "In 1880 the East Side had a population of 1,098 residents comprised mainly of German, Irish and Swedish families." William Erbe, *Local Community Fact Book: Chicago Metropolitan Area—Based on the 1970 and 1980 Censuses* (Chicago: Chicago Review Press, 1985), 138. The East Side was a small neighborhood within the larger Southeast Side region. The report continues, "In 1890, a year after annexation, the Calumet area, centered in South Chicago, had a population of 24,495, of which 13,083 were foreign born" (124). Note that the precise boundaries of "Calumet

area" are not specified. In *Calumet Beginnings*, Ken Schoon reports that in 1880, the population of South Chicago (another neighborhood in the region) was 1,962. "By 1889, the year that South Chicago, South Deering, and the East Side were annexed to the city of Chicago, there were mills, shipping facilities, several rail lines, a good sized business district, and a population of about 20,000." Schoon, *Calumet Beginnings: Ancient Shorelines and Settlements at the South End of Lake Michigan* (Indianapolis: Indiana University Press, 2013), 137.

35. David Bensman and Roberta Lynch, *Rusted Dreams: Hard Times in a Steel Community* (Berkeley: University of California Press, 1989).

36. In the 1930s, the company renamed Irondale as South Deering in honor of one of the other companies it had purchased. More than three-quarters of Wisconsin Steel laborers lived in South Deering. See the detailed history in Bensman and Lynch, *Rusted Dreams*; Lisbeth Cohen, *Making a New Deal: Industrial Workers in Chicago, 1919–1939* (Cambridge: Cambridge University Press, 2008); Keating, "Chicago's Harbors."

37. Cohen, *Making a New Deal.*

38. The four millgate communities were U.S. Steel South Works—South Chicago; Wisconsin Steel—South Deering; Republic Steel—East Side; Pressed Steel—Hegewisch. William Kornblum, *Blue Collar Community* (Chicago: University of Chicago Press, 1974); Mark J. Bouman, "A Mirror Cracked: Ten Keys to the Landscape of the Calumet Region," *Journal of Geography* 100, no. 3 (2001): 104–10.

39. James R. McIntyre, *The History of Wisconsin Steel Works of the International Harvester Company* (Chicago: Southeast Chicago Historical Museum, 1951).

40. There are a couple of maps in a 1925 publication, "The Iron and Steel Industry of the Calumet Region." One (p. 29) shows the location of existing steel mills in the Calumet (SE Chicago and NW Indiana) region. The other one (p. 41) shows the location of the materials used in the steelmaking process.

41. William Cronon, *Nature's Metropolis*, 25.

42. In the tradition of Polanyi and Bourdieu, agency is embedded in institutions, which form the core of social fields, define rules, roles, and expectations, and stabilize patterns of behavior; Karl Polanyi, "The Economy as Instituted Process," in *Trade and Market in the Early Empires*, ed.

Karl Polanyi, Conrad M. Arensberg, and Harry W. Pearson (Chicago: Henry Regnery Company, 1957); Pierre Bourdieu and Loïc J. D. Wacquant, *An Invitation to Reflexive Sociology* (Chicago: University of Chicago Press, 1992).

43. Linda Carlson, *Company Towns of the Pacific Northwest* (Seattle: University of Washington Press, 2014); Margaret Crawford, *Building the Workingman's Paradise: The Design of American Company Towns* (London: Verso, 1995); Nancy Fraser and Linda Gordon, "A Genealogy of Dependency: Tracing a Keyword of the U.S. Welfare State," *Signs: Journal of Women in Culture and Society* 19, no. 2 (1994): 309–36.

44. Sheldon Goldenberg and Gerda R. Wekerle, "From Utopia to Total Institution in a Single Generation: The Kibbutz and the Burderhof," *International Review of Modern Sociology* 2, no. 2 (1972): 224; Rosabeth Moss Kanter, "Commitment and Social Organization: A Study of Commitment Mechanisms in Utopian Communities," *American Sociological Review* 33 (1968): 499–517.

45. Local resident Russ Penrose's essay, "Montreal: The City Beautiful", was retrieved in hard copy at the Iron County Historical Society, Hurley, Wisconsin, in 1995. He wrote, "Within its boundaries the town was alive with character, a spirit, a deep sense of morality and it bubbled with goodness and decency of the people who live there. It was a place without turmoil and complexities. Life was simple and people were happy." Another resident, Mary Woitkielevicz Mossey, offered similar reflections in her biography, *The Iron Ore Miner's Daughter* (n.d.). A physical copy is located in the Iron County Historical Society, Hurley, Wisconsin.

46. Iris Marion Young, "House and Home: Feminist Variations on a Theme," in *Intersecting Voices: Dilemmas of Gender, Political Philosophy, and Policy* (Princeton, NJ: Princeton University Press, 1997), 134–64.

47. As Linda Carlson summarized in her book about company towns in the western United States, paternalistic companies were explicit in their desire "to create a better life for their employees: decent housing, good schools, and a 'morally uplifting' society. . . . In return, they expected stable, hard-working employees who would eschew the evils of drink and, most important, not fall prey to the blandishments of union organizers" (*Company Towns of the Pacific Northwest*, 190).

48. Nelson Lichtenstein, "It's Workers Who Should Determine When Their Workplace Is Safe," *The American Prospect*, April 29, 2020; Melina Ey, " 'Soft, Airy Fairy Stuff'? Re-Evaluating 'Social Impacts' in Gendered Processes of Natural Resource Extraction," *Emotion, Space and Society* 27 (May 2018): 1–8; Shannon Elizabeth Bell and Richard York, "Coal, Injustice, and Environmental Destruction: Introduction to the Special Issue on Coal and the Environment," *Organization and Environment* 25, no. 4 (2012); Marion Fourcade, "The Fly and the Cookie: Alignment and Unhingement in 21st-Century Capitalism," *Socio-Economic Review* 15, no. 3 (2017): 661–78; Stephanie Malin, "There's No Real Choice but to Sign: Neoliberalization and Normalization of Hydraulic Fracturing on Pennsylvania Farmland," *Journal of Environmental Studies and Sciences* 4, no. 1 (2014): 17–27.

49. Mining firms had a vested interest in keeping good workers close, housed, and as reserve labor for inevitable mining booms and busts. For example, even when the Montreal Mining Company furloughed most of its seven hundred permanent workers during the post–World War I iron ore price decline, the company did not evict them from company housing. Workers remained in matching white houses, paying low rents, until in 1922, the Company rehired all employees and increased wages. While this maneuver was certainly appreciated by employees, the mine itself benefited by retaining its trained workforce; *Ironwood Daily Globe*, August 27, 1923, 34; Phil S. Hanna, "Slant of a Visitor," *Ironwood Daily Globe*, August 12, 1932; *Ironwood Daily Globe*, "Eight Years Ago," June 9, 1931; *Ironwood Daily Globe*, "Montreal Mine Goes on One Shift," May 27, 1920; *Ironwood Daily Globe*, "Mine Pay Schedule Increased," May 15, 1922.

50. Oglebay Norton, *Oglebay Norton Company: Montreal Mine 1886–1962*.

51. Liesch, *Ironwood, Hurley, and the Gogebic Range*, 79.

52. Benzoni, *Beyond the Mine*, 158; Mossey, *The Iron Ore Miner's Daughter*. Montreal Mine went on strike only once. The Cary Mine (nearby but beyond the geographic range of Montreal, WI) went on strike several times because its managers offered fewer nonincome/paternalistic benefits and had less control over employees. In the 1960s, the Cary Mine had a contract agreement with the Montreal Mine to use the Montreal medical services but at a cost (much lower than elsewhere).

53. Why the Wisconsin iron ranges unionized five to seven years after the National Labor Relations Act (NLRA) was passed in 1935 remains unexplained in the archives. I presume the implementation of local unions was slowed for two reasons—first, the range's geographic distance from organizers made it hard to access, and second, matching the correct trade union to the right mine might've been challenging, as some of the Gogebic mines were owned by their steel manufacturing companies, making them eligible to join the U.S. Steelworkers Union. Others were independent mines more suited for Iron Workers or similar unions.

54. Perhaps age and time matters—unions were active for only twenty years on the Iron Range, between the early 1940s and the 1960s. But when compared with Chicago, we can see how little impact they seemed to make. And silences in historical data regarding unions challenge that view. Instead, unions seemed most weakened by company towns. In exchange for the privileges of living in a middle-class community— solid wages, consistent employment, and all economic, health, and social needs fulfilled within a several-mile radius of the anchor industry— workers were dissuaded from seriously unionizing.

55. Benzoni, *Beyond the Mine*, 254.

56. As historians have effectively traced, welfare capitalism reproduced gender roles. Company managers paid nurses to visit workers' wives and teach them about hygiene and childhood health. Gertrude Beeks, *National Civic Federation Review*, vols. 1 and 2 (Brooklyn, NY: Williams & Co., 1904), 5–6.

57. Ann Markusen et al., *Steel and Southeast Chicago: Reasons and Opportunities for Industrial Renewal, a Research Report to the Mayor's Task Force on Steel and Southeast Chicago* (Evanston, IL: Northwestern University, Center of Urban Affairs and Policy Research, 1985).

58. The first generation of Chicago steelworkers integrated into a city already churning from rapid industrialization, working-class poverty, and, to the consternation of steel mill management, a culture of union organizing. Yet even though violence between workers and police at the McCormick manufacturing plant in 1893 as well as labor revolts in Pullman in 1894 occurred only three miles from the nascent steel communities, steelworkers remained unorganized well into the twentieth

century. Notably, McCormick was incorporated into International Harvester a handful of years before the firm acquired Brown's mill. In 1902, Chicago's International Harvester—a new amalgamation of three Chicago-based agricultural machinery companies: McCormick, Deering, and Plano—purchased Brown's mill to serve as a captive source of steel bars for its reapers and tractors. "Fearing that (Carnegie's U.S. Steel) would use its market power to raise prices artificially . . . Harvester organized its own steel division" (Bensman and Lynch, *Rusted Dreams*, 43). International Harvester owned all components of the steel commodity chain: iron and coal mines, Great Lakes freighters, ironworks, steel mills, and final manufacturing sites. International Harvester controlled more than 80 percent of world production in grain harvesting equipment and, at its peak in the 1920s and 1930s, managed six major manufacturing facilities in the Chicago area in addition to its steel mill that employed nearly 20,000 workers.

The sheer size of this collection of companies, combined with the repercussions of the late-nineteenth-century labor conflicts, doubtless informed the careful way that International Harvester's Wisconsin Steel interacted with workers. Workers at Wisconsin Steel never joined the United Steelworkers Union. Rather, Wisconsin Steel initiated an employee-run "Works Council" shortly after the nationwide steel strike of 1919 (Bensman and Lynch, *Rusted Dreams*). This council offered a controlled venue for worker complaints, promoted community gardens on company land, community baseball teams, and operated a credit union to fund members' purchase of homes. Wisconsin Steel's organization was one of the first employee representation plans (ERP) in the region—an experimental form of non-union-based, participatory mechanisms aimed at institutionalizing a "system of industrial peace" (Jennifer Klein, *For All These Rights: Business, Labor, and the Shaping of America's Public-Private Welfare State* [Princeton, NJ: Princeton University Press, 2006], 18). Ideally, ERPs were voluntary associations, comprised of "joint committees made up of management and labor representatives [who] discussed issues brought to them by either party and made recommendations." In practice, these Committees "beat back early attempts" of unionization by addressing grievances on an individual basis (Reynolds and Dawson, *Iron Will*, 148–49).

Wisconsin Steel's ERP seemed to do just that. When the national 1919 steel strike was issued, the fledgling Works Council asked its members to stay home rather than picket. When Harvester called its men back to work three weeks later, 70 percent of their labor force returned with enthusiasm (Cohen, *Making a New Deal*).

Combining corporate paternalism and worker cooperation, the Wisconsin Steel Works Council became the independent Progressive Steelworkers Union in 1937 (very notably, two years after the NLRA was established). Progressive negotiated its own contracts with Harvester, brought individual cases to arbitration, and voiced opinions in promotions, job assignments, and hiring. Since Progressive was an independent union, Wisconsin Steel was not bound by industrywide labor agreements negotiated by the Steelworkers Organizing Committee or, later, the United Steelworkers. However, Harvester's Wisconsin Steel matched the wages and benefits achieved by the national unions in exchange for Progressive never striking. This informal deal assured continual steel supplies for Harvester's tractor manufacturing plants and consistent, paid employment for Wisconsin Steelworkers. Even though it was situated in one of the most organized steel communities in the United States, Wisconsin Steel did not experience strikes for forty years (Bensman and Lynch, *Rusted Dreams*, 41). The tight overlap of home and work in Wisconsin Steel's isolated millgate neighborhood of South Deering set the neighborhood and its mill on a path toward a history of industrial relations that more closely paralleled the company towns emerging in the iron ore ranges of the Lake Superior mining district (Cohen, *Making a New Deal*).

See Klein, *For All These Rights*, for a thorough discussion of unionization at Wisconsin Steel, and Bensman and Lynch, *Rusted Dreams*, for a deep history of the company; "National Labor Relations Act," 1935, OurDocuments.Gov, https://www.ourdocuments.gov/doc.php?doc =67&flash =old&page=transcript.

59. See Kornblum, *Blue Collar Community*, for a thorough discussion of race in the mills.

60. In a May 26, 2005 oral history at the Southeast Chicago Historical Society, Alfred described "the definite ethnic problem with Hispanics and Black people in the early days of the steel industry. They were

always channeled into either labor gang, coke plant, yard department or such. And as years went on, little by little, those things changed [with] more civil rights. [But] we never had a Black man in the boiler shop until probably . . . in the '70s, you know."

61. Roger Biles, "Race and Housing in Chicago," *Journal of the Illinois State Historical Society (1998-)* 94, no. 1 (2001): 31–38; Arnold R. Hirsch, *Making the Second Ghetto: Race and Housing in Chicago 1940–1960* (Chicago: University of Chicago Press, 2009). More broadly, see Richard D. Alba and John R. Logan, "Minority Proximity to Whites in Suburbs: An Individual-Level Analysis of Segregation," *American Journal of Sociology* 98, no. 6 (1993): 1388–427; Douglas S. Massey and Brendan P. Mullan, "Processes of Hispanic and Black Spatial Assimilation," *American Journal of Sociology* 89, no. 4 (1984): 836–73; Ann Owens, "Inequality in Children's Contexts: Income Segregation of Households with and without Children," *American Sociological Review* 81, no. 3 (2016): 549–74; Merle Zwiers, Maarten van Ham, and David Manley, "Trajectories of Ethnic Neighbourhood Change: Spatial Patterns of Increasing Ethnic Diversity," *Population, Space and Place* 24 (2018): e2094.

62. William Julius Wilson, *When Work Disappears: The World of the New Urban Poor* (New York: Vintage, 1997).

63. Until the passage of the NLRA in 1935, companies had little incentive to acquiesce to worker demands for shorter workdays, mill or mine safety mechanisms, or basic safety gear, such as hard-toed boots. In Chicago, late-nineteenth-century trade unions (which had been responsible for several powerful, city-wide strikes earlier that century) were puzzled as to how to effectively cultivate membership in mass production industries. In 1903, the Chicago Federation of Labor claimed more than half of the city's workers as members. However, steel was notably absent from their rosters. The standard model of unionization did not suit the massive scale of steel manufacturing comprised of lower-skill tasks performed by a constant stream of easily replaced workers. As multiple labor histories (which this book is not) document, a new model of large-scale unionization would come to center around steel workers' interests. By the first major strike by steel in 1919, labor on the Southeast Side was skilled at organizing work stoppages and altercations with management over unsafe working conditions or unpredictable wage cuts. Other

scholarly and historical reports thoroughly discuss the 1919 strike (David Brody, *Steelworkers in America: The Non-Union Era* [New York: Harper-Collins, 1970]); Klein, *For All These Rights*; Cohen, *Making a New Deal*. The NLRA envisioned a form of unionization that, unlike the craft unions of the prior century, was organized around entire industries, regardless of skill or trade (Barry Eidlin, "Class vs. Special Interest: Labor, Power, and Politics in the United States and Canada in the Twentieth Century," *Politics & Society* 43, no. 2 [2015]: 181–211). Enacted the same year as FDR's Social Security Act, the NLRA guaranteed the rights of certain private-sector employees to organize into trade unions that could collectively bargain with employers for better terms and conditions at work and take action, including striking, if negotiations were not forthcoming. The Act aimed to rebalance the "inequality of bargaining power between employees who do not possess full freedom of association or actual liberty of contract and employers who are organized in the corporate or other forms of ownership association." Employers were required to recognize labor unions that a majority of their workforce joined. These unions had to be independent (not managed by the employer) and organized by representatives of the members' own choosing; Geoff Eley and Keith Nield, "Farewell to the Working Class?" *International Labor and Working-Class History* 57 (2000): 1–30; Rod Sellers, *Chicago's Southeast Side Revisited* (Chicago: Arcadia, 2001).

64. Racial integration was stunted at times by national organizations; the American Federation of Labor (AFL) was notoriously racialized through the mid-twentieth century. This is not a focus of this project, but for contemporaneous analysis of this issue, see Herbert Hill, "Racism Within Organized Labor: A Report of Five Years of the AFL-CIO, 1955–1960," *The Journal of Negro Education* 30, no. 2 (1961): 109–18.

65. Chicago oral histories were conducted by Chicago-area high school students in 2005 and transcribed and stored at the Southeast Chicago Historical Society; Osborne Calvin Ferguson, Oral History, Pos. 219, from the Southeast Chicago Historical Museum, May 14th, 2005.

66. Courtesy of the Southeast Chicago Historical Society.

67. Brian Thiede and Tim Slack, "The Old Versus the New Economies and Their Impacts," in *Rural Poverty in the United States*, ed. Ann

R. Tickamyer, Jennifer Sherman, and Jennifer Warlick (New York: Columbia University Press, 2017), 231–49.

68. U.S. Department of Labor, "100 Years of U.S. Consumer Spending: Data for the Nation, New York City, and Boston," 2006, http://www.bls.gov/opub/uscs/1960-61.pdf. Iron and steel workers were part of a larger pattern—across all levels of education, job experience, and occupation, the American middle class expanded between 1940 and 1970.

69. Jefferson Cowie and Joseph Heathcott, eds., *Beyond the Ruins: The Meanings of Deindustrialization* (Ithaca, NY: ILR Press, 2003), 4.

70. Some of the earliest analyses of capitalism noted the shift from home-based work to the process of wage earners physically leaving the private sphere and entering the public arena of employment to sell their labor on the open market. Class relations encompass *economic production* and *social reproduction*, which are two sides of the same coin, functioning as a "system of interdependent parts" (Michael Burawoy, "Neoclassical Sociology: From the End of Communism to the End of Classes," *American Journal of Sociology* 106, no. 4 [2001]: 1107). Companies played a vital role in setting the tone and context for the reproduction of labor—a process usually relegated to domestic spheres alone (Silvia Federici, *Patriarchy of the Wage: Notes of Marx, Gender, and Feminism* (Oakland, CA: PM Press, 2021.). Karl Marx considered the divorce of home and work as both central to primitive accumulation and one of the unintended consequences of the capitalist system. Unpaid laborers are left behind to manage tasks vital for the perpetuation of humanity, if undervalued by capital—people caring for the household, tending the ill and aged, and raising the next generation of wage laborers. This division between paid and unpaid labor is inherently gendered—a patriarchy of wage, as feminist Federici put it; see Karl Marx, "The Costs of Circulation," in *Capital*, vol. II, trans. I. Lasker (Moscow: Progress Publishers, 1956).

71. Norwood B. Melcher and Jachin M. Forbes, "Iron Ore," in *Bureau of Mines Minerals Yearbook, Year 1950* (Reston, VA: U.S. Geological Survey, 1953), 613–43.

72. Schultz, *Wisconsin's Foundations*, 52; Catherine Techtmann, *Rooted in Resources* (Friendship, WI: New Past Press, 1993).

73. "Report of Fact Finding Committee Appointed to Investigate and Report on the Iron Mining Industry in the Gogebic," 1961. Hard copy accessed at the Iron County Historical Society, Hurley, WI.

74. Elsewhere, labor historians capably review how companies intentionally constructed nonincome, welfare capitalist benefits as an alternative to the "humiliation" of dependency upon "charitable expenditures . . . of the State and municipal governments" (see Beeks, 1909, quoted in Andrea Tone, *The Business of Benevolence: Industrial Paternalism in Progressive America* [Ithaca, NY: Cornell University Press, 1997], 41). Avoiding dependency on state-based welfare systems reiterates patterns of reliance on employment—on the very structures of capitalism that allowed the rise—and furthered the fall—of the blue-collar middle class.

75. Steel cohered the linkages between "the melting of ore in the blast furnace through to the production of bolts, metal shelves and buildings, boilers, engines, finished rail cars, tractors, and automobiles." Via rail and waterways, the report continued, "about 87 percent of raw steel produced locally is shipped within the east and west north-central regions." Markusen et al., *Steel and Southeast Chicago*.

76. Unionized workers not only earned higher wages but also received more nonwage benefits than did nonunion jobs. Value-added manufacturing (smelting, cutting, rolling, and design) work was better paid than extractive work in rural regions due to a combination of the skill level of the labor, higher costs of living in urban settings, and more effective union activity in Chicago than in many mining locations. Rebecca M. Blank, "Why Has Economic Growth Been Such an Ineffective Tool Against Poverty in Recent Years?" in *Poverty and Inequality: The Political Economy of Redistribution*, ed. Jon Neill (Kalamazoo, MI: W. E. Upjohn Institute for Employment Research, 1997): 27–42.

77. Bensman and Lynch, *Rusted Dreams*; Rod Sellers concurred and wrote me this note: "When I graduated from high school in 1964 many of my friends went to work in the mills. I went to college and drove a 1955 automobile while my friends were driving various "muscle cars."

78. "Ward 10: Table DP-1. Profile of General Demographic Characteristics," Census 2000, 2003, https://drive.google.com/drive/folders/0B9vdVdII oXSCTlYoc18yVFhuVG8. Real Estate Center. 2019. "South Deering."

Institute for Housing Studies at DePaul University. 2019. https://www.housingstudies.org/data-portal/geography/south-deering.

79. "About Us," USX Federal Credit Union, March 5, 2021, https://www.usxfcu.org/about-us/.

80. Victor Storino Oral History, Pos. 110, from the Southeast Chicago Historical Museum, May 14, 2005.

81. Henri Lefebvre, *The Production of Space* (Oxford: Basil Blackwell, 1991), 26.

82. Derek Gregory and John Urry, eds., *Social Relations and Spatial Structures* (London: Macmillan, 1985), 30.

2. HOME WITHOUT THE COMPANY: DEINDUSTRIALIZING THE AMERICAN MIDWEST

1. "Pickands Mather and company announced Tuesday that operation of the Cary mine in Hurley will be terminated on January 28, 1965 and the operation of the Geneva Mine will be terminated on February 19, 1965. The closing of the two mines will throw some 454 men in the Gogebic Range area out of work." White Binder 1985 Iron County Historical Society, p. 72, clipped and pressed newspaper article entitled "Mines Here Get Closing Notice" by Robert Kending.

2. William Julius Wilson, *When Work Disappears: The World of the New Urban Poor* (New York: Vintage, 1997), 29–30.

3. Lori G. Kletzer, "Globalization and Job Loss, from Manufacturing to Services," *Economic Perspectives* 29, no. 2 (May 2005): 38–47; Jack Metzgar, "Blue-Collar Blues: The Deunionization of Manufacturing," *New Labor Forum*, no. 10 (Spring–Summer 2002): 20–23; Lee E. Ohanian, "Competition and the Decline of the Rust Belt," Federal Reserve Bank of Minneapolis, December 20, 2014, www.minneapolisfed.org/article/2014/competition-and-the-decline-of-the-rust-belt; Justin R. Pierce and Peter K. Schott, "The Surprisingly Swift Decline of US Manufacturing Employment," *American Economic Review* 106, no. 7 (2016): 1632–62; John Wasik, "It's No Thanksgiving for Wisconsin Workers," *Daily Calumet*, November 27, 1980, Chicago History Museum, Lumpkin Papers.

4. Between 1958 and 1985, Chicago's Cook County, Illinois, and neighboring Gary, Indiana, home of U.S. Steel's headquarters, lost 187,000

steel-related jobs. By the end of the twentieth century, the region had whittled their steel workforce down by half.

Ann Markusen et al., *Steel and Southeast Chicago: Reasons and Opportunities for Industrial Renewal, a Research Report to the Mayor's Task Force on Steel and Southeast Chicago* (Evanston, IL: Northwestern University, Center of Urban Affairs and Policy Research, 1985); Teresa L. Córdova and Matthew Wilson, "Abandoned in Their Neighborhoods: Youth Joblessness amidst the Flight of Industry and Opportunity," January 2017, https://greatcities.uic.edu/2017/01/29/abandoned -in-their-neighborhoods-youth-joblessness-amidst-the-flight-of -industry-and-opportunity/.

5. The most prominent of these were the Kennedy Round (1963–67), the Tokyo Round (1973–79), and the Uruguay Round (1986–94). José Pallares oral history, from the Southeast Chicago Historical Museum, May 14, 2005

6. "America's Uneasy History with Free Trade," *Harvard Business Review*, April 28, 2016, hbr.org/2016/04/americas-uneasy-history-with-free-trade. In comparison, tariffs were at 2.7 percent in 2013.

7. John C. Raines, Lenora E. Berson, and David Gracie, eds., *Community and Capital in Conflict: Plant Closings and Job Loss* (Philadelphia: Temple University Press, 1982); Steven High, *Industrial Sunset: The Making of North America's Rust Belt, 1969–1984* (Toronto: University of Toronto Press, 2003).

Before 1950, midwestern manufacturing companies had managed costs through a combination of strategic company consolidation, the cross-pollination of company representatives on competitors' boards, and successfully lobbying for favorable tariffs or tax laws. Following the first round of GATT negotiations, the same European and Japanese economies that had received reconstruction aid from the United States after World War II began to offer lower-priced ores and steel to American buyers. Great Lakes manufacturers and mines struggled to match plummeting prices.

8. Jeffrey T. Manuel, *Taconite Dreams: The Struggle to Sustain Mining on Minnesota's Iron Range, 1915–2000* (Minneapolis: University of Minnesota Press, 2015).

9. The Department of Labor defines displaced workers as "persons 20 years of age and older who lost or left jobs because their plant or company closed or moved, there was insufficient work for them to do, or their

position or shift was abolished." In the twentieth and early twenty-first century, the displacement of industrial jobs coincided with the increase of low-wage jobs with fewer benefits or avenues for advancement.

Labor Market Information Glossary, Employment Development Department, State of California, https://labormarketinfo.edd.ca.gov/LMID/Glossary_of_Terms.html; Ann R. Tickamyer, Jennifer Sherman, and Jennifer Warlick, "Politics and Policy: Barriers and Opportunities for Rural People," in *Rural Poverty in the United States*, ed. Ann R. Tickamyer, Jennifer Sherman, and Jennifer Warlick (New York: Columbia University Press, 2017): 239–52.

10. Victor Storino oral history, from the Southeast Chicago Historical Museum, May 14, 2005.

11. William R. Freudenburg, Scott Frickel, and Robert Gramling, "Beyond the Nature/Society Divide: Learning to Think About a Mountain," *Sociological Forum* 10, no. 3 (1995): 369.

12. Holly Fellman, "'Everything's a Rustin,'" *Iron County Miner*, June 5, 1964.

13. From archives: White Binder 1985 Iron County Historical Society. *Iron County Miner*, August 31, 1962. Physical copy photographed by author from newspaper clipping entitled "Montreal Mine Closing Effects in Dollars and Cents"; no author included in clip ping. Also accessible at https://www.newspapers.com/image/358535090/?terms=non-magnetic&match=1.

14. Milton Friedman, "The Case for Free Trade," *Hoover Digest*, no. 4 (1997): 42–49; N. Gregory Mankiw, "Why Voters Don't Buy It When Economists Say Global Trade Is Good," *New York Times*, July 29, 2016.

15. Dan Fuller and Doris Gied-Stevenson, "Consensus Among Economists," *Journal of Economic Review* 34, no. 4 (2003): 369–87.

16. While criticism of both free trade and regulation aligns with Iron County's overwhelmingly Republican base, these two comments still hint at a surprising environmental consciousness. In a theme that will reemerge in chapter 5, residents recognize the value of regulation in protecting natural places even if they decry its dissuading effect on new extractive development in their own home region.

17. This view was predominant. "In a sense," argued the journalist James Fallows in a 1985 *Atlantic* essay, "the difference is merely symbolic: nearly 70 percent of employed Americans work in service industries,

and services have employed more people than manufacturing for at least a hundred years."

18. And even as a new wave of automation replaced certain manual labor jobs, proponents point out that technology created more jobs than it has replaced. Even during the height of the late-twentieth-century recession—between 1989 and 1992—nearly one and a half million job losses in blue-collar industries were corrected for by almost three million new occupations requiring social skills like health, education, or social services. However, in contrast to iron and steel work, service jobs typically required a high school or college degree even though they paid a fraction of what entry-level industrial positions had offered. Even today, service jobs often involve nonstandard employment arrangements such as subcontracting or part-time hours that keep employees from qualifying for pensions, health insurance, or paid time off. Service work emerged as the dominant employment sector because the same economic drivers that caused deindustrialization catalyzed industry's *economic displacement*—the permanent disappearance of an entire category of employment from a particular location. Without the option to return to these now-extinct jobs, only two-thirds of trade-displaced workers tend to find new work. When compared to people who lose jobs for other reasons, displaced workers tend to be older, less educated, and experience longer periods of unemployment before finding a new job if they find one at all. Reemployment is a challenge in part because not only do these workers have fewer transferable skills but also typically earned higher-than-average wages in the job they lost, making new, lower-wage jobs for which they are qualified less appealing.

Jennie E. Brand, "The Far-Reaching Impact of Job Loss and Unemployment," *Annual Review of Sociology* 41, no. 1 (2015): 359 75; Arne L. Kalleberg, "Precarious Work, Insecure Workers: Employment Relations in Transition," *American Sociological Review* 74 (2009): 1–22; Arne L. Kalleberg, Michael Wallace, and Robert P. Althauser, "Economic Segmentation, Worker Power, and Income Inequality," *American Journal of Sociology* 87, no. 3 (1981): 651–83; National Research Council (US) and Institute of Medicine (US) Committee on the Health and Safety Needs of Older Workers, "The Role of the Changing Labor Market and the Changing Nature of Work in Older Workers' Work

Experiences and Health Outcomes," in *Health and Safety Needs of Older Workers*, ed. D. H. Wegman and J. P. McGee (Washington, D.C.: National Academies Press, 2004).

19. The economic efficiencies of capital mobility sound good to "people who are confident they'll always end up being winners," as the journalist Neil Irwin mused: "How a Quest by Elites Is Driving 'Brexit' and Trump," *New York Times*, July 1, 2016.

20. Federally backed pension guarantees were instituted in 1974, as part of the Employee Retirement Income Security Act of 1974. Not all pensions are backed or guaranteed. See https://www.pbgc.gov/about for more information.

21. Victor Sterino oral history, from the Southeast Chicago Historical Museum, May 5, 2005.

22. For more than sixty years, International Harvester was both owner and primary customer of Wisconsin Steel, steadily ordering steel rods and sheeting needed for Harvester's tractors, combines, and hay balers. Beginning in the late 1960s, Harvester was shaken by significant international competition and declines in American farming.

23. See David Bensman and Roberta Lynch, *Rusted Dreams: Hard Times in a Steel Community* (Berkeley: University of California Press, 1989), for an excellent history of Wisconsin Steel and Walley (2013) for an autoethnography of Wisconsin Steel's closure.

24. Mike Giocondo, "Wisconsin Workers Fight to Reopen Mill," *Daily World*, April 10, 1980. Chicago History Museum, Lumpkin box 3, folder 1.

25. Selling the mill was a good financial bet for International Harvester. After more than a decade, a suit between International Harvester and the federal government compelled the company to pay workers $14.8 million in delayed pension claims—a mere fraction of the money Envirodyne lost in the purchase of the mill. In 1995, the company was forced to issue one-tenth of backpay in the form of stocks (Wasik, "It's No Thanksgiving for Wisconsin Workers"; R. C. Longworth, "Chicago Wisconsin Steel Workers Still Seeking What's Theirs," *Chicago Tribune*, June 30, 1982, Southeast Chicago History Museum, Lumpkin box 4, folder 2; R. C. Longworth, "Wisconsin Steel Deal May End Ex-Workers' Agony: After 15 Years, Stock Offered to Pensioners," *Chicago Tribune*,

December 9, 1995, http://articles.chicagotribune.com/1995-12-09/news
/9512090180_1_workers-wisconsin-steel-pension-claims.

26. Jacob Kaplan, "South Works—Forgotten Chicago: History, Architecture, and Infrastructure," Forgotten Chicago History Architecture and Infrastructure RSS, last updated on December 28, 2008, forgottenchicago.com/articles/south-works/.

27. Economists have also observed the role of powerful labor unions, such as the United Steelworkers, in intentionally limiting a competitive labor market—that is, the market wage rate determined through the interaction of supply and demand in the labor market (see Kristoffer Smemo, Samir Sonti, and Gabriel Winant, "Conflict and Consensus: The Steel Strike of 1959 and the Anatomy of the New Deal Order," *Critical Historical Studies* [Spring 2017]: 39–73.) There is a popular narrative that high wage rates contributed significantly to the collapse of the American steel industry. Certainly, unions effectively negotiated higher wages through the use of labor strikes and strike threats, thus enabling the average Rust Belt worker to enjoy a 12 percent wage premium when compared with other U.S. workers of similar education, experience, and gender. Some economists argue that union-negotiated wages made certain manufacturing industries underprepared to respond to economic shifts with agility and creativity. However, the view that wage rates caused the collapse of the nation's steel industry has been largely debunked. Labor cost differentials are reported on national levels but may, in fact, misrepresent regional differences.

In a report for the city of Chicago, Markusen et al., in *Steel and Southeast Chicago*, point out, "Chicago steelworker earnings are lower than those in competitor regions." Steelworker base pay did respond to economic crises and company negotiations for wage concessions, dropping from $12 an hour to $10 in 1985. With additional incentive pay, overtime, and shift differentials, the report authors observed, "In 1985, steelworkers' average hourly earnings, adjusted for inflation, were below what they had been in 1977." American steelmaking wage rates were higher than those in other steelmaking nations, although a major portion of the differential is accounted for by bias in exchange rates. "This figure (of $26/hour) is inflated because U.S. firms, who are free to lay off or retire workers during downturns, add the costs of unemployment benefits, pensions, and insurance for these displaced workers into the hourly compensation figure. These figures sometimes include the white-collar salaries and benefits, estimated to be 50 percent of total employment costs." Labor costs may have increased the financial strain of companies, but they were not the straw that broke the camel's back.

28. Steven High and David W. Lewis, *Corporate Wasteland: The Landscape and Memory of Deindustrialization* (Ithaca, NY: Cornell University Press, 2007). United Steelworkers lost 105,000 members and disbanded more than one thousand local branches between 1979 and 1983.

29. Lumpkin papers, Chicago History Museum. The Wisconsin Steel's Progressive Steel Workers Union (PSWU) was an independent union, often called a "company union." Raises and benefits won by this union unaffiliated with the United Steelworkers' Union were pegged to USW's raises. This is another reason that Frank Lumpkin and the Save Our Jobs Committee worked independently from USW.

30. Matthew Liesch, *Ironwood, Hurley, and the Gogebic Range* (Chicago: Arcadia, 2006); Jeffrey T. Manuel, *Taconite Dreams: The Struggle to Sustain Mining on Minnesota's Iron Range, 1915–2000*, 2015.
    Iron Mining Association of Minnesota, "Minnesota's Iron Mining Industry," (Duluth: Iron Mining Association of Minnesota, 2014).

31. "Oglebay Norton Company History," Funding Universe: International Directory of Company Histories, 1997, http://www.fundinguniverse.com /company-histories/oglebay-norton-company-history/.

32. Oglebay Norton Company 1961 letter from physical archives, Iron County Historical Society, Hurley, Wisconsin.

33. Della E. Rucker, "National Register of Historic Places Registration Form: Plummer Mine Headframe," OMB No. 10024–0018. Iron County Historical Society Records. Green Bay, WI, 1992.

34. Citizenship rights include workplace benefits, or access to material goods provided by the company according to Fred Block and Margaret R. Somers, *The Power of Market Fundamentalism: Karl Polanyi's Critique* (Cambridge, MA: Harvard University Press, 2014), 111.

35. James Simmie and Ray Brady, "Middle Class Decline in Post-Industrial Society," *Long Range Planning* 22, no. 4 (1989): 52–62.

36. Barry Bluestone and Bennett Harrison, *The Deindustrialization of America: Plant Closings, Community Abandonment, and the Dismantling of Basic Industry* (New York: Basic Books, 1982);.

37. According to the CPI Inflation Calculator (https://www.bls.gov/data /inflation_calculator.htm), $70,000 in 1984 is worth $179,920.89 in 2023, and $7,000 is worth $17,992.

38. According to the 1985 Federal Poverty Income Guidelines, the poverty line for Richard's family of five was $12,450. Their household income was $4,450 less. See "The 1985 Federal Poverty Income Guidelines," *Social Security Bulletin* 48, no. 7 (1985): 48.

39. Michelle Lamont, *The Dignity of Working Men: Morality and the Boundaries of Race, Class and Immigration* (Cambridge: Cambridge University Press, 2000).

40. For instance, these studies include Alanen's work on mining towns (Alanen, Arnold. "The Planning of Company Communities in the Lake Superior Mining Region." Journal of the American Planning Association 45, no. 3 (1979): 256–78.); Steven High's overview of deindustrialization across North America (*Industrial Sunset: The Making of North America's Rust Belt, 1969–1984.* [Toronto, Buffalo, London: University of Toronto Press, 2003]; and Kathryn Marie Dudley's study of manufacturing closure in Wisconsin (*End of the Line: Lost Jobs, New Lives in Postindustrial America.* [Chicago: University of Chicago Press, 1994]). Research on the Farm Crisis also speaks to similar issues; see Kathryn Marie Dudley, *Debt and Dispossession: Farm Loss in America's Heartland* (Chicago: University of Chicago Press, 2000).

41. Christine J. Walley, "Deindustrializing Chicago: A Daughter's Story," in *The Insecure American: How We Got Here and What We Should Do About It*, ed. Hugh Gusterson and Besteman, Catherine Lowe, (Oakland, CA: University of California Press, 2010), 113–39; Christine J. Walley, *Exit Zero: Family and Class in Postindustrial Chicago* (Chicago: University of Chicago Press, 2013).

42. Pierce and Schott, "The Surprisingly Swift Decline of US Manufacturing Employment."

43. Markusen et al., *Steel and Southeast Chicago.*

44. Standing, "The Precariat," 10–12.

45. Lori G. Kletzer, "Globalization and Job Loss, from Manufacturing to Services," *Economic Perspectives* 29, no. 2 (May 2005): 38–47.

46. Amanda Weinstein, "When More Women Join the Workforce, Wages Rise—Including for Men," *Harvard Business Review*, January 31, 2018.

47. For decades, Southeast Chicago steel companies had negotiated expansions of nonincome benefits with unions—not exactly paternalism, like in Wisconsin, but benefits like pensions, loans from company credit unions, training programs, and insurance. Nonincome benefits were negotiated by unions and offered by companies seeking to reward people for multiyear, loyal employment. As benefits accrued over time, workers were motivated to being working at the mills straight out of high school with the expectation of living in the same neighborhood and working with their company until retirement. The structure of nonincome benefits encouraged residential stability.

48. William R. Freudenburg, "Addictive Economies: Extractive Industries and Vulnerable Localities in a Changing World Economy," *Rural Sociology* 57, no. 3 (1992): 305–32; Tomas Havranek, Roman Horvath, and Ayaz Zeynalov, "Natural Resources and Economic Growth: A meta-analysis," *World Development* 88 (December 2016): 134–51; J. Tom Mueller, "Natural Resource Dependence and Rural American Economic Prosperity from 2000 to 2015," *Economic Development Quarterly* 36, no. 3 (2022): 160–76.

49. White Binder 1985 Iron County Historical Society (p. 30). "Montreal Mine Closing Effects in Dollars and Cents," August 31, 1962, in *Iron County Miner*, 1.

50. Michael Hout, "How Class Works: Objective and Subjective Aspects of Class Since the 1970s," in *Social Class: How Does It Work*, ed. A. Lareau and D. Conley (New York: Russell Sage Foundation, 2008), 25–65; Michèle Lamont, "Addressing Recognition Gaps," 419–44; Benjamin Sosnaud et al., "Class in Name Only: Subjective Class Identity, Objective Class Position, and Vote Choice in American Presidential Elections," *Social Problems* 60, no. 1 (2013): 81–99; Marc W. Steinberg, "'The Labour of the Country Is the Wealth of the Country': Class Identity, Consciousness, and the Role of Discourse in the Making of the English Working Class," *International Labor and Working-Class History* 49, no. 49 (1996): 1–25; Loic Wacquant, "Symbolic Power and Group-Making: On Bourdieu's Reframing of Class," *Journal of Classical Sociology* 13, no. 2 (2013): 274–91.

51. Alan Abramowitz and Ruy Teixeira, "The Decline of the White Working Class and the Rise of a Mass Upper Middle Class," *Political Science*

Quarterly 124, no. 3 (2009): 391–422; Guy Standing, "The Precariat," *Contexts* (2014): 10–13; Erik Olin Wright, "Is the Precariat a Class?" *Global Labour Journal* 7, no. 2 (2016): 123–35.

52. Pierce and Schott, "The Surprisingly Swift Decline of US Manufacturing Employment,"; Anne Case and Angus Deaton, *Deaths of Despair and the Future of Capitalism* (Princeton, NJ: Princeton University Press, 2020); Lawrence King, Gábor Scheiring, and Elias Nosrati, "Deaths of Despair in Comparative Perspective," *Annual Review of Sociology* 48 (2022): 299–317; Michèle Lamont, *The Dignity of Working Men: Morality and the Boundaries of Race, Class, and Immigration* (Cambridge, MA: Harvard University Press, 2000); Seth Abrutyn and Anna S. Mueller, "Toward a Cultural-Structural Theory of Suicide: Examining Excessive Regulation and Its Discontents," *Sociological Theory* 36, no. 1 (2018): 60

53. Kai Erikson, *Everything in Its Path: Destruction of Community in the Buffalo Creek Flood* (New York: Simon & Schuster, 1976), 200.

54. Ann Swidler, "Culture in Action: Symbols and Strategies," *American Sociological Review* 51, no. 2 (1986): 273–86; Stephen Vaisey, "Motivation and Justification: A Dual-Process Model of Culture in Action," *American Journal of Sociology* 114, no. 6 (2009): 1675–715.

Pierre Bourdieu and Loïc Wacquant wrote that "rational choice may take over" in "times of crisis" when "the routine adjustment of subjective and objective structures is brutally disrupted"—rational choice referring to nonhabitual and explicit problem-solving: "Symbolic Capital and Social Classes," *Journal of Classical Sociology* 13, no. 2 (2013): 292–302.

55. Aliza Luft, "Theorizing Moral Cognition: Culture in Action, Situations, and Relationships," *Socius: Sociological Research for a Dynamic World* 6 (2020): 1–15.

3. HOW TO STAY IN THE RUST BELT: WORK, CHOICE, AND HOME IN THE DECADE AFTER COMPANY CLOSURE

1. Lee Huskey, Matthew Berman, and Alexandra Hill, "Leaving Home, Returning Home: Migration as a Labor Market Choice for Alaska Natives," *The Annals of Regional Science* 38, no. 1 (2004): 75–92.

2. U.S. Census Bureau, "Iron County, Wisconsin," QuickFacts. 2015, http://www.census.gov/quickfacts/table/PST045215/55051; Timothy Smeeding, Julia Isaacs, and Katherine Thornton, *Wisconsin Poverty Report*, Institute for Research on Poverty, May 2014; State of Wisconsin Department of Workforce Development, 2015 Annual Report, https://dwd.wisconsin.gov/dwd/pdf/annual-report-2015.pdf.

3. This is likely conservative, taking into account net out-migration, rate of in-migration across decades, rates of homeownership, rates of free-and-clear (mortgage paid off) homeownership. See the introduction for more details.

4. Kelly Main and Gerardo Francisco Sandoval, "Placemaking in a Translocal Receiving Community: The Relevance of Place to Identity and Agency," *Urban Studies* 52, no. 1 (2015): 71–86.

5. Rebecca Elliot, *Underwater: Loss, Flood Insurance, and the Moral Economy of Climate Change in the United States* (New York: Columbia University Press, 2021); Aliza Luft, "Theorizing Moral Cognition: Culture in Action, Situations, and Relationships," *Socius: Sociological Research for a Dynamic World 6* (2020): 2378023120916112.

6. William Julius Wilson, *When Work Disappears: The World of the New Urban Poor* (New York: Vintage, 1997), 142–43.

7. Interviewees discussed only legal informal work with me, but these side hustles were likely extralegal in some cases. Emily J. Wornell, Leif Jensen, Ann R. Tickamyer, "The role of informal work in the livelihood strategies of U.S. households," in *The Informal Economy: Exploring Drivers and Practices*, ed. Ioana A. Horodnic, Peter Rogers, Colin C. Williams, and Legha Momtazian, 117–38 (London: Routledge Publishing, 2017).

   Leif Jensen, Ann R. Tickamyer, and Tim Slack, "Rural-Urban Variation in Informal Work Activities in the United States," *Journal of Rural Studies* 68 (2019): 276–84; Jennifer Sherman, *Those Who Work, Those Who Don't: Poverty, Morality, and Family in Rural America* (Minneapolis: University of Minnesota Press, 2009); Tim Slack et al., "Social Embeddedness, Formal Labor Supply, and Participation in Informal Work," *International Journal of Sociology and Social Policy* 37, nos. 3–4 (2017): 248–64.

8. Today, the few paper mills left in northern Wisconsin no longer require debarked aspen.

9. Stewart Lockie, Maree Franettovich, Vanessa Petkova-Timmer, John Rolfe, Galina Ivanova. "Coal Mining and the Resource Community Cycle," *Environmental Impact Assessment Review* 29, no. 5 (2009): 330–39; Hudson Ray and David Sadler, "Contesting Works Closures in Western Europe's Old Industrial Regions: Defending Place or Betraying Class?" in *Reading Economic Geography*, ed. T. J. Barnes, J. Peck, E. Sheppard, and A. Tickell (Oxford: Blackwell, 2004); Cecily Neil, Markku Tykkyläinen, and John Bradbury, *Coping with Closure—An International Comparison of Mine Town Experiences* (London: Routledge, 1992), xvii, 427.

10. Commutes long and short brought locations that were once unimaginable to millgate or company town residents into the practical decisions of everyday life. The newly unemployed echoed trends across the United States. Beginning in 1970, the U.S. Census observed that both the time spent commuting and the distance traveled to access work increased by several percentage points. Since the turn of the twenty-first century, commuting trends have leveled out as workers adjust to driving an average twenty-five minutes to their workplaces. Since 1990, the time spent commuting has increased by three minutes. Since 1980, the number of people driving alone (rather than in carpools or on a bus) has increased by little more than 10 percent. Between 1980 and 2000, commuting by public transit and by walking decreased by several percentage points and never recovered. Brian McKenzie, "Commuting Patterns," https://web.archive.org/web/20210329130228/https://www.census.gov/newsroom/cspan/2013/commuting.html.

11. Rural counties comprise the majority of U.S. counties classified as farming-dependent (92 percent), mining-dependent (88 percent), manufacturing-dependent (65 percent), and federal- and state-government-dependent (55 percent) (U.S. Economic Research Service as cited in Tim Slack, "Work in Rural America in the Era of Globalization," in *Rural America in a Globalizing World: Problems and Prospects for the 2010s*, ed. C. Bailey, L. Jensen, and E. Ransom (Morgantown: West Virginia University Press, 2014), 573–90).

12. Researchers note that long commutes divert energy from the very activities employed workers often seek to preserve. Stephan J. Goetz et al., "U.S. Commuting Networks and Economic Growth: Measurement and Implications for Spatial Policy," *Growth and Change* 41, no. 2 (2010):

276–302; Daniel T. Lichter and David L. Brown, "Rural America in an Urban Society: Changing Spatial and Social Boundaries," *Annual Review of Sociology* 37, no. 1 (2011): 565–92; Robert Putnam, in *Bowling Alone: The Collapse and Revival of American Community* (New York: Simon & Schuster, 2000), 213, notes that "each additional ten minutes in daily commuting time cuts involvement in community affairs by 10 percent."

13. Another narrative: Julian, who took over his dad's small logging business in the woods behind the company town, ended up traveling to look for new buyers when their primary customer—the iron mine—closed. While the work was inherently place-based, the markets weren't. "I forget what year—someplace in the mid-1970s—I was falling short of markets on pulpwood, so I told the wife, 'We're going to take a ride. We're going to make a U-ey [U-turn] in Wisconsin, visit the pulp mills, tell them our situation—that we've been logging almost all our lives, and here we've got no markets.' " The entrepreneurial commute brought in a handful of far-flung customers hours south who soon expected regular deliveries from Julian's forest plot.

14. Shawn Malia Kanaiaupuni, "Sustaining Families and Communities: Nonmigrant Women and Mexico-U.S. Migration Processes," *Center for Demography and Ecology* 41 (2000), https://cde.wisc.edu/wp-2000-13/.

15. Manufacturing employers were disproportionally located on the Southeast Side of the city. For those who could get long-term and well-paying jobs, employment in this new generation of work was rarely available locally. The sociologist William Julius Wilson observed that one of the biggest consequences of deindustrialization for the working class—and African Americans in particular—was the spatial mismatch between the newly suburbanized sites of employment and the residential neighborhoods where the former workers lived. Hampered by the implicit requirement to own a personal vehicle for commuting due to severely limited public transportation between the city and certain suburbs and often dissuaded by explicit racism, rates of unemployment among African America blue-collar workers outpaced their white peers. William Julius Wilson, *The Truly Disadvantaged: The Inner City, the Underclass, and Public Policy* (Chicago: University of Chicago Press, 1987).

Theresa Córdova and Matthew Wilson suggest that in Chicago, like in many locations, "joblessness is a function of structural changes in the economy that date back several decades." In 1957, large numbers of jobs were located throughout Chicago's zip codes with an expansive area making up Chicago's central area. By 2015, jobs became centralized toward the Loop, and the South and West Sides of Chicago in particular had fewer jobs. Teresa L. Cordova and Matthew Wilson, "Abandoned in Their Neighborhoods: Youth Joblessness amidst the Flight of Industry and Opportunity," January 2017, https://greatcities.uic.edu/2017/01/29/abandoned-in-their-neighborhoods-youth-joblessness-amidst-the-flight-of-industry-and-opportunity/.

16. David Bensman and Roberta Lynch, *Rusted Dreams: Hard Times in a Steel Community* (Berkeley: University of California Press, 1989).

17. These forms of movement made Iron County and Southeast Chicago gender-segregated in new ways, as left-behind family members—typically women—worked to create continuity for children, invested in extended family relationships, and maintained the house and home to which men returned. Michael Burawoy, "The Functions and Reproduction of Migrant Labor: Comparative Material from Southern Africa and the United States," American Journal of Sociology 81, no. 5 (1976): 1050–87.

18. Laurent Gobillon, Harris Selod, and Yves Zenou, "The Mechanisms of Spatial Mismatch," *Urban Studies* 44, no. 12 (2007): 2401–27; Seth King, "President Signs Job Training Bill, Calling It an End to Boondoggle," *New York Times*, October 14, 1982.

19. Chicago Metropolitan Agency for Planning, "Commute Time Trends," December 3, 2015, https://www.cmap.illinois.gov/updates/all/-/asset_publisher/UIMfSLnFfMB6/content/commute-time-trends-in-the-cmap-region.

20. Gordon Lafer, *The Job Training Charade* (Ithaca, NY: Cornell University Press, 2004).

As both cause and consequence of closure, the machinery that miners managed for deep shaft iron mining grew obsolete as industrial engineers perfected new strip-mining methods. And in the steel industry, automation supplanted the team-based millwork that produced metals products through the twentieth century. In both cases, a handful of interviewees took advantage of the government-subsidized retraining programs; these programs have been a bipartisan center-piece of federal responses to economic crisis ever since rural vocational education employed out-of-work men in the Great Depression. Each iteration of jobs training support echoed Reagan's vision of a federal program that "will train more than one million Americans every year in skills they can market."

Transitional assistance to those who experience job loss due to economic restructuring may also be of more value in areas where other job opportunities are more limited. When there are fewer jobs available, it takes longer to find the next job. For instance, unemployment spells are longer in rural areas due to differences in job growth rates and in personal skill characteristics. Reemployment problems may be particularly severe when the primary local industry experiences economic difficulties and large numbers of people are displaced from jobs. These locations are exactly the ones that might benefit most from extended unemployment insurance payments or targeted job loss assistance such as Trade Adjustment Assistance. In rural areas with limited alternative employment options, support for unemployed and displaced workers may need to be differently designed as well as available for a longer period of time.

21. White Binder 1985 ICHS (p. 30)—"Montreal Mine Closing Effects in Dollars and Cents." Based, in part, on the results of the test and educational information provided by state representatives, some miners returned to school through federal funding provided by the short-lived Area Redevelopment Administration (ARA).

22. Mitchell was one of five interviewees from both cases who recalled using government-funded retraining programs intended to aid "trade-displaced workers"—those in the working class unlikely to find a new job in their old occupation due to the trade-driven contraction of an industry. The Kennedy administration funded several programs: the Job Corps for the youngest workers, the Area Development Act for retraining efforts in "depressed areas" like Iron County, and, through the Labor Department, the Trade Adjustment Assistance fund to pay for retraining for workers whose jobs were moving overseas. Personal communication with the industrial historian Jeff Manuel suggests

that the job retraining in the early 1960s in Iron County was likely the result of the Area Development Act of 1961, which created the ARA. While this program was short-lived, it provided federal funds for job retraining efforts in 'depressed areas' through the auspices of local or state-level agencies. "In essence," Manuel advised me, "it was an attempt to revive the New Deal regional planning model in the postwar era."

23. These programs were aimed at solving the mismatch between workers' skills and their geographical location. Beginning with the Kennedy administration, every presidential administration has pushed through legislation funding retraining programs. Rather than address the macroeconomic causes of permanent closures of blue-collar industrial facilities, historians show, policymakers on both sides of the aisle consistently argued that mass job losses was evidence of the lack of agility of American workers to meet changing, occupational demands of a globalizing economy. But federally funded job retraining programs were often as short-lived and sporadically funded as their political contexts, and they aimed to fix skill problems in aggregate without addressing the geographic dislocation of employment. For these reasons, only a handful of my interviewees utilized these federally subsidized job training programs.

To address the growing problem of mass unemployment among dislocated workers who were unlikely to return to their previous industry or occupation due to the permanent closure of a plant or facility, the Nixon administration updated legislation to aid trade-displaced workers in the 1970s, and the Reagan administration passed the Job Training Partnership Act (JTPA) in 1982. In 1973 and 1974, Nixon signed Congress's Comprehensive Employment and Training Act to train workers for jobs in public service and enacted Trade Adjustment Assistance with the Trade Act of 1974 to help trade-affected workers find reemployment at suitable wages. More recent attempts to address limitations to existing programs include the Clinton administration formally repealing the Act and replacingd many of its provisions with the Workforce Investment Act of 1998.In his administration, Obama attempted to consolidate the forty-seven federal job training programs across nine agencies in the Workforce Innovation and Opportunity

Act; Jeffery Selingo, "The False Promises of Worker Retraining," *Atlantic*, January 8, 2018.

24. Peter M. Blau and Otis Dudley Duncan, *The American Occupational Structure* (New York: Wiley, 1967).

25. Selingo, "The False Promises of Worker Retraining." Ronald D'Amico and Peter Z. Schochet, The Evaluation of the Trade Adjustment Assistance Program: A Synthesis of Major Findings, U.S. Department of Labor, Washington, DC, December 2012;

26. Lafer, *The Job Training Charade*.

27. David Ventura, oral history, Position 100, Southeast Chicago Historical Museum, February 17, 2006.

28. Wilson, *When Work Disappears*.

29. Andrew Hurley, *Environmental Inequalities: Class Race and Industrial Pollution in Gary, Indiana 1945–1980* (Chapel Hill: University of North Carolina Press, 1995).

30. It is possible that interviewees benefited indirectly from this programming when, for instance, a new employer used federal funding to subsidize the costs of their on-the-job training. But this did not come up in interviews, suggesting that study participants did not experience job training as a memorable tool for strategizing next steps for employment.

31. In his study of blue-collar job loss in an African American neighborhood only a few miles north of the steel mill region, William Julius Wilson traced the roots of this geographic mismatch to the pernicious blend of residential segregation, economic restructuring, and the suburbanization of employment. In his 1997 book, he said, "Over the last two decades, 60 percent of the new jobs created in the Chicago metropolitan area have been located in the northwest suburbs of Cook and du Page counties. African Americans constitute less than 2 percent of the population in these areas. . . . One result of these changes for many urban blacks has been a growing mismatch between the suburban location of employment and minorities' residence in the inner city" (*When Work Disappears*, 37).

32. Christopher added that his certified apprenticeship made it "it easy to get jobs." Within a month of losing his position at U.S. Steel, he was

driving to manufacturing plants an hour away in the suburbs with his certification as an industrial electrician in hand. Just before his unemployment benefits ran out, he found work. That first position didn't last long—macroeconomic changes were undermining manufacturing sectors across the United States by the 1990s. But every time a manufacturing plant made his position redundant, he would apply for unemployment or pick up shifts at the local McDonald's and wait for the next job opening.

33. While there is certainly a wage premium for a college education, less than one-third of all jobs require a degree. Lafer writes, "In the two-thirds of the labor market where college degrees are not required, the relationship between education and wages is extremely weak" (*The Job Training Charade*, 12–13). Although most participants of the JTPA came from manufacturing, Lafer finds that only about 7 percent of eligible workers took advantage of free retraining programs, and those few who participated faced disappointing wages symptomatic of a nationally declining economy. While in aggregate, 69 percent of trainees funded by the federal government in 1987 got jobs in their fields, they were paid lower wages than similar jobs the previous decade. According to William J. Gainer, Nixon- and Reagan-era job training programs funded aptitude tests, classes at nearby colleges, and certification programs for the newly unemployed aimed at teaching skills for a new economy. City economic development officials quickly realized that the best training programs were agile enough to change tack and alter educational offerings that mirrored the rapidly changing needs of a region. William J. Gainer, "Statement of William J. Gainer, Associate Director, Human Resources Division before the Subcommittee on Employment Opportunities House Committee on Education and Labor on the Job Training Partnership Act, Title III Dislocated Worker Program," Washington, DC, November 8, 1985, https://www.gao.gov/assets/110/101191.pdf.

34. People with strong levels of place attachment are less willing to learn new employment-related skills which enable them to relocate elsewhere. See N. A. Marshall et al., "Transformational Capacity and the Influence of Place and Identity," *Environmental Research Letters* 7, no. 3 (2012): 034022.

4. STORIES OF HOUSE, LANDSCAPE, COMMUNITY: NARRATING THE DECLINING ACTION OF DEINDUSTRIALIZATION

1. As contemporary interviewees' narratives continued beyond the 1980s and 1990s, many explained their motivation to continue living in Iron County and Southeast Chicago in increasingly abstract terms. While I do not presuppose that residential stability is always motivated—some people stayed because of layers upon layers of intentional decisions and great reflection, while others seemed to have remained in place out of habit or coincidence—I found interviewees intentionally motivated their persistence in place with language defining their affection for both their geographies and their remnant social worlds. For more analysis of motivations, consider the range of motives studied by sociologists: intuitive motives (see Stephen Vaisey, "Motivation and Justification: A Dual-Process Model of Culture in Action," *American Journal of Sociology* 114, no. 6 [2009]: 1675–715; dispositional motives (*Pierre Bourdieu, Outline of a Theory of Practice* [Cambridge: Cambridge University Press, 1977]); habitual motives (John Dewey, *Human Nature and Conduct: An Introduction to Social Psychology* [New York: Holt, 1922]); and Alfred Schutz, "Tiresias, or Our Knowledge of Future Events," in *Collected Papers*, vol. 2: *Studies in Social Theory*, ed. A. Brodersen [The Hague: Martinus Nijhoff, 1964], 277–93).

2. Southeast Chicago (zip code 60617) is currently 56 percent owner-occupied, with nearly half of those homeowners (45 percent) living free and clear of mortgage payments. 43 percent of the housing stock on the Southeast Side is rental. "Ward 10: Table DP-1. Profile of General Demographic Characteristics," Census 2000, 2003. "ZCTA60617, DP04 Selected Housing Characteristics." US Census Bureau, Washington, D.C., 2021. https://data.census.gov/table?t=Homeownership%20Rate&g=860XX00US60617. Today, nearly 90 percent of houses in Iron County are owner-occupied and 50 percent of Iron County homeowners have paid off their mortgages. This contrasts with the Wisconsin state-wide homeownership rate of 68 percent and the national average of only 35 percent. "Iron County, Wisconsin DP04 Selected Housing Characteristics." US Census Bureau, Washington, D.C., 2021. https://data.census.gov/cedsci/profile?g=0500000US55051.

3. J. W. Duyvendak, *The Politics of Home: Belonging and Nostalgia in Europe and the United States* (Basingstoke, UK: Palgrave Macmillan, 2011).

4. The proportion of owner-occupied houses has also lingered above regional and national averages, suggesting that this localized buyers' market might be dissuading residents from selling their undervalued house. Poverty and unemployment rates in both Southeast Chicago and northern Wisconsin have remained unabated in the double digits, even as national rates dropped to record lows in the 2010s. "Iron County, Wisconsin Profile," 2021, Washington, DC, https://data.census.gov/cedsci /profile?g=0500000US55051, Chicago Census Tract Data.

5. "Time Series/Trend Charts: Current Population Survey/Housing Vacancy Survey." United States Census Bureau, 2023, Washington, DC, https://www.census.gov/econ/currentdata/dbsearch?programCode =HV&startYear=1956&endYear=2023&categories[]=RATE&dataType =HVR&geoLevel=MW&adjusted=0&notAdjusted=1&errorData=0#t able-results.

6. Alexander Bogin, William Doerner, and William Larson, "Local House Price Dynamics: New Indices and Stylized Facts," 2016. Working Paper 16–01. Annual House Price Indexes: States and Five-Digit ZIP Codes, https://www.fhfa.gov/DataTools/Downloads/Pages/House-Price -Index-Datasets.aspx#atvol.

7. As of November 2023, the median home value in Chicago is $287,337. The median price of homes currently listed in South Deering is $122,170, in The Bush is $105,879, and in South Chicago is $131,915. Data gathered from Zillow.com in November 2023.

8. Staying in their house simply made sense to Richard and Penelope. As the couple relayed this life history to me, it was not clear how much of their choice to stay in their steel mill neighborhood was voluntary or forced due to circumstances outside of their control. Until the late 1980s, African American families across the United States faced racial bias from realtors, banks, and neighbors when attempting to purchase houses. Black military veterans faced roadblocks in their pursuit of the same housing loans and benefits offered to their white compatriots. In the largely African American neighborhoods of South Chicago, federally backed loans were unavailable for purchasing houses in certain neighborhoods that were "redlined," or marked as high-risk investments. This would have made it harder for Richard and Penelope to

sell their house. And through the late 1980s, the residues of racially restrictive covenants—neighborhood or subdivision agreements that restricted African Americans and other non-whites from moving into the community—relegated many out-migrating Black families to more distant or less desirable neighborhoods. Racial restrictive covenants were adopted for set periods, often ranging from ten to twenty years, after which they would be reapproved. Thus, while racial restrictive covenants were outlawed in 1968, most of them, including those reapproved shortly before 1968, remained until they expired a decade or two later in 1980. The language of racial restrictive covenants remains in some deeds to date, although they are no longer legally enforceable. ("Racial Restriction and Housing Discrimination in the Chicagoland Area," *Digital Chicago*. Lake Forest College in partnership with the Chicago History Museum. https://www.digitalchicagohistory.org/exhibits /show/restricted-chicago/history. While Richard, Penelope, and other African American interviewees didn't explicitly discuss these limitations to their residential mobility, any conversation about housing in Chicago needs to acknowledge the often-unsaid role played by institutionalized racism in structuring their options in the postindustrial era. In addition, residential integration in the Trumbull housing project was violently protested in a western neighborhood in this region in the 1950s. American Friends Service Committee, "Trumbull Park, A Progress Report." (Chicago: Southeast Chicago History Museum, 1959).

9. Daniel T. Lichter and David L. Brown, "Rural America in an Urban Society: Changing Spatial and Social Boundaries," *Annual Review of Sociology* 37, no. 1 (2011): 565–92; Larry Long, *Migration and Residential Mobility in the United States* (New York: Russell Sage Foundation, 1988); Timothy M. Smeeding, "Middle Class in America," *Focus: University of Wisconsin-Madison Institute for Research on Poverty* 27, no. 1 (2010): 1–43.

10. The median home value in Wisconsin is $186,400. Wisconsin home values have gone up 6.5 percent over the past year (2022–2023). The median price of homes currently listed in Wisconsin is $209,900 while the median price of homes that sold is $178,400. The median price of homes currently listed in Iron County is $165,000—this number

includes the southern half of the county, which was not impacted by the iron mine closure. In Montreal and Hurley, the two incorporated towns impacted by iron mine closure, the median price of homes currently listed on Zillow is $50,000 and $90,000, respectively.

11. More than half of homeowners in Iron County own their houses outright today. U.S. Census Bureau, "DP04: Selected Housing Characteristics: Iron County, Wisconsin, 2010–2015," American Community Survey 5-Year Estimates (Washington, DC), 2015. Accessed online January 6, 2017 from https://factfinder.census.gov.

12. Robert Merton, *Sociological Ambivalence and Other Essays* (New York: Free Press, 1976), 5, 9. Ambivalence is a state we live in—one that recognizes complexity. Ambivalence, in Michael Carolan's view, is a "product of our sociological and ecological embeddedness" and thus "an unavoidable condition of being a social actor" in modern environmental and socioeconomic contexts ("Sociological Ambivalence and Climate Change," *Local Environment* 15 [2010]: 320).

13. Michael Mayerfeld Bell, "Ghosts of Place," *Theory and Society* 26, no. 6 (1997): 813–36; David M. Hummon, "Community Attachment—Local Sentiment and Sense of Place," in *Place Attachment*, ed. I. Altman and S. M. Low (Boston: Springer): 253–78; T. R. Sarbin, "Place Identity as a Component of Self: An Addendum," *Journal of Environmental Psychology* 3, no. 4 (1983): 337–42.

14. Harvey Motlotch, William Freudenburg, and Krista E. Paulsen, "History Repeats Itself, But How? City Character, Urban Tradition, and the Accomplishment of Place," *American Sociological Review* 65 (2000): 791–823; Christopher M. Raymond et al., eds., *Changing Senses of Place: Navigating Global Challenges* (Cambridge: Cambridge University Press, 2022).

15. Iron County, "Iron County Comprehensive Plan, Element 8—Land Use," Hurley, WI, 2005, http://www.nwrpc.com/DocumentCenter.

16. Kai Erikson, *Everything in Its Path: Destruction of Community in the Buffalo Creek Flood* (New York: Simon & Schuster, 1976), 191.

17. Edward C. Relph, *Place and Placelessness* (London: Pion, 1976), 1; original emphasis.

18. Lewis Mumford, *The City in History: Its Origins, Its Transformations, and Its Prospects* (New York: Harcourt Brace, 1961), 287.

19. See discussions of "belonging networks" in Anita Puckett, *Seldom Ask, Never Tell: Labor and Discourse in Appalachia* (Oxford: Oxford University Press, 2000).

20. Alfred Fleischer oral history, Southeast Chicago Historical Museum, May 26, 2005.

21. Bell, "Ghosts of Place," 813–36.

22. Michael Mayerfeld Bell, *City of the Good: Nature, Religion, and the Ancient Search for What Is Right* (Princeton, NJ: Princeton University Press, 2018).

23. This program requires historically accurate maintenance to the exterior of the house and allows exemptions to more modern safety codes. Any costs for keeping up these small houses in early-twentieth-century facades are aided by the eligibility of homeowners for certain tax benefits and federal grants for historic preservation. Benefits of being listed on the National Register of Historic Places: Owners of properties listed in the National Register may be eligible for a 20 percent investment tax credit for the certified rehabilitation of income-producing certified historic structures such as commercial, industrial, or rental residential buildings. This credit can be combined with a straight-line depreciation period of 27.5 years for residential property and 31.5 years for nonresidential property for the depreciable basis of the rehabilitated building reduced by the amount of the tax credit claimed. Federal tax deductions are also available for charitable contributions for conservation purposes of partial interests in historically important land areas or structures (Della E. Rucker, "National Register of Historic Places Registration Form: Plummer Mine Headframe," OMB No. 10024–0018. Iron County Historical Society Records. Green Bay, WI, 1992).

24. Like other communities with low population levels, longevity of residence, and overlapping social networks, Iron County is characterized by a high density of acquaintanceship—a phrase termed by the environmental sociologist Bill Freudenberg. Most applications of this concept are applied to rural settings. Its suitability to Southeast Chicago highlights how rural this community really is—a low population density, millgate neighborhoods creating a close-knit sense of village life, even today, and natural and industrial heritage areas drawing repeat, local visitors. William R. Freudenburg, "The Density of Acquaintanceship:

An Overlooked Variable in Community Research?" *American Journal of Sociology* 92, no. 1 (1986): 27–63.
25. Kai Erikson, *Everything in Its Path*, 213–14.
26. Home is a place "to which one withdraws and from which one ventures forth" (Y.-F. Tuan, "Geography, Phenomenology, and the Study of Human Nature," *Canadian Geographies* 15, no. 3 [1971]: 189).

5. NATURAL RESOURCE FUTURES: IRON COUNTY

1. "Iron County, Wisconsin Profile," United States Census Bureau, 2021, https://data.census.gov/cedsci/profile?g=0500000US55051; United States Census Bureau, "QuickFacts: Wisconsin," 2023. https://www.census.gov/quickfacts/fact/table/WI,ironcountywisconsin/PST045222
2. United States Census Bureau, Migration Patterns, "Young Adult Migration," 2022, https://migrationpatterns.org/.
3. Iron County, "Iron County Comprehensive Plan, Element 8—Land Use," http://www.nwrpc.com/DocumentCenter; Iron County Forestry and Parks Department, "Iron County Outdoor Recreation Plan 2016–2020," 2016, https://www.nwrpc.com/965/Iron-County-Outdoor-Recreation -Plan-2016; see analysis of these general trends in Thomas L. Daniels and Mark B. Lapping, "Small Town Triage: A Rural Settlement Policy for the American Midwest," *Journal of Rural Studies* 3, no. 3 (1987): 273–80.
4. My use of the term "menu of options" echoes other frameworks for understanding unequal access to resources due to local power structures and social relations. For instance, Edward R. Carr draws upon Foucault's concept of power/knowledge to explore how people's actions "are rationalized as part of or as productive of a field of possible action" ("Placing the Environment in Migration: Environment, Economy, and Power in Ghana's Central Region," *Environment and Planning* 37, no. 5: 930); see also A. Giddens, *The Constitution of Society: Outline of the Theory of Structuration* (Berkeley: University of California Press, 1984), for the idea of "structuration," which also discusses the coconstitution of agency and structures.
5. For analysis of other postindustrial towns that have utilized local government as a tool for advancement, see Braden T. Leap, *Gone Goose: The Remaking of an American Town in the Age of Climate Change*

328 • 5. NATURAL RESOURCE FUTURES

(Philadelphia: Temple University Press, 2018); Michelle Wilde Anderson, *The Fight to Save the Town: Reimagining Discarded America* (New York: Simon & Schuster, 2022).

6. "Report of Fact Finding Committee Appointed to Investigate and Report on the Iron Mining Industry in the Gogebic," 1961. Hard copy accessed at the Iron County Historical Society, Hurley, WI.

7. Today, the ICRDA manages utilities for the industrial park and sets businesses up with grants and tax breaks to make opening their doors there more feasible. See Iron County Resource Development Association, "Hurley Industrial Park," n.d, https://ironcountywi.com/hurley -industrial-park/; Tom Stankard, "Iron County Development Zone Aims to Help Businesses," *Ironwood Daily Globe*, August 7, 2015, https://www .yourdailyglobe.com/story/2015/08/07/news/iron-county-development -zone-aims-to-help-businesses/5234.html.

8. Iron County Forestry and Parks Department, "Iron County Outdoor Recreation Plan 2016–2020," 2016; Iron County Forestry Department, "Iron County, Wisconsin Outdoor Recreation Plan 2010–2015," http:// www.nwrpc.com/DocumentCenter.

9. Timber comprises 13 percent of the county's total labor income and totals $12 million in labor income; report on timber and tourism from personal correspondence with ICRDA entitled "Iron County: Economic Contribution of Forest Products in 2017 Dollars."

The forests themselves benefit private property owners and the local county government alike. Annually, the county coordinates a timber sale for purchase by pulp manufacturers across the state. County-owned lands have consistently brought $3 million dollars to the county per year for decades. But the local timber industry only benefits landowners with forests. More than 60 percent of the forests in the county are owned by the government.

10. Brian Thiede and Tim Slack, "The Old Versus the New Economies and Their Impacts," in *Rural Poverty in the United States*, ed. Ann R. Tickamyer, Jennifer Sherman, and Jennifer Warlick (New York: Columbia University Press, 2017), 238.

11. NorthStar Economics, Inc. "The Economic Impact of the Gogebic Taconite Mine," April 5, 2011, http://legis.wisconsin.gov/eupdates/Sen17 /GTAC Impact FINAL.pdf.

12. Chris Hubbuch, "Census: Half of Wisconsinites Over 40; White Majority Continues to Shrink," *Wisconsin State Journal*, June 20, 2019, https://madison.com/wsj/news/local/census-half-of-wisconsinites-over-40-white-majority-continues-to-shrink/article_88aa4779-05bb-5b31-9d31-02d2e7580f69.html.

13. Cortney Ofstad, "Iron County Celebrates Storied History," *Daily Globe*, July 29, 2013, https://www.yourdailyglobe.com/story/2013/07/29/news/iron-county-celebrates-storied-history/1027.html.

14. Cortney Ofstad, "Iron County Celebrates Storied History," *Daily Globe*, July 29, 2013; Cortney Ofstad, "Gogebic Taconite: 'We've Learned a Lot Talking to People': One-on-One Meetings Offered by G-Tac in Iron, Ashland Counties," *Daily Globe*, January 9, 2014, https://www.yourdailyglobe.com/story/2014/01/09/news/gogebic-taconite-weve-learned-a-lot-talking-to-people/2075.html.

15. M. D. Kittle, "Mining Conversation: GTAC Spokesman Sits Down with Wisconsin Reporter," *Wisconsin Reporter Townhall*, June 5, 2014, https://townhall.com/watchdog/wisconsin/2014/06/05/mining-bob-seitz-gogebic-taconite-n5109; Bill Williams, "Gogebic Taconite, LLC, October 2014: Corporate Structure," https://higherlogicdownload.s3.amazonaws.com/SMENET/1b517024-bb1c-4b2c-b742-0136ce7a009c/UploadedImages/TCjointConference/Bill Williams_Gogebic Taconite.pdf.

16. Danielle Kaeding, "Mine Can't Be Built in Iron County Until Zoning Laws There Change," *Wisconsin Public Radio*, November 7, 2014, http://www.wpr.org/mine-cant-be-built-iron-county-until-zoning-laws-there-change.

17. Danielle Kaeding, "GTAC Officially Withdraws Taconite Mine Plans: Northern Wisconsin Land Is Now Once Again Open to Public," *The Chronotype*, March 30, 2015, https://www.apg-wi.com/rice_lake_chronotype/news/gtac-officially-withdraws-taconite-mine-plans/article_ofcb46d0-d714-11e4-9e35-33d520d6b233.html.

18. Anthony Stella, "GTAC Deal Is a Bad One for Iron County, Residents," *Daily Globe*, February 10, 2015, https://www.yourdailyglobe.com/story/2015/02/10/opinion/gtac-deal-is-a-bad-one-for-iron-county-residents/4331.html; Al Gedicks, "GTac Mine Never Made Sense Here," *Wausau Daily Herald*, March 19, 2015, https://www.wausaudailyherald.com/story/opinion/2015/03/19/gogebic-taconite-mine-never-made-sense-wisconsin/25005443/.

19. Lee Bergquist, "Mining Firm Gogebic Taconite Has Role in Drafting Bill," *Journal Sentinel*, January 30, 2013, http://archive.jsonline.com/news /wisconsin/mining-firm-has-role-in-drafting-bill-9h8invg-189008511 .html/.

20. Quote from Steven Verburg, "Huge Mine May Shrink Away from Ashland County, Gogebic Taconite Says," *Wisconsin State Journal*, September 5, 2014, http://host.madison.com/wsj/news/local/environment /huge-mine-may-shrink-away-from-ashland-county-gogebic-taconite /article_0a3bebbe-6794-52f8-bd4e-36d7330d55cf.html; Lee Bergquist, "Mining Company, Allies Spent Freely to Get Bill Approved," *Journal Sentinel*, September 1, 2014, http://archive.jsonline.com/news/state politics/mining-company-allies-spent-freely-to-get-bill-approved -mining-company-allies-spent-freely-to-get—b-273488581.html/; Lee Bergquist, "Gogebic's Formal Request for Iron Ore Mine to Be Delayed," *Journal Sentinel*, August 26, 2014, http://www.jsonline.com /news/gogebics-request-for-mining-permit-to-be-delayed-gogebics -request-for-mining-permit-to-be-delayed-b9-272796301.html; Todd Richmond, "Tribe Voices Opposition to Northern Wisconsin Mine, Meets with Walker," *Wisconsin State Journal*, September 21, 2011, https:// madison.com/wsj/news/local/environment/tribe-voices-opposition-to -northern-wisconsin-mine-meets-with-walker/article_49ceoae2-e4ac -11eo-8eee-001cc4c002eo.html; Ron Seely, "Mining in Wisconsin: 'Everybody Wants a Decent Living,'" *Wisconsin State Journal*, October 10, 2011, http://host.madison.com/news/local/environment/mining -in-wisconsin-everybody-wants-a-decent-living/article_6fe257de-f32e -11eo-93a6-001cc4c002eo.html#ixzz3E4iXPbb6; Ron Seely, "Mining in Wisconsin: Promise or Peril?" *Wisconsin State Journal*, October 9, 2011, http://host.madison.com/news/local/environment/mining-in-wisconsin -promise-or-peril/article_a41d450d-bcd4-5b10-abd5-06982ac2bf57. html#ixzz3E4iy6lqK%oA; Ron Seely, "Legislative Committee Looks to Simplify Permit Process," *Wisconsin State Journal*, October 9, 2011, https:// madison.com/wsj/news/local/environment/legislative-committee -looks-to-simplify-permit-process/article_65a3f64e-f2a5-11eo-b527 -001cc4c03286.html; Todd Richmond, "Tribe Voices Opposition to Northern Wisconsin Mine, Meets with Walker," *Wisconsin State Journal*, September 21, 2011, https://madison.com/wsj/news/local/environment

/tribe-voices-opposition-to-northern-wisconsin-mine-meets-with-walker
/article_49ceoae2-e4ac-11e0-8eee-001cc4c002e0.html.

21. "Minutes from the Iron County Board of Supervisors November 12, 2019 Meeting," Hurley, WI, http://www.co.iron.wi.gov/meetings_notes .asp?thismeeting=37731.

22. "Mining," Iron County Economic Development Zone, 2015, http:// ironcountywi.com/mining-2/.

23. Thomas R. Huffman, "Enemies of the People: Asbestos and the Reserve Mining Trial," *Minnesota History* 59, no. 7 (Fall 2005): 292–306.

24. Dan Kaufman, "The Fight for Wisconsin's Soul," *New York Times*, March 29, 2014, http://www.nytimes.com/2014/03/30/opinion/sunday/the -fight-for-wisconsins-soul.html.

25. John Myers, "Gogebic Taconite Ready to Drill Test Holes in Northern Wisconsin," *Superior Telegram*, April 18, 2011, https://www.superior telegram.com/news/1948712-gogebic-taconite-ready-drill-test-holes -northern-wisconsin.

26. Katherine J. Cramer, *The Politics of Resentment: Rural Consciousness in Wisconsin and the Rise of Scott Walker* (Chicago: University of Chicago Press, 2016).

27. Lee Bergquist, "Open-Pit Mine Proposed in Ashland and Iron Counties," *Milwaukee Wisconsin Journal Sentinel*, November 17, 2010, http:// archive.jsonline.com/news/wisconsin/108584724.html; Lee Bergquist and Patrick Marley, "Legislation Would Ease Environmental Regulations on New Mines," *Milwaukee Wisconsin Journal Sentinel*, December 8, 2011, http://www.jsonline.com/news/wisconsin/legislation-would-ease -environmental-regulations-on-new-mines-bg3c04a-135279043.html; Cory McDonald et al., *Taconite Iron Mining in Wisconsin: A Review* (Madison: Wisconsin Department of Natural Resources, Bureau of Science Services, 2013); Patti Wenzel, "Mining for Compromise: Bill Favors GTac, Promises New Jobs," *Urban Milwaukee*, December 19, 2011, http:// urbanmilwaukee.com/2011/12/19/mining-for-compromise-bill-favors -gtac-promises-new-jobs/.

28. In response to concerns about polluted water runoff, the president of the GTac explained to a newspaper journalist, "The company can build a mine that minimizes pollution problems." If an environmental problem did emerge, he argued, "We have to engineer our way out of it"

(Seely, "Legislative Committee Looks to Simplify Permit Process"). The president of GTac likewise argued, "There are standards we have to live up to. These standards will be part of the permitting process. If we can't meet these, then we won't have a mine" (Richmond, "Tribe Voices Opposition to Northern Wisconsin Mine"). Similarly, a leader in the state's manufacturing industry trade group stated that the company's commitment to gathering as much data as possible "shows there is a very robust environmental process. People who talk about the company getting a free pass to pollute, it's just absurd" (Bergquist, "Mining Company, Allies Spent Freely to Get Bill Approved"; Bergquist, "Gogebic's Formal Request for Iron Ore Mine to Be Delayed"). Certainly, the influence of the company on shaping revisions to Wisconsin mining law calls into question GTac's commitment to regulatory rigor. The historical legacies of mining, combined with the local need for economic revitalization, spurred immediate support from many local residents and politicians.

29. For other examples of this nature-as-resource view, see Justin Farrell, *The Battle for Yellowstone: Morality and the Sacred Roots of Environmental Conflict* (Princeton, NJ: Princeton University Press, 2017); Charles C. Geisler, "Estates of Mind: Culture's Many Paths to Land," *Society & Natural Resources* 13, no. 1 (2000): 51–60; Colin Jerolmack and Edward T. Walker, "Please in My Backyard: Quiet Mobilization in Support of Fracking in an Appalachian Community," *American Journal of Sociology* 124, no. 2 (2018); Thomas K. Rudel et al., "Changing Drivers of Deforestation and New Opportunities for Conservation," *Conservation Biology* 23, no. 6 (2009): 1396–405; Thomas R. Vale, "The Myth of the Humanized Landscape: An Example from Yosemite National Park," *Natural Areas Journal* 18, no. 3 (1998): 231–36.

30. Jessica D. Ulrich-Schad et al., "Preferences for Economic and Environmental Goals in Rural Community Development in the Western United States," *Rural Sociology* 87, no. 2 (2022).

31. Cortney Ofstad, "Gogebic Taconite Officials Discuss Mine with County Board," *Daily Globe*, April 24, 2013, 22–24; Anthony Stella, "GTAC Deal Is a Bad One for Iron County, Residents," *Daily Globe*, February 10, 2015, https://www.yourdailyglobe.com/story/2015/02/10/opinion/gtac-deal-is-a-bad-one-for-iron-county-residents/4331.html.

32. Patti Wenzel, "Mining for Compromise: Bill Favors GTac, Promises New Jobs," *Urban Milwaukee*, December 19, 2011; NorthStar Economics Inc., "The Economic Impact of the Gogebic Taconite Mine."

33. For more analysis of GTac's discourse, see Erik Kojola and Amanda McMillan Lequieu, "Performing Transparency, Embracing Regulations: Corporate Framing to Mitigate Environmental Conflicts," *Environmental Sociology* 6, no. 4 (2020): 364–74; Steven Verburg, "Locals Fear Gogebic Taconite Pullout as Mine Work Drops into Slow Gear," *Wisconsin State Journal*, February 1, 2015.

34. M. D. Kittle, "Mining Conversation: GTAC Spokesman Sits Down with Wisconsin Reporter," *Wisconsin Reporter Townhall*, June 5, 2014, 1–6.

35. Rupert spent hours of his own time campaigning on behalf of the new mine at community meetings. He was embarrassed that GTac refused to pay its bills. But his disappointment in the company started before it withdrew its permit application. "I think GTac didn't do a good job at selling it. They made some big mistakes. I'm in business, [so] I would know how to handle the public a little bit better. They were in over their head."

36. "Climate Hurley—Wisconsin," U.S. Climate Data, 2021, https://www.usclimatedata.com/climate/hurley/wisconsin/united-states/uswi0335; Keith Uhlig, "You Call That Snow? In Hurley, the Snow Capital of Wisconsin, They Get 16 Feet per Year," *Wausau Daily Herald*, January 19, 2019, https://www.wausaudailyherald.com/story/news/2019/01/08/hurley-snowiest-city-wisconsin-snow-capital-winter-tourism/2192873002/; "Climate Aspen—Colorado," U.S. Climate Data, 2021, https://www.usclimatedata.com/climate/aspen/colorado/united-states/uscoo016.

37. Uhlig, "You Call That Snow?"

38. Edna Ferber, *Come and Get It* (New York: Vintage, 1933).

39. Iron County Resource Development Association, "ATV Trails," Iron County Economic Development Zone, https://ironcountywi.com/recreation/atv-trails/; Iron County Resource Development Association, "Lake and Flowages," Iron County Economic Development Zone, https://ironcountywi.com/recreation/lakes-and-flowage; Wisconsin Department of Natural Resources, "Public Access Lands Mapping Tool," Bureau of Facilities and Land, https://dnrmaps.wi.gov/H5/?Viewer=Public_Access_Lands.

40. Iron County Forestry and Parks Department, "Iron County Outdoor Recreation Plan 2016–2020."

41. Iron County Economic Development, "Recreation," accessed February 8, 2023, https://ironcountywi.com/Recreation/.
42. Iron County Economic Development, "Outdoor Recreation Map," accessed February 10, 2023, https://ironcountywi.com/recreation/outdoor -recreation-plan/.
43. Danielle Kaeding, "GTAC Officially Withdraws Taconite Mine Plans," *Chronotype*, March 30, 2015, https://www.apg-wi.com/rice_lake_chronotype /news/gtac-officially-withdraws-taconite-mine-plans/article_ofcb46d0 -d714-11e4-9e35-33d520d6b233.html.
44. The building holds its own collection of century-old photographs and mining records.
45. Iron County Forestry Department, "Iron County, Wisconsin Outdoor Recreation Plan 2010–2015."
46. Report entitled "Total Tourism Impacts—2019–2020." accessed via personal correspondence with representatives of the Iron County Resource Development Association.

This assessment is based on the proportion of employment and income derived from tourist-oriented services—entertainment and recreation, accommodations, eating and drinking establishments, and hospitality—and the share of vacant housing units used for seasonal use. The United States Department of Agriculture's Economic Research Service (USDA ERS) has a set of typology codes identifying whether a county's economy is particularly dependent on specific sectors: recreation, manufacturing, mining, or government (https://www.ers.usda .gov/data-products/county-typology-codes). The Recreation typology is determined from three components: the share of employment in entertainment and recreation, accommodations, eating and drinking establishments, and real estate; the share of personal income from these same categories; and the share of vacant housing units used seasonally. Income and employment in these categories are averages for 2010–2012 from the Bureau of Economic Analysis. Seasonal housing is from the 2010 Census. Counties with the highest scores are identified as Recreation counties. The ERS classification system does not directly identify particular amenities that attract people but rather identifies the economic characteristics of recreation-dependent communities. The economic measures of recreation do serve as a strong proxy for natural amenities: an analysis of geographic variables shows that recreation-dependent counties are significantly correlated with cooler summer temperatures, a larger share of public land and protected public land, and a larger part of the county in lakes, rivers, and oceanfront.

47. Visitor spending in neighboring counties of Ashland and Bayfield is nearly double that of Iron County's $20 million. But those counties also support three times as many permanent residents (Iron County Forestry and Parks Department, "Iron County Outdoor Recreation Plan 2016–2020"; Megan Lawson, "Recreation Counties Attracting New Residents and Higher Incomes," January 2019, https://headwaterseconomics.org/economic-development/trends-performance/recreation-counties-attract/.

48. Secondary homeownership refers to housing units that are not occupied full-time.

49. "Time Series/Trend Charts: Current Population Survey/Housing Vacancy Survey." United States Census Bureau, 2023, Washington, DC, https://www.census.gov/econ/currentdata/dbsearch?programCode=HV&startYear=1956&endYear=2023&categories[]=RATE&dataType=HVR&geoLevel=MW&adjusted=0&notAdjusted=1&errorData=0#table-results. Bayfield and Ashland, to the west of Iron County, claimed 47 percent and 30 percent vacant housing, respectively. Gogebic County, Michigan, to the east, has 37 percent vacant housing (U.S. Census Bureau, "DP04: Selected Housing Characteristics: Iron County, Wisconsin, 2010–2015," American Community Survey 5-Year Estimates, Washington, DC, 2015. Accessed online January 6, 2017, from: https://factfinder.census.gov.). Of the approximately three thousand full-time, occupied housing units in Iron County, approximately six hundred residents moved into their housing unit between 1990 and 1999 and nearly one thousand moved in between 2000 and 2009 (U.S. Census Bureau, 2009).

50. As of 2021, Iron County homes are 83.7 percent owner occupied; overall in Wisconsin, homes are 67 percent owner occupied. United States Census Bureau, "QuickFacts: Iron County, Wisconsin," 2021. https://www.census.gov/quickfacts/fact/table/ironcountywisconsin/HSG445219#HSG445219. United States Census Bureau, "QuickFacts: Wisconsin," 2023. https://www.census.gov/quickfacts/fact/table/WI,ironcountywisconsin/PST045222.

51. Jeremy Bryson and William Wyckoff, "Rural Gentrification and Nature in the Old and New Wests," *Journal of Cultural Geography* 27, no. 1 (2010): 53–75; Susan Charnley, Rebecca J. McLain, and Ellen M. Donoghue, "Forest Management Policy, Amenity Migration, and Community Well-Being in the American West: Reflections from the Northwest Forest Plan," *Human Ecology* 36, no. 5 (2008): 743–61; Chris R. Colocousis, "'It Was Tourism Repellent, That's What We Were Spraying': Natural Amenities, Environmental Stigma, and Redevelopment in a Postindustrial Mill Town," *Sociological Forum* 27, no. 3 (2012): 756–76; Gary Paul Green, "The Opportunities and Limits of Economic Growth," in *Rural Poverty in the United States*, ed. Ann R. Tickamyer, Jennifer Sherman, and Jennifer Warlick (New York: Columbia University Press, 2017), 416–38; J. T. Mueller, "Natural Resource Dependence and Rural American Economic Prosperity from 2000 to 2015," *Economic Development Quarterly* 36, no. 3 (2022), 160–76; Richelle Winkler et al., "Social Landscapes of the Inter-Mountain West: A Comparison of 'Old West' and 'New West' Communities," *Rural Sociology* 72, no. 3 (2007): 478–501.

52. J. Dwight Hines, "The Post-Industrial Regime of Production/Consumption and the Rural Gentrification of the New West Archipelago," *Antipode* 44, no. 1 (2012): 74–79; Meaghan L. Stiman, "Discourses of Resource Dependency: Second Homeowners as 'Lifeblood' in Vacationland," *Rural Sociology* 85, no. 2 (2020): 468–94.

53. All but three of the other Wisconsin counties also support at least twice as many permanent residents than does Iron County (Iron County Forestry and Parks Department, "Iron County Outdoor Recreation Plan 2016–2020").

54. Richard J. Reeder and Dennis M. Brown, *Recreation, Tourism and Rural Well-Being* (Washington, DC: United States Department of Agriculture, Economic Research Service, August 2005).

55. Iron County Forestry and Parks Department, "Iron County Outdoor Recreation Plan 2016–2020."

56. Dwight J. Hines, "The Post-Industrial Regime of Production/Consumption and the Rural Gentrification of the New West Archipelago," *Antipode* 44, no. 1 (2012): 74–97.

57. That amounted to thirty jobs; personal correspondence and report from ICRDA entitled "Total Tourism Impacts—2019–2020."

58. Iron County boasts Wisconsin's largest ATV trail system, starting in the Hurley area, with more than 250 miles of trails and routes to take riders deep into the heart of Iron County. Along the routes, motorists will find a variety of pit stops offering food, beverages, gas, lodging, and scenic outlooks. The Iron County Forestry Department, along with the Iron County ATV Association, maintains 118 miles of ATV trails throughout the county. The Forestry Department also contracts with the White Thunder Riders and Mercer SnoGoers to maintain 165 miles of winter ATV trails. "ATV UTV Trails," Iron County Forestry & Parks. https://ironcountyforest.org/atv-utv-trails/.

6. TANGLED LANDSCAPES: SOUTHEAST CHICAGO

The chapter epigraphs are from Thomas F. Gieryn, "A Space for Place in Sociology," *Annual Review of Sociology* 26, no. 1 (2000): 465; Corli Jay et al., "Stories and Lessons from Inside the Stop General Iron Hunger Strike," *South Side Weekly*, November 11, 2021, https://southsideweekly.com/stories-and-lessons-from-inside-the-general-iron-hunger-strike/.

1. What to do with all this land is not a recent question. More than a century ago, Daniel Burnham, the key architect of the city's 1893 World's Fair, suggested two models of development for the marshland in this region. On one page of his 1909 *Plan of Chicago*, Burnham suggested constructing six dock extensions into Lake Michigan from the Calumet River to accommodate even more bulk steamers. A few pages later, however, Burnham reflected on the natural beauty of the area: "On the banks of the Calumet in the neighborhood of 103rd street are large swamps capable of being developed into fine parks; the country is gently undulating with plenty of woodland and the view across Lake Calumet is fine." Daniel Burnham, "Plan of Chicago (Chicago: The Commercial Club)," 1909, https://publications.newberry.org/makebigplans/plan_images/sketch-diagram-docks-suggested-mouth-calumet-river-1909.

2. Colleen Connolly, "Get to Know Your Ward: 10th Ward," *NBC Chicago and Ward Room*, January 27, 2015, https://www.nbcchicago.com/news/local/chicago-politics/get-to-know-your-ward-10th-ward/97973/.

3. University of Illinois at Chicago Great Cities Institute, *10th Ward Data, 2015*, 2015, http://www.pbchicago.org/uploads/1/3/5/3/13535542/10th_ward _data_sheet.pdf.

4. Michael Greenberg and M. Jane Lewis, "Brownfields Redevelopment, Preferences and Public Involvement: A Case Study of an Ethnically Mixed Neighbourhood," *Urban Studies* 37 (2000): 2501–14.

5. Since the 1980s, Waste Management had been using the southern wards as landfills for the city's waste—now, those dumps are capped. David N. Pellow, *Garbage Wars: The Struggle for Environmental Justice in Chicago* (Boston, MA: MIT Press, 2004).

6. Illinois Institute of Technology Institute of Design and Calumet Collaborative, *The Future of Brownfields: Critical Paths for Redeveloping the Calumet Region* (Chicago: Illinois Institute of Technology Institute of Design and Calumet Collaborative, 2018).

7. "Overview of EPA's Brownfields Program," United States Environmental Protection Agency, https://www.epa.gov/brownfields/overview-epas -brownfields-program. See also Jessica Higgins, "Evaluating the Chicago Brownfields Initiative: The Effects of City-Initiated Brownfield Redevelopment on Surrounding Communities," *Northwestern Journal of Law & Social Policy* 3 (Spring 2008): 240–62.

8. Christine J. Walley, *Exit Zero: Family and Class in Postindustrial Chicago*. Chicago: University of Chicago Press, 2013, 126; Arcadis G&M, "Steel Production Area Remedial Action Plan," (Chicago: Former Wisconsin Steel Works, 2006); Jim Schwab, *Deeper Shades of Green: The Rise of Blue-Collar and Minority Environmentalism in America* (San Francisco: Sierra Club, 1994), 170–71.

9. Phil Birge-Liberman, "(Re)Greening the City: Urban Park Restoration as a Spatial Fix," *Geography Compass* 4 (2010): 1392–1407.

10. Due to financial constraints and the geographic remoteness of the Southeast Side from downtown, only the most polluted properties were quickly remediated. Smaller brownfields lay vacant, contributing to localized economic hardships in the region.

11. "Youth Employment Data: Employment to Population Ratios for 16 to 19 and 20 to 24 Year Olds by Chicago Community Area, 2005–2009 to 2010– 2014," 2016, https://ycharts.com/indicators/chicago_il_unemployment _rate; "Illinois & Chicago Metropolitan Area Unemployment Rates," Illinois Department of Employment Security, https://ides.illinois.gov

/resources/labor-market-information/laus/chicago-metropolitan-area
-unemploymentrates.html.

12. Manufacturing was a significant part of Chicago's economy in 1960, employing 57.8 percent of working Hispanic or Latino 20- to 24-year-olds. In Chicago in 1960, compared to the United States as a whole, larger concentrations of 16- to 19-year-olds and 20- to 24-year-olds worked in manufacturing and saw larger declines over time, suggesting that Chicago was disproportionally impacted by the decline in manufacturing. Among 16- to 19-year-olds and 20- to 24-year-olds, Hispanic or Latinos, who had the largest concentration in manufacturing employment, have also seen the largest decline over time. For Blacks and Latinos, their percentage decline in manufacturing is paralleled by their percentage increase in retail and services, while whites increased employment in higher-paying professional and related service jobs (Teresa L. Córdova and Matthew Wilson, "Abandoned in Their Neighborhoods: Youth Joblessness Amidst the Flight of Industry and Opportunity," Great Cities Institute, January 2017, https://greatcities.uic .edu/2017/01/29/abandoned-in-their-neighborhoods-youth-joblessness -amidst-the-flight-of-industry-and-opportunity/, figures 19 and 20).

13. See other examples of nonprofits stepping into the lacunas left by politics in Jeremy R. Levine, *Constructing Community: Urban Governance, Development, and Inequality in Boston* (Princeton, NJ: Princeton University Press, 2021).

14. Beatriz Ponce de León, "Planning, Activism Bring Changes to Bush," LISC Chicago's New Communities Program, 2005, http://www.new communities.org/news/articleDetail.asp?objectID=212.

15. Some, but certainly not all, organizations making change on the Southeast Side are Southeast Youth Alliance (http://southeastyouthalliance .org/); Southeast Environmental Task Force (http://setaskforce.org/); Alliance of the Southeast (https://asechicago.org/who-we-are/); Claretian Associates (https://www.claretianassociates.org/); Metropolitan Family Services (https://www.metrofamily.org/); and People for Community Recovery (https://www.metrofamily.org/).

Maria Maynez, "Reclaiming the Sacrifice Zone: The Youth-Led Campaign for Environmental Justice on the Southeast Side," *Borderless*, May 6, 2021, https://borderlessmag.org/2021/05/06/reclaiming-the -sacrifice-zone-stop-general-iron-environmental-justice/.

16. City of Chicago Department of Planning and Development, "Calumet Area Land Use Plan," 2005, https://www.chicago.gov/content/dam/city/depts/zlup/Sustainable_Development/Publications/Calumet_Design_Guidelines_Land_Use/Calumet_Area_Land_Use_Plan.pdf.

17. Richard M. Daley and Alicia Mazur Berg, "Chicago Brownfields Initiatives: Recycling Our Past, Investing in Our Future," Departments of Environment and Planning and Development, 2003, accessed at the Southeast Chicago Historical Museum; James R. Elliott and Scott Frickel, "Urbanization as Socioenvironmental Succession: The Case of Hazardous Industrial Site Accumulation," *American Journal of Sociology* 120 (2015): 1767.

18. Joel Rast, "Curbing Industrial Decline or Thwarting Redevelopment?" Center for Economic Development, November 24, 2005, http://www4.uwm.edu/ced/publications/pmdstudy1.pdf.

19. "About," 2nd City Zoning. Accessed February 10, 2023, https://secondcityzoning.org/about/; also see City of Chicago Department of Planning and Development, "Zoning and Land Use Map," City of Chicago: Zoning Website. Accessed February 10, 2023, https://gisapps.chicago.gov/ZoningMapWeb/?liab=1&config=zoning.

20. Stephen H. Linder, "Coming to Terms with the Public-Private Partnership: A Grammar of Multiple Meanings," *American Behavioral Scientist* 43 (1999): 35; Faranak Miraftab, "Public-Private Partnerships: The Trojan Horse of Neoliberal Development?" *Journal of Planning Education and Research* 24 (2004): 89–101.

Policymakers coordinate with private capital to create employment; ironically, the neoliberal policies that caused deindustrialization also caused disinvestment in public infrastructures, rendering cities more reliant on capital to help local communities function. Due to the systematic defunding of city government agencies, the remediation and reuse of these brownfields relies once again on private capital through public-private partnerships (PPP)—cooperation between the state and private business that leverage capital's interest in competition and capacity for investment to solve public problems. When this cost-sharing approach is applied to brownfield remediation, proponents argue that public incentivization of private investment in marginalized land allows governments to transform liabilities into revenue-building opportunities.

21. The geographer David Harvey observed that, as industrial economic powerhouses collapsed in the 1980s, political entities in cities across the United States began adopting strategies of economic management that prioritized market mechanisms, rather than publicly funded systems, as a solution to social, economic, and environmental problems. These strategies took the form of tax breaks, incentives, and aggressive marketing campaigns intended to lure capital back to shrinking cities. David Harvey, "From Managerialism to Entrepreneurialism: The Transformation in Urban Governance in Late Capitalism," *Geografiska Annaler. Series B, Human Geography* 71, no. 1 (1989): 3–17.

    Emily Lorance Rall and Dagmar Haase, "Creative Intervention in a Dynamic City: A Sustainability Assessment of an Interim Use Strategy for Brownfields in Leipzig, Germany," *Landscape and Urban Planning* 100 (2011): 770.

22. Jack Lyne, "$63 Million in Incentives, Last-Second Space Deal Help Chicago Land Boeing," Incentives Deal of the Month from *Site Selection's Exclusive New Plant Database*, June 2001, https://siteselection.com/ssinsider/incentive/tio106.htm.

23. "Business Incentive Programs: The Chicago Loop," Loop Chicago, https://loopchicago.com/d business/invest/incentive-programs/.

24. Chicago Department of Planning and Development, "Intergovernmental Agreement Will Support Infrastructure Work at Illinois International Port District," 2019, https://www.chicago.gov/content/dam/city/depts/mayor/PressRoom/PressReleases/2019/July/VariousApproved.pdf.

    This pool is known as tax increment financing (TIF), which is a funding tool used by the city of Chicago to promote public and private investment across the city. Funds are used to build and repair roads and infrastructure, clean polluted land, and put vacant properties back to productive use, usually in conjunction with private development projects. Funds are generated by growth in the equalized assessed valuation (EAV) of properties within a designated district over a period of twenty-three years. When an area is declared a TIF district, the amount of property tax the area generates is set as a base EAV amount. As property values increase, all property-tax growth above that amount can be used to fund redevelopment projects within the district. The increase, or increment, can be used to pay back bonds issued to pay upfront costs or can be used on a pay-as-you-go basis for individual projects. These development initiatives direct part of a neighborhood's property taxes into a fund that supports private development projects.

Jeffrey Kleeger, "Flexible Development Tools: Private Gain and Public Use," *Urban Lawyer* 46, no. 2 (2014): 377–411; Higgins, "Evaluating the Chicago Brownfields Initiative," 240–62.

25. Associated Press, "Work Begins on Southeast Side Industrial Development," *Chicago Tribune*, February 8, 2019, https://www.chicagotribune.com /business/ct-biz-southeast-side-chicago-industrial-park20190208-story.html.

26. "Illinois Enterprise Zone Program," Illinois Department of Commerce, https://www2.illinois.gov/dceo/ExpandRelocate/Incentives/taxassistance /Pages/EnterpriseZone.aspx; "Boundaries of Enterprise Zones," Chicago Data Portal, https://data.cityofchicago.org/Community-Economic -Development/Boundaries-Enterprise-Zones/64xf-pyvh.

27. As a whole, the city of Chicago actually experienced job growth in the last few decades of the twentieth century as service and retail jobs emerged in the city center and the northern end. But those entry-level jobs were distant dreams in the neighborhoods where steel mills used to stand on the edge of the city. Polluted residues from industry, geographical distance from large consumer populations, and intentional policies dissuaded the development of retail or service industries in the Southeast Side—that was the geographical unevenness that William Julius Wilson referred to.

28. This information is taken from interviews with several local government leaders and from digital ethnographic observation at a community meeting.

29. "Worldwide Locations," Ford Corporate, https://corporate.ford.com /operations/locations/global-plants/chicago-assembly-plant.html.

30. Environmental Protection Agency (EPA), "Environmental Issues in Southeast Chicago." Accessed February 10, 2023, https://www.epa.gov /il/environmental-issues-southeast-chicago.

31. James R. Elliott and Scott Frickel, "Urbanization as Socioenvironmental Succession: The Case of Hazardous Industrial Site Accumulation," *American Journal of Sociology*, 120, no. 6 (2015): 1736–77.

32. Christine J. Walley, *Exit Zero: Family and Class in Postindustrial Chicago*. Chicago: University of Chicago Press, 2013, 127.

33. Brett Chase, "City Knew of Youth Baseball Field Contamination a Year Ago but Didn't Tell Residents," *Chicago Sun Times*, September 17, 2020, https://chicago.suntimes.com/2020/9/17/21443814/baseball-babe-ruth-field -little-league-hegewisch-epa-contamination-manganese-southeast-side.

34. David N. Pellow, *Garbage Wars: The Struggle for Environmental Justice in Chicago* (Cambridge, MA: MIT Press, 2004).

35. Steve Lerner, *Sacrifice Zones: The Front Lines of Toxic Chemical Exposure in the United States* (Cambridge, MA: MIT Press, 2012); Maria Maynez and Mike Centeno, "Reclaiming the Sacrifice Zone," *Borderless Magazine*, May 6, 2021, https://borderlessmag.org/2021/05/06 /reclaiming-the-sacrifice-zone/; Dorceta E. Taylor, *Toxic Communities: Environmental Racism, Industrial Pollution, and Residential Mobility* (New York: New York University Press, 2014); Ava Tomasula y Garcia, "Possible Landscapes," *Belt Magazine*, January 6, 2020, https://beltmag .com/steelworkers-park-chicago-landscape/.

36. Editorial Board, "A Bonanza for the North Side, but What About the South Side?" *Chicago Tribune*, July 19, 2018, https://www.chicago tribune.com/opinion/editorials/ct-edit-lincoln-yards-north-branch -20180719-story.html.

37. Considering how much land is available in Southeast Chicago, it's hard to know whether or not companies would have moved to sites without these incentives. Likewise, tax increment financing, which freezes taxes on businesses that expand or locate in a specific area, often have a negative impact on schools and services that are funded primarily through property taxes.

38. Editorial Board. "Editorial: On Chicago's Southeast Side, the Peril of Living in a 'Toxic Donut,' " *Chicago Tribune*, August 25, 2020, https:// www.chicagotribune.com/opinion/editorials/ct-editorial-general-iron -southeast-side-toxic-donut-20200825-outmryzwynayrmytzjkfhfq5vq -story.html.

39. Christine J. Walley, *Exit Zero: Family and Class in Postindustrial Chicago*. Chicago: University of Chicago Press, 2013.

40. Lincoln Park is 76.5 percent white and has a per capita income of $73,965, leading observers to flag General Iron's movement as an act of

344 • 6. TANGLED LANDSCAPES

environmental racism, with the facility leaving a wealthy white area for a poorer Hispanic location.

41. Smaller industries can slip through the cracks, as environmental regulation is on a plant-by-plant basis rather than assessed for accumulated environmental burdens across a region. Thus, each new plant adds a little more pollution. Already, the region is defined as "environmentally overburdened" by the U.S. EPA. James R. Elliott and Matthew Thomas Clement, "Natural Hazards and Local Development: The Successive Nature of Landscape Transformation in the United States," *Social Forces* 96, no. 2 (2017): 851–76.

42. Brett Chase, "Activists Vow Hunger Strike to Protest General Iron Move to Southeast Side," *Chicago Sun Times*, February 4, 2021, https:// chicago.suntimes.com/2021/2/4/22267209/general-iron-hunger-strike -southeast-side-george-washington-high-school-chuck-stark; Jim Daley, "Hunger Strikers Seeking Environmental Justice Win Air-Pollution Delay," *Scientific American*, March 24, 2021, https://www.scientificamerican .com/article/hunger-strikers-seeking-environmental-justice-win-air -pollution-delay/.

43. Quinn Meyers, "Permit for Southeast Side Metal Shredding Facility Paused After EPA Steps In," *WTTW PBS Chicago*, May 15, 2021, https:// news.wttw.com/2021/05/15/permit-southeast-side-metal-shredding -facility-paused-after-epa-steps.

44. Centers for Disease Control and Prevention, "CDC—Immediately Dangerous to Life or Health Concentrations (IDLH): Graphite (Natural)— NIOSH Publications and Products," May 1994, https://www.cdc.gov /niosh/idlh/7782425.html.

45. The U.S. EPA notes that metals manufacturing can release cancer-causing levels of chemicals, like benzene and glycol ethers, into the air (U.S. Environmental Protection Agency, "2002 TRI Factsheet: Industry Sector: Fabricated Metals, 332," TRI Explorer, May 2023, https://enviro .epa.gov/triexplorer/industry.html?pYear=2002&pLoc=332&pParent =TRI&pDataSet=TRIQ1).

In Southeast Chicago, tolerance for the uneven distribution of environmental harms across space and demographics decreased as the industry began to crumble at the same time that knowledge about the long-term impacts of air and water pollution on bodies became more widely available in the 1970s. Through what came to be known as the environmental justice movement, residents across industrial communities began to lobby local and federal governments to increase legal consequences for the pollution of steel. Robert J. Brulle and David N. Pellow, "Environmental Justice: Human Health and Environmental Inequalities," *Annual Review of Public Health* 27 (2006): 103–24; Robert Bullard, *Dumping in Dixie: Race, Class, and Environmental Quality* (Boulder, CO: Westview, 1990); Raoul S. Liévanos, Pierce Greenberg, and Ryan Wishart, "In the Shadow of Production: Coal Waste Accumulation and Environmental Inequality Formation in Eastern Kentucky," *Social Science Research* 71 (January 2018): 37–55.

46. While the fullness of acquiescence to harm is difficult to quantify, particularly within the context of a powerful large-scale industry and otherwise economically bereft local community, to this day, researchers consistently find that some people are willing to bear the environmental burdens of industry if economic gains are sufficient. John Gaventa, *Power and Powerlessness: Quiescence and Rebellion in an Appalachian Valley* (Chicago: University of Illinois Press, 1982); Colin Jerolmack and Edward T. Walker, "Please in My Backyard: Quiet Mobilization in Support of Fracking in an Appalachian Community," *American Journal of Sociology* 124, no. 2 (2018); Matthew E. Kahn, "The Silver Lining of Rust Belt Manufacturing Decline," *Journal of Urban Economics* 46, no. 3 (1999): 360–76.

47. See the excellent reporting by Brett Chase on the sacrifice zone of the Southeast Side of Chicago ("Year in Review: How I Report on Chicago's 'Sacrifice Zones'—through the Eyes of Those Who Live in Our Most Polluted Neighborhoods," *Chicago Sun Times*, December 19, 2022).

48. Southeast Environmental Task Force, "About Us," accessed February 10, 2023, http://setaskforce.org/about-us-2/.

49. This article explains her insistence that a metals recycling company install pollution-control equipment to minimize particulate matter if and when they moved operations to an existing recycling site on the Southeast Side: Michael Hawthorne, "Citing Environmental Racism, Southeast Side Activists File Civil Rights Complaint against Chicago: 'We've Been a Dumping Ground for Too Many Years,'" *Chicago Tribune*, August 13, 2020.

50. National Audubon Society, "State Line/Calumet Region," accessed on January 18, 2022, https://www.audubon.org/important-bird-areas/state-linecalumetregion; Mark Bouman, "Calumet Region: A Line in the Sand," in *City of Lake and Prairie: Chicago's Environmental History*, ed. Kathleen A. Brosnan, William C. Barnett, and Ann Durkin Keating (Pittsburgh: University of Pittsburgh Press, 2020), 286–300; Ann Durkin Keating, *Chicago Neighborhoods and Suburbs: A Historical Guide* (Chicago: University of Chicago Press, 2008).

51. "The Story of Big Marsh," Friends of Big Marsh, accessed September 15, 2021, https://bigmarsh.org/history.

52. Chicago Park District. "Chicago Southeast Side Parks," https://www.chicagosesideparks.com/.

53. "More Than 100 Acres of Wetlands to Be Restored on Southeast Side of Chicago," Audubon, February 24, 2020, https://gl.audubon.org/news/more-100-acres-wetlands-be-restored-southeast-side-chicago.

54. Erika Slife, "Southeast Side to Get 556 Acres of Parkland," *Chicago Tribune*, January 10, 2011, https://www.chicagotribune.com/news/ct-xpm-2011-01-10-ct-met-park-district-land-0111-20110110-story.html.

55. Brett Chase, "Toxic Southeast Side Site Should Be Turned Into Park, Group Says," *Chicago Sun Times*, September 13, 2020, https://chicago.suntimes.com/2020/9/13/21433181/acme-steel-coke-redevelopmenttoxic-cleanup-environment-southeast-side-site-deering.

56. Millennium Reserve Organization (now Calumet Collaborative), "Explore the Millennium Reserve and Greater Calumet Region: A Natural and Cultural Guide to the Region from Bronzeville to the Indiana Dunes," 44. http://web.archive.org/web/20160330182758/http://www.millennium-reserve.org/globalassets/guides/millennium-reserveandcalumetguidebook_october2014.pdf.

57. Jeremy Ross, "'It's A Hidden Gem': New Pump Track Opens at Big Marsh Park On Southeast Side; 'Huge for the Bike Enthusiast,'" *CBS Chicago*, October 10, 2020, https://chicago.cbslocal.com/2020/10/10/big-marsh-park-pump-track-grand-opening-south-deering-southeast-side/.

58. Dan Wheeler, "What Four Big Walls Can Offer Chicago's South Side," *Chicago Tribune*, August 8, 2017, https://www.chicagotribune.com/opinion/letters/ct-walls-south-works-steel-chicago-south-side-20170808-story.html.

59. This idea isn't new; beginning in the 1990s, eastern Europe was turning ore walls, old factories, and other postindustrial sites into large-scale jungle gyms. Joseph Giordono, "Duisburg: Urban Decay Now a Family Climbing Getaway in Germany," *Stars and Stripes*, August 30, 2005, https://www.stripes.com/travel/duisburg-urban-decay-now-a-family -climbing-getaway-in-germany-1.38946.

60. Azam Ahmed, "Swamped by a Past of Steel," *Chicago Tribune*, March 19, 2007.

61. Matthew Wilson, Anish Tailor, and Alex Linares, "2017 Chicago Community Area Economic Hardship Index," Great Cities Institute, December 13, 2019, https://greatcities.uic.edu/2019/12/13/fact-sheet-chicago -community-area-economic-hardship-index-2017/.

62. James R. Elliott, Elizabeth Korver-Glenn, and Daniel Bolger, "The Successive Nature of City Parks: Making and Remaking Unequal Access Over Time," *City and Community* 18 (2019): 109–27; Kevin Loughran, "Urban Parks and Urban Problems: An Historical Perspective on Green Space Development as a Cultural Fix," *Urban Studies* 57 (2020): 2321–38; Ken Gould and Tammy Lewis, *Green Gentrification: Urban Sustainability and the Struggle for Environmental Justice* (New York: Routledge, 2016); Jonathan Essoka, "The Gentrifying Effects of Brownfields Redevelopment," *Western Journal of Black Studies* 34 (2010): 299–315.

63. U.S. Census Bureau, "Ward 10: Table DP-1. Profile of General Demographic Characteristics," Census 2000, retrieved August 20, 2021, https://drive.google.com/drive/folders/0B9vdVdIIoXSCTlYoct8yV FhuVG8; Institute for Housing Studies at DePaul University, "Cook County Housing Price Index," retrieved January 20, 2022, https://price -index.housingstudies.org/.

64. Chicago Park District, "Chicago Southeast Side Parks."

65. "The Story of Big Marsh."

66. Chicago Park District. "Ford Calumet Environmental Center (FCEC)," https://www.chicagoparkdistrict.com/FCEC.

67. Contemporary reindustrialization collides with these marginal, "unintentional landscapes" of historical capitalism, as the geographer Matthew Gandy put it, to create issues of infrastructure and access for residents on the Southeast Side. But these aren't entirely unintentional

landscapes—they are the residues of past integration of millgate neighborhoods and workplaces ("Unintentional Landscapes," *Landscape Research* 41 [2016]: 433–40).

68. Carolyn Finney, *Black Faces, White Spaces: Reimagining the Relationship of African Americans to the Great Outdoors* (Chapel Hill: University of North Carolina Press, 2014), 47.

69. Joshua Singer, "Environmental Issues in Southeast Chicago," U.S. Environmental Protection Agency, updated on April 24, 2018, https://www.epa.gov/il/environmental-issues-southeast-chicago.

70. Since 2015, a collaboration of more than a dozen regional nonprofits have worked together to nominate the Illinois/Indiana steel region to the National Parks Service for designation and funding as a National Heritage Area. This designation—which as of publication is still pending—would bring in more consistent funding for maintenance of walking and biking trails, establishment or expansion to steel buildings and volunteer-run museums, and annual events designed to attract more visitors.

CONCLUSION

1. Angel Adams Parham, *American Routes: Racial Palimpsests and the Transformation of Race* (New York: Oxford University Press, 2017), 296.

2. William H. Sewell, "A Theory of Structure: Duality, Agency, and Transformation," *American Journal of Sociology* 98, no. 1 (1992): 1–29.

3. For instance, researchers focused on domestic life show how uneven power dynamics at home, as both physical location and social arrangement, can impoverish people's options and actions e.g. Gillian Rose, *Feminism & Geography: The Limits of Geographical Knowledge* (Minneapolis: University of Minnesota Press, 1993); Iris Marion Young, "House and Home: Feminist Variations on a Theme," in *Intersecting Voices: Dilemmas of Gender, Political Philosophy, and Policy* (Princeton, NJ: Princeton University Press, 1997), 134–64.

4. W. Neil Adger et al. defines resilience as the ability of communities to absorb external changes in stresses while maintaining the sustainability of their livelihoods ("Migration, Remittances, Livelihood Trajectories, and Social Resilience," *Ambio* 31, no. 4 [2002]: 358).

For examples of resilience narratives permeating urban/community planning contexts, see: Richard Florida, *The Rise of the Creative Class* *(New York: Basic Books, 2019); Richard Florida,* "Returning to the Rust Belt," *Bloomberg,* August 31, 2017, https://www.citylab.com/life/2017/08 /returning-to-the-rust-belt/538572/; "Richard Florida on the Resiliency of Cities," April 26, 2023, *DataSmart* podcast, Bloomberg Center for Cities, Harvard University. https://datasmart.hks.harvard.edu /exclusive-richard-florida-resiliency-cities; also see "Build Your Strong Town," Strong Towns, https://www.strongtowns.org/. Julian Reid noted concerns that discourses on resilience may place a disproportionate responsibility for self-help onto vulnerable or marginalized communities and people ("Interrogating the Neoliberal Biopolitics of the Sustainable Development-Resilience Nexus," *International Political Sociology* 7, no. 4 [2013]: 353–67).

5. For instance, see J. D. Vance, *Hillbilly Elegy* (New York: HarperCollins, 2017); in counterpoint, see Anthony Harkins and Meredith McCarroll, Appalachian Reckoning: A Region Responds to Hillbilly Elegy. (Morgantown: West Virginia University Press, 2019). Elizabeth Catte, *What You Are Getting Wrong About Appalachia* (Cleveland, OH: Belt, 2018).

6. See Kai Erikson's later work (*A New Species of Trouble: Explorations in Disaster, Trauma, and Community* [New York: Norton, 1994]), as well as climate change research by Rebecca Elliot, *Underwater: Loss, Flood Insurance, and the Moral Economy of Climate Change in the United States* (New York: Columbia University Press, 2021); Summer Gray, *In the Shadow of the Seawall Coastal Injustice and the Dilemma of Placekeeping* (Oakland: University of California Press, 2023).

7. Amanda McMillan Lequieu, "Birdwatching on Brownfields: Contradictory Contexts and Ambivalence in the Neoliberal City" *Environmental Justice* 16, no. 1 (2023): 72–81.

8. Robert Merton, *Sociological Ambivalence and Other Essays* (New York: Free Press, 1976), 5, 9; Michael Carolan, "Sociological Ambivalence and Climate Change," *Local Environment* 15, no. 4 (2010): 320.

9. Jan W. Duyvendak, *The Politics of Home: Belonging and Nostalgia in Europe and the United States* (Basingstoke, UK: Palgrave Macmillan, 2011); Per Gustafson, "Meanings of Place: Everyday Experience and

Theoretical Conceptualizations," *Journal of Environmental Psychology* 21, no. 1 (2001): 5–16.

10. Jane L. Collins, "New Directions in Commodity Chain Analysis of Global Development Processes," *Research in Rural Sociology and Development* 11 (2005): 1–15.

11. Manuel Castells, *The Informational City: Economic Restructuring and Urban Development* (Oxford: Blackwell, 1989).

12. Katherine Roberts frames actions to perpetuate land tenure, negotiate resources, or maintain social links as "self-positioning strategies," which involve critical choices, "including those that appear to be inaction." "The Art of Staying Put: Managing Land and Minerals in Rural America," *Journal of American Folklore* 126, no. 502 (2013): 408.

13. Wendell Berry, "How to Be a Poet (to remind myself)," *Poetry*, January 2001.

14. Christiane von Reichert, John B. Cromartie, Ryan O. Arthun, "Impacts of Return Migration on Rural U.S. Communities," *Rural Sociology* 79, no. 2 (2013): 200–26.

15. Matthew Hall and Jonathan Stringfield, "Undocumented Migration and the Residential Segregation of Mexicans in New Destinations," *Social Science Research* 47 (2014): 61–78; Daniel T. Lichter et al., "Residential Segregation in New Hispanic Destinations: Cities, Suburbs, and Rural Communities Compared," *Social Science Research* 39, no. 2 (2010): 215–30; Amon S. Emeka, "Poverty and Affluence Across the First Two Generations of Voluntary Migration from Africa to the United States, 1990–2012," *Sociology of Race and Ethnicity* 2, no. 2 (2016): 162–85.

16. Current research on Rust Belt cities suggests that while immigrants are reshaping urban landscapes, local immigration policies are directly shaping where immigrants come to call home in cities across the United States. Tomas R. Jimenez, *Replenished Ethnicity: Mexican Americans, Immigration, and Identity* (Berkeley: University of California Press, 2010); Yolande Pottie-Sherman, "Rust and Reinvention: Im/migration and Urban Change in the American Rust Belt," *Geography Compass* 14, no. 3 (2020): 1–13.

Chicago is a sanctuary city, meaning the city will not ask about immigration status, disclose that information to authorities, or, most importantly, deny access to city services based on immigration status. Heather Cherone,

"What Does It Mean That Chicago Is a Sanctuary City? Here's What to Know," *WTTW PBS news*, October 20, 2023. https://news.wttw.com/2023/10/20/what-does-it-mean-chicago-sanctuary-city-here-s-what-know.

17. Arlie Russell Hochschild, *Strangers in Their Own Land: Anger and Mourning on the American Right* (New York: New Press, 2016); Jennifer M. Silva, *We're Still Here: Pain and Politics in the Heart of America* (Oxford: Oxford University Press, 2019).

18. Philip Stoker, Danya Rumore, Lindsey Romaniello, and Zacharia Levine, "Planning and Development Challenges in Western Gateway Communities," *Journal of the American Planning Association* 87, no. 1 (2021): 21–33.

19. Richelle Winkler, Donald R. Field, A. E. Luloff, Richard S. Krannich, Tracy Williams, "Social Landscapes of the Inter-Mountain West: A Comparison of 'Old West' and 'New West' Communities," *Rural Sociology* 72 (2009): 478–501; Kevin E. McHugh and Robert C. Mings, "The Circle of Migration: Attachment to Place in Aging," *Annals of the Association of American Geographers* 5, no. 3 (1996): 530–50; Anastasia Christou, *Narratives of Place, Culture and Identity: Second-Generation Greek-Americans Return "Home"* (Amsterdam: Amsterdam University Press, 2006). Judy Gillespie, Catherine Cosgrave, Christina Malatzky, Clarissa Carden, "Sense of place, place attachment, and belonging-in-place in empirical research: A scoping review for rural health workforce research," *Health and Place* 74 (2022).

APPENDIX A: NOTES ON METHODS

1. Coal Camp USA, Western PA, Irwin Gas Coalfield, Herminie. http://www.coalcampusa.com/westpa/gas/herminie/herminie.htm.

2. Virtual Museum of Coal Mining in Western Pennsylvania, Ocean No. 1 Mine (Herminie Mine), https://web.archive.org/web/20140414025504/http://patheoldminer.rootsweb.ancestry.com/ocean.html.

3. bell hooks, *Teaching to Transgress: Education as the Practice of Freedom* (New York: Routledge, 1994), 126.

4. Bryant Keith Alexander, "Fading, Twisting, and Weaving: An Interpretive Ethnography of the Black Barbershop as Cultural Space," *Qualitative Inquiry* 9, no. 1 (2003): 109.

5. Gökçe Günel, Saiba Varma, and Chika Watanabe, "A Manifesto for Patchwork Ethnography," Member Voices, *Fieldsights*, June 9, 2020, https://culanth.org/fieldsights/a-manifesto-for-patchwork-ethnography.
6. Susan E. Bell, *DES Daughters: Embodied Knowledge and the Transformation of Women's Health Politics* (Philadelphia: Temple University Press, 2009).
7. Mario L. Small and Jenna M. Cook, "Using Interviews to Understand Why: Challenges and Strategies in the Study of Motivated Action," *Sociological Methods & Research* 52, no. 4 (2021): 1591–1631.
8. Thomas K. Rudel, "How Do People Transform Landscapes? A Sociological Perspective on Suburban Sprawl and Tropical Deforestation," *American Journal of Sociology* 115, no. 1 (2009): 129–54; Colleen Crystal Hiner, *Changing Landscapes, Shifting Values: A Political Ecology of the Rural-Urban Interface* 3544835 (2012); J. Tom Mueller and Ann R. Tickamyer, "A More Complete Picture: Rural Residents' Relative Support for Seven Forms of Natural Resource-Related Economic Development," *Rural Sociology* 85, no. 2 (2020): 376–407.
9. Scott Peters and Nancy Franz, "Stories and Storytelling in Extension Work," *Journal of Extension* 50, no. 4 (2012); William L. Bland and Michael Mayerfeld Bell, "A Holon Approach to Agroecology," *International Journal of Agricultural Sustainability* 5, no. 4 (2007): 262.
10. Small and Cook, "Using Interviews to Understand Why."
11. Patricia Ewick and Susan S. Silbey, "Subversive Stories and Hegemonic Tales: Toward a Sociology of Narrative," *Law & Society Review* 29, no. 2 (1995): 197–226; Donileen R. Loseke, "The Study of Identity as Cultural, Institutional, Organizational, and Personal Narratives: Theoretical and Empirical Integrations," *Sociological Quarterly* (2007): 661–88.
12. Charles Tilly, *Why? What Happens When People Give Reasons . . . and Why* (Princeton, NJ: Princeton University Press, 2008), 16. See also Francesca Polletta et al., "The Sociology of Storytelling," *Annual Review of Sociology* 37 (2011): 109–130 and Richard E. Nisbett and Timothy D. Wilson, "The Halo Effect: Evidence for Unconscious Alteration of Judgments," *Journal of Personality and Social Psychology* 35, no. 4 (1977): 249.

INDEX

migration (*continued*)
out-migration, 4, 6, 15, 20, 96–98, 273n3, 276n11, 286n47. *See also* mobility, residential
Millennium Reserve, 213–14
Mill Fairs, 62–63
millgate communities, 45, 53–59, 64, 294n38, 299n58. *See also* company towns
mobility, economic, 59–60, 70, 77, 92–93, 96, 118, 126, 165, 184, 277n12, 308n19
mobility, residential, 11–13, 115, 135, 231, 233, 236–37, 243, 263, 266, 276n10, 280n21, 292n23, 324n8. *See also* migration
Montreal, Wisconsin, 40–41, 49–52, 137–38, 178, 180–82, 289n14; Montreal Mining Company, 61, 74–75, 82–84, 137, 145, 153–54, 184–85, 291n19, 296n49, 296n52; *Montreal: The City Beautiful* (Penrose), 295n45
Morello, Julie, 259, xi
Mumford, Lewis, 128, 148

National Audubon Society, 211
National Labor Relations Act (NLRA) (1935), 51, 54, 297n53, 300n63
National Register of Historic Places, 153, 181, 326n23
natural resources. *See* future, of Iron County
Natural Resources Defense Council, 207

navigational equipment, 145
New Keynesians, 75–76
North Chicago Rolling Mill, 44

Oglebay Norton Company, 40–41, 51, 82–84, 290nn19–20, 310n32. *See also* Montreal, Wisconsin
oil prices, 72
Ojibwe, 37, 38, 167, 288n10; Red Cliff Band of Lake Superior Chippewa, 172–73, 175
Open Lands, 199
OpenStreetMap, 19, 24
out-migration, 4, 6, 15, 20, 96–98, 273n3, 276n11, 286n47
overqualification, 113–14

parks. *See* tourism and outdoor recreation, in Southeast Chicago
patchwork ethnography, 28
paternalism, of companies, 39, 46, 51–53, 61, 82, 84, 295n47, 296n52, 299n58, 312n47; welfare capitalism, 53, 297n56, 303n74, 312n47. *See also* capitalism, role in home
pensions, 61, 76, 78–79, 81, 84, 89, 93, 102, 113–14, 137, 168, 308n20
Peters, Scott, 258
Pierce, Justin, 88
place attachment, 140, 142, 179, 192. *See also* landscapes and place attachment
placemaking, 36–37, 66–67. *See also* capitalism, role in home

Printed and bound by CPI Group (UK) Ltd, Croydon, CR0 4YY

09/05/2024

14499836-0003